THE CARE
OF ANTIQUES
AND HISTORICAL
COLLECTIONS

AMERICAN ASSOCIATION FOR STATE AND LOCAL HISTORY BOOK SERIES

Series Editor

Sandra Sageser Clark
Michigan Historical Center

Editorial Advisory Board

Robert R. Archibald, Missouri Historical Society
Charles F. Bryan, Jr., Virginia Historical Society
Lonnie G. Bunch, Smithsonian Institution
George F. MacDonald, Canadian Museum of Civilization
George L. Vogt, South Carolina Department of Archives and History

About the Series:

The American Association for State and Local History Book Series publishes technical and professional information for those who practice and support history and addresses issues critical to the field of state and local history. To submit a proposal or manuscript to the series, please request proposal guidelines from AASLH headquarters: AASLH Book Series, 530 Church Street, Suite 600, Nashville, Tennessee 37219. Telephone: (615) 255-2971. Fax: (615) 255-2979.

About the Organization:

The American Association for State and Local History (AASLH) is a non-profit educational organization dedicated to advancing knowledge, understanding, and appreciation of local history in the United States and Canada. In addition to sponsorship of this book series, the association publishes the periodical HISTORY NEWS, a newsletter, technical leaflets and reports, and other materials; confers prizes and awards in recognition of outstanding achievement in the field; and supports a broad educational program and other activities designed to help members work more effectively. Current members are entitled to discounts on AASLH Series books. To join the organization, contact the Membership Director, AASLH, 530 Church Street, Suite 600, Nashville, Tennessee 37219.

The Care
of Antiques
and Historical
Collections

by

Per E. Guldbeck

With Revisions, an Introduction,
a Chapter on Photographs
and an Index
by
A. Bruce MacLeish

Second Edition, Revised and Expanded

ALTAMIRA
PRESS

A Division of Sage Publications, Inc.
Walnut Creek • London • New Delhi

For information contact:

AltaMira Press
A Division of Sage Publications, Inc.
1630 North Main Street, Suite 367
Walnut Creek, California 94596 U.S.A.

Sage Publications Ltd.
6 Bonhill Street
London EC2A 4PU United Kingdom

Sage Publications India Pvt. Ltd.
M-32 Market
Greater Kailash 1
New Delhi 110 048 India

PRINTED IN THE UNITED STATES OF AMERICA

Library of Congress Cataloging-in-Publication Data

Guldbeck, Per E. (Per Ernst)
　　The care of antiques and historical collections / by Per E.
　　Guldbeck : with revisions, an introduction, a chapter on
　　photographs, and an index by A. Bruce MacLeish.—2nd ed.,
　　rev. and expanded.
　　　　p. cm. — (American Association for State and Local
　　History book series)
　　　　Includes bibliographical references and index.
　　　　ISBN 0-7619-9135-2 (pbk.)
　　　　1. Art objects—Conservation and restoration. 2. Antiques—
　　Conservation and restoration. I. MacLeish, A. Bruce. II. Title.
　　III. Series.
　　NK1127.5.G8　　　1995
　　069'.5—dc20　　　　　　　　　　　　　　　　　　　95-46056
　　　　　　　　　　　　　　　　　　　　　　　　　　　　CIP

Designed by Gary Gore. Originally published by the American Association for State and Local History.

Publication of this book was made possible in part by funds from the sale of the Bicentennial State Histories, which were supported by the National Endowment for the Humanities.

　　　　　　1995　　　1996　　　1997　　　1998　　8　7　6　5　4

To the memory of
Per Guldbeck,
who provoked many of us
to improve,
and to continue improving,
our efforts and our knowledge.

The material in this book, based upon the decades of study and practical experience in conservation brought to the first edition by its author, Per Ernst Guldbeck, has been reconsidered, revised, and brought up to date by A. Bruce MacLeish, Curator of Collections for the New York State Historical Association, in light of the changes in techniques, materials, points of view, and methods of training that have taken place since the book's first appearance. This revised, expanded version, says Mr. MacLeish, is "an adaptation to the more conservative viewpoint . . . Its goal . . . is to help start—and maintain—sound programs of storage, display, and environmental control that will benefit historical artifacts. . . . the text enumerates the safest possible methods of caring for objects and . . . implores all concerned to consider the well-being of each object before dashing headlong into an indiscriminate program of gluing and polishing."

With complete confidence in Mr. MacLeish's sound professional judgment, the American Association for State and Local History, as publisher, asked other conservation experts in specialized fields to serve as critical readers as the manuscript took shape, and we have been well pleased with their encouragement. However, because the results obtained by following the suggestions given in the text will depend to a great extent upon individual judgment, skill, accuracy, and caution, the Association cannot guarantee results, nor can we assume responsibility for any damage to property or injury to any person arising from use of any material in this book.

—The Editors, AASLH Press

Contents

Preface

This book is a revised edition of *The Care of Historical Collections: A Conservation Handbook for the Nonspecialist*, written by the late Per E. Guldbeck and published by the American Association for State and Local History in 1972. In the years that have intervened since publication of the original work, a good many changes in techniques, materials, points of view, and methods of training in the care of artifacts have taken place. This revision was undertaken to fill in a few of the gaps, modify a few approaches, and generally bring up to date the comprehensive body of information in the earlier edition.

"The philosophy of proper museum functions has changed, over the years, and will continue to change," Per Guldbeck wrote, in the original work; and so it has, in the past decade. This recasting of Per's work in the earlier book is therefore not a refutation of it, but an adaptation to the more conservative viewpoint prevailing today—the general view that, in many instances, both expert and nonspecialist may be able to do more for their collections by taking few active measures with objects, protecting them more by providing proper environment and handling.

The purpose of this book is to provide a reliable basis for caring for an assortment of historically significant materials, such as may be found in a small museum or a private collection. Its goal, therefore, is to help start—and maintain—sound programs of storage, display, and environmental control that will benefit historical artifacts, and, as part of that help, to aid in the identification of problems that may be safely handled on the spot and those that require the attention of a trained conservator.

As one might expect, this book is intended more as a starting point than as an encyclopedic reference that will always yield the right answer for cherished collections.

While it is not designed to endow the reader with finished expertise, the kinds of treatment suggested in it are intended to be as helpful as possible to the kinds of objects usually found in museums or private collections, and its recommendations should effect some worthwhile result in cleaning or repair. Though it is very difficult to make such recommendations—and many conservators and curators refuse to endorse treatments or commercial products to the nonspecialist—the text enumerates the safest possible methods of caring for objects and—

again—implores all concerned to consider the well-being of each object before dashing headlong into an indiscriminate program of gluing and polishing. Those who would make no recommendations for treatments argue that a little knowledge is a dangerous thing; since the alternative is no knowledge, however—or the traditional, rather than more recent, more informed, ways of handling objects—the risk seems worthwhile. It is problematical whether all the information presented here may be considered the best possible advice, but it is an honest attempt in that direction.

*   *   *   *   *

C. R. Jones, conservator for the New York State Historical Association, provided a great deal of information for this revision, as did Christopher Tahk, Cathleen Baker, and Jonathan Thornton of the Department of Conservation of Historic and Artistic Works, State University College at Buffalo. The author assumes all responsibilities for errors in fact or judgment in the writing of this revised edition.

September 1983   A. BRUCE MACLEISH

Preface to the First Edition

It was with some diffidence that this manual was undertaken, since there already exist excellent books on the conservation of historic materials. But as a result of speaking on the subject at a number of history museum meetings, I began to realize that often there were more questions raised than answered.

Many of the people who have responsibility for the care of artifact collections come from small historical societies. They are uncertain as to how to proceed, what they can safely undertake, or where to buy the necessary equipment and supplies. In addition, they are often overwhelmed by the technical literature and are not sure that they can understand it or translate it into practical use. Thus, this work has been prepared with the idea of providing small historical societies with an introduction to the problems of conservation and what can safely be done by the serious amateur.

Although this book was conceived primarily to aid the small historical society or museum—ranging in size from a one-man operation to a staff of five or six—it would be a mistake to assume that sheer numbers of staff guarantee that a collection will be cared for. Large institutions may put their energies into exhibition, education, or other activities at the expense of the basic collections which are the core of the institution's validity. The question then is not how large or small a staff you have, but how much time is devoted to the care of collections—and whether the people involved in the job have proper grounding in the philosophy of conservation and in the correct procedures.

This manual approaches the complex subject of conservation in three parts. The first consideration is for the health and safety of the total collection. What essential physical facilities will provide for the maximum life of a museum's collections? What requirements for storage and security are basic to the primary care of artifacts?

Regardless of how conducive the physical environment may be to the well-being of historic materials, sooner or later the museum staff will need to take more active and immediate measures to conserve a specific object. Section II considers two preliminaries to any conservation efforts. The nature and composition of the artifact must be identified and documented before the proper treatment can be determined; and the workshop area must provide a safe and controlled laboratory for that treatment. The final section of the manual discusses specific problems and methods in the conservation of artifacts and what first aid and repairs a nonspecialist dare undertake.

Bibliographies and supply lists are included at the end of each chapter. An introductory work like this does not pretend to cover the subject, lest the general reader become overwhelmed by detail. Furthermore, other bibliographies, such as the New York State Historical Association's *Guide to Historic Preservation, Historical Agencies, and Museum Practices*, have been published for those concerned with delving more deeply into specific problem areas. The materials included here indicate sources the author personally has found helpful for guiding the director who has neither the time nor the staff to pursue a problem in depth. A work that attempts to précis the field of conservation encounters not only the possibility of errors, but of contrary opinions in approach to and methods of treating artifacts. For this reason I emphasize again that readers should and must make use of the reading lists and keep abreast of new literature.

Reading over the manuscript in galley proof, I was suddenly aware of how much of it was inadvertently a rephrasing of advice and lectures from many of my colleagues of the IIC and of how much I owe to them. Particular thanks for their inspiration and help over the years go to Dr. Robert Feller of the Mellon Institute, and Dr. Nathan Stolow of the National Gallery of Canada, whose fundamental scientific researches have contributed so much to the field of conservation.

I acknowledge real thanks to my friend and colleague, H. J. Swinney, director of the Margaret Woodbury Strong Museum, Rochester, New York, who edited this manuscript and recast it into clear language. I am also grateful to Harold Peterson of the U.S. National Park Service and to Mr. and Mrs. Sheldon Keck, noted conservators, who read and criticized various chapters. But any errors in fact or judgment are mine alone.

The philosophy of proper museum functions has changed over the years and will continue to change. At one time collecting and scholarship were considered most important. Then came the concept of expanded exhibitions, with popular lectures, traveling shows, school visits, and an increasing emphasis on interpretation and greater utilization of tactile senses. None of these approaches is in itself wrong. But so often in our attempt to win popularity with the public, the artifact becomes merely a pawn in the game, suffering attrition, damage, or loss. In considering the practice of conservation, remember that no matter what the present interpretative philosophy of your museum, the collection is its core. Only by proper concern for your artifacts will you be able to maintain your integrity as a professional.

March 1972   PER E. GULDBECK

THE CARE
OF ANTIQUES
AND HISTORICAL
COLLECTIONS

Introduction

In these times, when valuable artifacts are being collected by more people and institutions than ever before, it is coming to the attention of many collectors and workers in small museums that their precious objects will not always be there if some sort of basic care is not given them.

Finding out how to provide such care is no simple matter. In fact, that subject is extremely complex, and often the specialists in a given field of conservation—the science of repairing and caring for objects— disagree sharply on the kinds of treatment that may be considered proper. The mere identification of an object and its materials can be a task requiring the assistance of experts with scientific training. Combine with that difficulty the myriad ills that can attack all artifacts and the combinations of materials that are the rule, rather than the exception—few items are made entirely of one material—and the problems of preserving objects in a collection may seem insurmountable. At times there is no easy answer to repairing damage already done or stopping the degradation of an object. The only way one may be sure of taking the right steps in beginning is to know what one is dealing with.

Carefully describing and recording the condition of an object usually raises more questions than it answers, but at least then the answers may be sought in an organized way. What is the object? What is it made of, exactly? Does it have joints, repairs, broken parts, glue, solder, or paint that indicate the need for extra attention in researching or caring for it? Will treatment to one material endanger another material? If these questions are answered conscientiously for each object in one's care, the limitations of what may be done without expert help should become obvious.

In actively treating any artifact, one must be willing to admit one's own limits of knowledge and skill, to avoid ruining the very object that should be saved. Even trained conservators are expected to recognize and concede their own limitations—since no individual can be expert in *all* areas—and call on specialists for assistance whenever necessary.

No matter how conscientiously the information in this book was prepared, or how carefully its instructions may be followed, it is inevitable that some attempts at cleaning or repair of some objects will *fail*. Even conservators who have devoted years to working with one single kind of material occasionally run into failures through some quirk in treatment; but they usually test carefully while working, to preclude a major disaster, and they have the accumulated knowledge about many kinds of treatment to fall back on. *Anyone who is inexperienced in the scientific treatment of objects had best be quite circumspect in treating any object—test carefully and proceed slowly, because you usually have no alternative to try.* If you test a cleaning method and just *begin* to soften the finish of a *tiny* test area on a table, don't panic; that is not anything like so unfortunate as attacking the whole piece at once and finding yourself with a large, sticky mess. Bearing in mind that any technique may fail at some time, you should be able to keep the failure small, rather than monumental: test, *first*, in a very small, inconspicuous area of the artifact—and if you are not *sure* about what you are doing, call a conservator at once.

When the time comes that conservation advice or treatment is needed, it should not be an impossible task to find an expert. One first step, for a private collector, would be to ask local museums for suggestions about conservators; or the administrator of a small museum might get in touch with a museum that deals in the kind of object needing attention. Specialized help with conservation problems is offered through the conservation program of the State University of New York at Buffalo, as well as through summer work projects at New York University and Winterthur. Another approach would be to obtain a membership list from the American Institute for Conservation (AIC, Klingle Mansion, 3545 Williamsburg Lane, Washington, D.C. 20008) and seek help there; the Professional Associates and Fellows of that organization are all qualified conservators, and although the AIC is not the only conservation group in the country, it is probably the best place to look for help. An important bonus to be found in the *AIC Directory* is the code of ethics for conservators; the elements of that code are extremely important considerations in treating any collection object. Any trustworthy conservator should know and adhere to the AIC code of ethics—ask for that assurance for any work you have done. If the first attempt does not come up with a conservator who can answer your questions, perhaps at least you will find someone to steer you in the right direction. There are many specialties in the profession, and the person you need may be far from your area. Do not be discouraged if you have to go far afield, for there is no substitute for the right information or the right treatment.

1

The Artifact
and Its Documentation

Relics of the past are important to many people, for varying
reasons. Many of us cherish them as the keepsakes of times past,
as inherited family treasures, or in remembrance of beloved
relatives. To the historian, however, tangible objects preserved from
earlier days shed revealing and valuable light on the lives, ideas,
activities, and attitudes of our predecessors. Old things are equally vital
to artists, writers, laboratory scientists, medical researchers, and connoisseurs of antiques, as tangible bits of evidence in continuing studies
of aesthetic values or the understanding of earlier technologies. And
there is, today, an additional reason for the appreciation of antiquities:
private individuals enjoy *collecting* them. Serious collectors keep that in
mind, because the number of authentic documents of the past is limited,
and the number of collectors is growing, daily.

Such a situation produces a humming sellers' market, and spurious,
"improved," and "cheered-up" artifacts purporting to be genuine
antiques come to light continually. It therefore behooves even the
informed collector to be always careful about acquiring new pieces for a
collection.

Whether the serious buyer of historical artifacts be private collector,
dealer, or museum professional, he or she should know something of
the materials, techniques of manufacture, and styles of the past, to deal
intelligently with the identification of the objects sought. A working
knowledge of technology of the past will help, not only in the identification of types of artifacts, but in the detection of spurious or altered
pieces.

Collectors for museums must be certain that museum resources are
used in the right way; very few institutions today enjoy the luxury of
being able to acquire anything that looks interesting—and checking its
authenticity later. The museum typical of the past may have been the
community attic; but collectors for institutions today, aware that the

5

museum has a specific story to tell, that it usually has limited storage space, and that it always carries the obligation to preserve the valid artifacts that it owns, must be more discriminating about objects that are accepted than their predecessors were, years ago.

Not all artifacts can be easily documented, unfortunately; one must therefore often rely on an acquired background of experience and scholarship in assessing—and accepting—an object as valid, of its type. That is no simple requirement. As an example of the myriad identification problems one may encounter, some carpenters' tools have not changed shape in the last several hundred years; a traditional type of try square made within the past ten years may look much the same as one of the same type that is fifty years old—or a hundred and fifty.

Reliable antique dealers offering expensive pieces or items of major importance should provide good documentation or a guarantee for such pieces; and reputable dealers in rural areas are just as aware of price levels as are city dealers—if they have a good piece, it will usually go for a fair market price. Beware of bargains, unless you want to be fooled: most of us know that genuine antique harpsichords and Hepplewhite chairs are not usually found in old barns and sold for a song. Your only defense in acquiring objects for a sound historical collection is scholarship and experience; learn all you can about styles, techniques, materials, and tools. There is no short cut to knowing the real from the spurious. What is necessary is a long apprenticeship in studying old pieces, thumbing through style and hallmark books, acquiring a workable knowledge of decorative hardware, brasses, turnings, carvings, and designs, and a good idea of the technology of the period represented by any item you may consider buying.

Scientific tools will help in making decisions about an object's authenticity only if one knows what to look for: detecting the presence of Prussian blue in a painting, for instance, is of no importance at all unless one knows when that color came into use, or whether its presence on the painting being examined is part of the original painting or a bit of later repair work. Similarly, the presence of square nails in a piece of furniture may really prove nothing about the age of the piece, since square nails have been made and used by artisans and craftsmen from Roman times up to the present. (See the section on "Fastenings for Wooden Artifacts," below, for more on this.)

There is no one book or piece of scientific apparatus that will give you all the answers or keep you from being fooled occasionally by a clever fraud. An old saw among serious collectors is the saying that "The expert who says he has never been stung is either lying or just doesn't realize it yet." Reading, technical examination, comparison, and handling many historical artifacts are sound ways to acquire a usable body of knowledge of the field.

Many well-known books that discuss furniture styles and touchmarks in silver and pewter are generally available. A brief list of them appears at the end of this chapter, among the selections recommended for further reading.

If you are interested in an artifact but unsure about its authenticity, consult an art historian who is expert in that particular field. To determine the object's current market value, get an estimate or an opinion from a reputable appraiser.

Museum people, for the most part, do not make monetary appraisals of artifacts on a free-lance basis for people outside the museum. For one thing, that involves a fundamental issue of professional ethics and legal liability; also, administrative policy at many museums forbids staff members to assign monetary value to any object, except for notation in the museum's own records. And, since museum people do not usually make extensive knowledge of over-all pricing and price fluctuations a first priority, they do not ordinarily accumulate the amount of reliable, precise information needed to keep up with current pricing generally.

Appraisers of antiques and artifacts, on the other hand, are specialists, professionals, with detailed knowledge about current prices of such objects. On request, they will exchange an informed opinion about an object's monetary worth for a nominal fee or for a percentage of the object's market value. They are impartial outsiders, and their comments and opinions are usually worth the money they charge for the information they provide.

Other Points To Consider before Buying

In addition to an object's authenticity and market value, there are other questions that should be considered before one accepts a piece: What is the physical condition of the object? Is there enough of the artifact left to justify its acceptance, and what would be the approximate cost of its repair or conservation? Is its value historical, aesthetic, or spiritual? Is the piece really germane to the purposes of your collection?

Do the worn places on the item appear in logical areas? Has the piece been "upgraded" by additions not germane to its period or type? One should expect to find signs of wear on old objects, but there should be no intrusions on the normal accumulation of old scratches and abrasions. If paint, glaze, or other decorations appear to have been applied

Fig. 1.1, Fig. 1.2, and Fig. 1.3. Although the platter and its decoration shown in full in Fig. 1.1 may appear to be old, genuine, and "all of a piece," careful examination proves otherwise: a close-up of the eagle's claw and left wing tip makes obvious the fact that the eagle decoration was applied over scratches and crazing in the original glaze. The platter is old, but the decoration is not.

over some good indications of age, then you have found a recently decorated antique piece. If engraved lines on wood, horn, ivory, or metal interrupt old scratches and worn patches, then the engraving was done recently—and carefully polished after placement, so as not to appear new. Sometimes a barely discernible difference in materials used will call attention to improper repairs, or perhaps a look at a questionable area under ultraviolet light will indicate that closer scrutiny is needed for unexplained differences in the appearance of the finish, or odd drips of glue, here and there.[1] Labels on furniture, signatures on some objects, and even hallmarks on silver may have been altered or added dishonestly, and any sign of that sort of activity always indicates the need for the closest possible examination.

We mentioned earlier that dating by nails and screws alone is not definitive, because they might have been used to make legitimate, necessary modern repairs to the piece; and handmade nails can still be

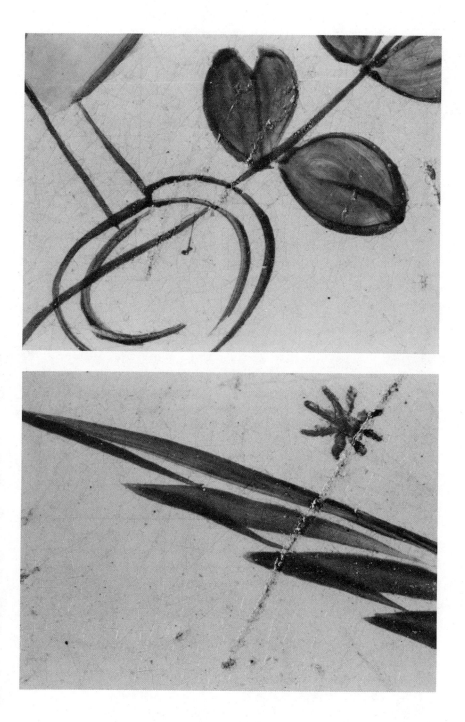

acquired or made on a home forge. At any event, always use a hand lens and look closely at all nails, screws, and hardware in any piece you are considering buying. (And see "Fastenings for Wooden Artifacts," below.) Check for evidence of corrosion, as well as accumulated dirt, varnish, and paint layers; and always look carefully at the scratches and scuffs in areas showing what should be normal wear from the object's appropriate use.

These kinds of evidence are generally of the negative sort, and may not necessarily reveal much that is significant about the object examined. They do raise questions, however, and invite further investigation to determine whether one is dealing with normal repairs to an object, or deliberate attempts to camouflage a bogus item as a genuine antique. Often, one must simply decide how much unexplained alteration—not always of the duplicitous kind—one can accept in an "authentic" object. The tale of Daniel Boone's knife, which has had one new blade and two new handles, is the extreme, but be prepared for the fact that very few antiques have reached the present day without being changed in structure or finish to some degree.

The information on the next few pages concerns tools and tool marks, hardware, firearms, and some materials of which historic objects are made. The data offered should serve as a limited introduction to *some* of the problems encountered in identification and may indicate *some* of the vast lore one needs to accumulate to know more about the materials in one's collection.

Lumber and Furniture

Genuinely old lumber can be distinguished from modern by the great variation in thickness of all old planks and studding. Modern two-by-four wall studs will not vary more than one-sixteenth of an inch in size, in lumber yards all across the country—the size is standarized and must be maintained within those limits by the people who produce and sell lumber. *Old* wall studding, however, was not made to conform to a strict, specific standard size—the size was approximate. Genuinely old wall studs, even those from a single building, will show a variety of measurements. Old lumber generally has clear grain, with few knots in it, and it has an even, cloudy, slightly opaque patina that modern oil stains cannot duplicate. Fakers, who sometimes use pieces of old boards to "improve" an existing antique, run into difficulty when sawing an old board, since the exposed wood will be a color different from the weathered surface. And since end-grain wood takes stain and dyes quite readily, it is almost impossible to "age" new saw marks to match the old surface.

Fig. 1.4. The wood of this "old" wooden molding plane is indeed old—but the worm holes that appear in it were made before the plane was shaped from it. They intrude into the working surfaces of the tool and make it clear that the piece is not genuine.

There are a variety of ways of "distressing" the wood used to make reproductions of historic objects, to make it look old— application of oil and chemical stains, the use of sulphur and ammonia vapors, pouring burning shellac on the wood's surface, beating the surface with tire chains, strewing on carpet tacks and beating them with a board, rasping edges for a worn effect, sand-blasting or charring and scraping the wood, making shotgun-pellet holes in it, burning it with acid, and so on—the list of methods is almost endless. The collector's only defense is sound scholarship, a sharp eye, and constant watchfulness.

Wood analysis can be helpful in answering *some* questions about wooden objects. Successful analysis can reveal not only the type of tree used to make the lumber involved, but possibly also where that type of tree commonly grew. Be sure to consult with those who will make the analysis *before* taking a sample of the wood; if the sample is not properly obtained, it may be useless. (For sources on wood analysis, see the bibliography at the end of this chapter.)

Fastenings for Wooden Artifacts

Wooden pins. Wooden pins or tree-nails—called "trunnels"—are often considered by the layman to be "old-timey," and the crude forerunners of metal nails. Wooden nails and dowels may indeed have come before metal ones, but they have also held their own, up to the present time, in house and furniture construction.

Traditional trunnels were irregular-looking and roughly octagonal in cross-section, rather than circular, as modern dowels are. Their irregular, octagonal shape was not accidental—they were made that way because, contrary to the old saying, square (or at least polygonal) pegs *do* fit better in round holes than round pegs do—for purposes of holding things together, anyway. Trunnels were made slightly oversize, so that when one was driven into a round hole of somewhat smaller diameter, the shoulders or edges of the trunnel bit into the wood of the hole and made a tight fit. These old fasteners were also made of tough, seasoned hardwood, and the wood they were driven into was usually greener than they. As the greener wood seasoned, it shrank slightly and held the trunnel even tighter. For that reason, pins and joints in old houses and well-made furniture did not need glue for a tight bond.

Metal nails and hardware. The earliest nails and hardware came to America from abroad, but by the mid-1600s, production of spikes, nails, brads, and tacks had begun in this country; and, by the beginnning of the 1800s, the first machine-made nails were being turned out.[2] Despite the distinctive characteristics of nails of different periods, a point must be made about using nails for establishing the date of an object. *While machine-made nails appeared at the end of the eighteenth century, handmade nails continued to be produced and used for specialized purposes. Therefore, the presence or absence of a certain type of nail is not itself definitive in dating a piece.* Machine-made *cut* nails—or "square nails"—are still being produced; and a careful examination, using a hand lens, if necessary, should reveal the difference between them and the earliest machine-made or handwrought nails. There remains the possibility that anyone could add genuine antique nails or modern handmade items to an object to lend it unwarranted appearance of authenticity.

Screws. While the principle of the screw has been known from antiquity, it was not until the 1600s that screws were used for fastenings. By the 1700s, screws were used with table hinges, clockworks, and firearms. The slots in these early screws were sometimes off-center and narrow, the threads generally coarse, and the small ends were flat. In the early nineteenth century, machine-made screws appeared, and by

1846, the modern, gimlet-pointed screw had followed. About the same time, modern nuts and bolts with standardized threads were introduced; but because many blacksmiths still had their old taps, hand-wrought bolts were made until quite recent times.

Bogus screws may be easy to detect, since the labor involved in making the handwrought kind makes their manufacture unprofitable; and "antiqued" modern screws are often easy to spot, because of their large, altered slots, saw and file marks, and smooth finishes. There is still no guarantee that old genuine fasteners might not be used for nefarious purposes, however.

Woodworking Tools and Tool Marks

Saws

The pit saw. The traditional two-man pit saw—an enormous hand saw used to cut logs lengthwise into planks—became obsolete in most areas of the United States soon after the earliest pioneering days, though its use persisted in England into the present century. To use it, one man stood above or on top of the log to be sawn, and his mate stood facing him, but below, in a pit, under the log. As the cut progressed, the pitman moved closer and closer to the topman, until the saw was almost vertical, whereupon both men stepped backward—away from each other—and the saw assumed an angle again. Thus, the pit saw ordinarily left a very distinctive mark: a series of fan-shaped scars along the side of a plank, each individually formed and quite unlike the mechanical regularity of a power saw.

The sash saw. The power-driven up-and-down saw or sash saw was the standard sawmill saw until the mid-nineteenth century. A type in which the blade was not under tension was called a "muley saw." The sash saw produced a regular pattern of parallel tooth marks, as every tooth went past the plank with every reciprocating stroke. Thus, the pattern of marks repeats itself about every half-inch or so down the plank.

The band saw. The modern band saw, an endless ribbon of edge-toothed steel, makes a similar mark. However, the "repeats" of the band saw pattern are several inches apart, because, due to the great length of the band saw blade, any damaged or odd tooth goes past the plank at widely spaced intervals.

The circular saw. The circular saw leaves a regular series of interlocking curved lines. Since it came into general use in this country about the time of the Civil War, circular saw marks can be used to help date a piece of sawed lumber. But beware: in some places, circular saws were used quite early, while in other places, the old-fashioned up-and-down (sash) saw was still in operation well toward the end of the nineteenth century. Even the pit saw continued to be used in England into the twentieth century, and a few shipyards in the United Sates clung to it, too. All these different kinds of saw marks, therefore, if they are viewed with care and discrimination, *are* good indicators of the time period in which a piece of lumber was made—but they *can* be deceptive.

Hand Planes

Hand-planed boards are characterized by a series of long, shallow, concave valleys along their length. Carpenters put a shallow curve on the fore-plane blades in order to eliminate the ridges or long scratches that resulted from using a square-edged blade to dress rough lumber. One can sometimes see this effect by looking at the wood's surface in a raking light, or feel it by running the fingers at right angles to the grain of the wood. However, the ridged effect is usually to be found only on drawer bottoms or the back sides of furniture, since it is only the first step in dressing a wood surface. *Finished* wood surfaces are often very smooth and free of tool marks.

Wood-Boring and Hewing Tools

Wood-boring tools had a variety of points and cutting edges, which have their own sequential development. Various boring tools were used for making holes of different sizes and depths in wood; and different types of tools were also selected according to the hardness of the wood being worked on and whether one was boring across or straight into end grain.[3] Even if one studies the technology of these tools, it is usually difficult to find an accessible bored hole in a test object and then to examine the bottom of that hole to determine the kind of tool that formed it. Nevertheless, if the evidence is available, by direct inspection or X-ray, it may prove useful in dating a piece.

Axe, broadaxe, and adze marks and the study of which tool was used when, and how, comprise another entire field beyond the scope of this discussion. However, there is one bit of popular lore about adze marks that should be suppressed. People sometimes exclaim in delight at "crude adze marks" found on old beams that have been exposed inadvertently—or sometimes purposefully, with the intent of "earlying up" a house. *Timbers that were meant to be hidden were usually only roughly dressed, square, with a broadaxe, since the tool marks on them would be covered*

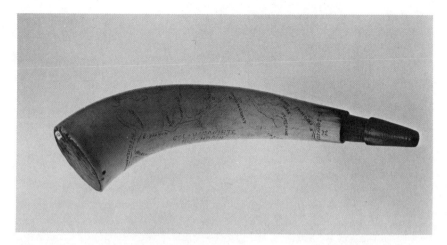

Fig. 1.5. Lettering styles and the type of cattle horn used to make this fraudulent powder horn are inconsistent with the date inscribed on it. Wear marks on it are not natural, and occasionally the inscription goes through old scratches in the surface.

over with plaster or paneling. But timbers that were to be exposed were frequently dressed with an adze, for a smooth surface: the adze is a finishing tool and cannot easily be used to remove much stock, let alone produce the gouged appearance that is popular today. Our ancestors did not *want* a rough-hewn effect; they wanted their homes to look as smoothly finished as possible. Old timbers that were meant to be exposed were often so smooth one would think they had been planed.

Firearms and Powderhorns

Unless you are a real expert on firearms and their accessories, do not spend good money for these items unless you can get a money-back guarantee or a clear understanding of the conditions under which the item has been sold. There is a tremendous market for firearms and their accounterments; unfortunately, there is an equally tremendous number of people toggling together old odds and ends and "improving" existing legitimate pieces with new engravings and false signatures. It has been said that if all of "Pancho Villa's pistols" in private collections were brought together in one place, there would be enough firearms there to equip the entire Mexican army.

Reputable arms dealers charge a tidy price for their goods; but most of them sell on an "examination-and-return-if-unsuitable" basis: the buyer may pay for the piece and take it with him, to examine for a specified number of days, and may return it for refund if he wishes, so long as the return is made within the specified time.

Engraved powderhorns and scrimshaw sell for quite high prices, by any standard. Remember, however, that new whale's teeth are still to be found, and cow horns are easily purchased; and a good engraver with no scruples can deliver almost any scene one may order. Be wary, therefore, of these small artifacts, and consult experts before you buy. You can make up money lost on a bad bargain, but it takes a long time to get over the sense of chagrin one feels about mistakes in judgment that leave one badly stung.

If you *should* find that you have bought a fake, do not display it with historical objects—do not make yourself party to falsehood. It may seem difficult not to display such a piece, especially if it is so well made as to escape detection as a fraud, early on—and especially also if you have paid good money for it. Making mistakes is human, however; and admitting and learning from that is one of the marks of a professional. And there is this footnote to such an experience: there is today a growing interest, in some circles, in collecting known fakes, so you might be able to recoup your financial loss by selling your bogus acquisition to an informed and willing purchaser.

NOTES

1. Harold L. Peterson, *How Do You Know It's Old?* (New York: Charles Scribner's Sons, 1975), pp. 10–14, 68–73.
2. Lee H. Nelson, *Nail Chronology as an Aid to Dating Old Buildings,* Technical Leaflet 48 (Nashville: The Amercian Association for State and Local History, 1968).
3. R. A. Salaman, *Dictionary of Tools Used in the Woodworking and Allied Trades, c. 1700–1970* (New York: Charles Scribner's Sons, 1980).

SUGGESTED READING

The following brief list of books represents general discussions of the identification and preservation of some kinds of artifacts important to collectors. This list is only a beginning point for research, and the curator or collector is urged to make his own list as he goes along.

Bullock, Orin M., Jr. *The Restoration Manual: An Illustrated Guide to the Preservation and Restoration of Old Buildings.* Norwalk, Conn.: Silvermine Publishers, 1966.

The hows, ifs, whats, and whys of restoring historical buildings. Heavily illustrated. Chapters on "The Architect," development of programs, selecting the period to be restored, historical research, execution of restoration, specifications, postrestoration maintenance; bibliography, glossary, and appendixes with notes on restoration of masonry, heating, etc. This book is a basic part of the library of anyone interested in this field.

Cescinsky, Herbert. *The Gentle Art of Faking Furniture*. New York: Dover Publications, 1968. Deals predominantly with fine English and Continental pieces, but contains much valuable specific advice and has philosophical approach to knowing furniture.

Chronicles of the Early American Industries Association. Bound reprints of the first twenty-five years of the *Chronicle* are available, as are other back issues and a lending library; these are some of the members' services of EAIA, c/o John S. Kebabian, Washington Mt. Road, Becket, Massachusetts 01223.

Comstock, Helen, ed. *Concise Encyclopedia of American Antiques*. New York: Hawthorn Books, 1965. Exemplary of the general books on antiques, this reference should help one begin to identify many sorts of objects; each section concludes with a list of books for further reading.

Keck, Caroline K. *A Handbook on the Care of Paintings*. Nashville, Tenn.: The American Association for State and Local History, 1965.

Mayer, Ralph. *Dictionary of Art Terms and Techniques*. New York: Thomas Y. Crowell Company, 1969. One of the most helpful references of its type; giving attention to materials, tools, and processes of the arts.

Mayhew, Edgar de N., and Minor Myers, Jr. *A Documentary History of American Interiors from the Colonial Era to 1915*. New York: Charles Scribner's Sons, 1980. Concise narrative and documentary evidence about floor coverings, furnishings, and household objects of all kinds.

Mercer, Henry C. *Ancient Carpenter's Tools*. 3rd ed. Doylestown, Penn.: Bucks County Historical Society, 1960. **Note:** The Bucks County Historical Society also puts out a reprint of one of Mercer's early monographs, on the dating of old houses, which contains a section on nails, hinges, etc.

Noel Hume, Ivor. *Martin's Hundred*. New York: Alfred A. Knopf, 1982. A detailed but entertaining account of historical archaeology at Carter's Grove in Virginia; fascinating insight into the methods of archaeology, historical research, and conservation.

Peterson, Harold L. *How Do You Know It's Old?* New York: Charles Scribner's Sons, 1975. Comprehensive introduction to looking at objects with a critical eye; attention in particular to signs of age, indications of alterations or new materials.

Rath, Frederick L., Jr., and Merrilyn Rogers O'Connell, eds. *Bibliography on Historical Organization Practices: Vol. 2, Conservation of Collections*. Nashville: American Association for State and Local History, 1977.

_____. *Bibliography on Historical Organization Practices: Vol. 4, Documentation of Collections*. Nashville: American Association for State and Local History, 1979.

The works in this series are extremely helpful for getting started in research or background information; large numbers of resources are listed by subject area, making it simpler for one to organize the search for further readings.

Salaman, R. A. *Dictionary of Tools Used in the Woodworking and Allied Trades, c. 1700–1970.* New York: Charles Scribner's Sons, 1980.
Probably the most comprehensive reference of its kind, encompassing British and American tools of the period, though some associated trades may not be found on the author's list.

Seale, William. *Recreating the Historic House Interior.* Nashville: The American Association for State and Local History, 1979.
A conscientious guide to the documentation and preparation of architectural elements, furnishings, and objects in historic buildings.

Studies in Conservation, Abstracts, IIC News. Published periodically by the International Institute for Conservation of Historic and Artistic Works, 608 Grand Bldgs., Trafalgar Square, London, WC 2N, 5HN, England.

Underwater Archaeology: A Nascent Discipline. Paris: UNESCO, 1972.
Descriptions of numerous sites, various methods and techniques by a large group of authors; an excellent introduction to the subject.

WOOD ANALYSIS

Forest Products Laboratory, Center for Wood Anatomy, Madison, Wisconsin.
Provides analysis of wood samples at no charge.

Michael R. Palmer, Wood Anatomist, Wood Analysis Laboratory, Winterthur Museum, Winterthur, Delaware.
Analysis of wood samples. Fee for each sample.

2

Controlled Environment Vital for Collections' Conservation

Proper control of the environment in which a collection is kept is one of the most important conservation measures collectors may take to slow down deterioration of artifacts.

Several disparate factors interact to influence the collection environment. Major components are temperature, humidity, lighting, atmospheric cleanliness, and—odd though it may seem—simple good housekeeping.

Less critical environmental factors that some artifacts may need protection from include inappropriate or poorly constructed display cases; some kinds of glues, paints, or fabrics used to make repairs; some types of carpets and carpet backings, and various kinds of adhesives used to anchor them in place; some pest control substances and their method of application; and the kinds of cleaning materials—and methods—used throughout the main building, as well as those used on the artifact itself, its case, or the room in which it is housed.

Temperature and Humidity

Temperature and humidity are prominent among the major factors that can cause serious damage to artifacts. They are interacting and unavoidable, and collectors often feel that they must be the first environmental problems dealt with for the safety of a collection.

Effects of temperature/humidity fluctuations. Ideally, for artifacts, temperature and humidity levels should vary as little as possible, the year round. Sudden and frequent fluctuations in levels of temperature and humidity safe for artifacts can cause serious damage throughout a collection. Even gradually escalating changes caused by mechanical breakdowns or improper adjustment of controls can be damaging if not soon corrected. Poor maintenance or undetected malfunctioning of control mechanisms can, within a fairly short time, allow damaging build-ups of

19

extreme heat or extreme dryness, or too little heat and too much moisture, or combinations of those conditions—all of them bad for artifacts.

Periodic, rapid, or long-term fluctuations in relative humidity, for example, from extremes of 15 percent in winter up to 80 percent in summer, as part of a daily or seasonal cycle, lead to sweating—condensation of moisture—on metal objects or hard surfaces. In such an environment, the paint layers on objects covered by several applications of paint begin to flake and crack. So do wood veneers and marquetry work. And the alternate raising and lowering of the amount of moisture in the air causes stress in wooden objects and furniture, as the differences in the moisture levels cause repeated expansion and contraction of the wood.

Heat and Moisture Combinations

High heat, low humidity. Air too hot and too dry causes brittleness in objects made of paper and leather and weakens the fibers in textiles. Wooden objects react to it by shrinking and checking. As shrinking occurs, frames and joints of wooden furniture tend to grow loose, come open, and sometimes pull apart. Paintings made on wooden panels "cup" or warp, and may crack. Inadvertent placement of some objects too near such potential sources of heat as incandescent light fixtures, radiators, and vents or ducts for a central heating system can cause damage to those objects in an area otherwise considered safe for their storage.

Heat, high humidity, and stagnant air. Warmth and *high* humidity, combined with weak lighting or none, are an open invitation to the growth of bacteria. Mold, mildew, fungus, and dry rot flourish under those conditions, especially when any artifact of organic—and nutritive—material is available: paper objects are eaten up, or soon begin to show foxing and mold growth; starch pastes lose their strength and their holding power; leather weakens.

And when high humidity is combined with air stagnation, leather, wood, and textiles are all destroyed. Often, under these conditions, metallic corrosion is also accelerated, and some bacteria can attack metal.

High humidity. Although figures often given for high humidity may vary, one should not, as a rule, let the humidity level around artifacts go much above 65 percent. In air containing more than 65 percent humidity, mold growths form on organic materials, wooden objects swell, wood veneers may peel, oxidation of metals is increased, and—if industrial vapors or salt air are also present—deterioration of almost all materials is accelerated.

Recognizing the Enemy

In bringing temperature and humidity within safe bounds for your collection, it helps to be aware of what the terms mean, the way they work, and some of the methods for controlling them.

Temperature, of course, is the degree of hotness or coldness in anything—a body, an engine, a planet, the atmosphere—measured on any of several arbitrary scales, usually a thermometer, usually either Fahrenheit or Centigrade (Celsius).[1] The temperature of the surrounding atmosphere, whatever its degree of hotness or coldness, affects and interacts steadily with the amount of moisture in the atmosphere, which is where humidity comes in.

Humidity has to do with the moisture content of the atmosphere, although there are more ways of considering the amounts of it present than is true of temperature. In addition to *high humidity* (lots of moisture in the air) and *low humidity* (less of it), there are *absolute humidity, relative humidity,* and *specific humidity,* all having to do with different ways of measuring the amount of water vapor in the atmosphere.

Specific humidity does not apply here; nor does absolute humidity, except in its bearing on relative humidity. Relative humidity is what the weather forecasters name as chief villain on especially muggy, steamy days—and relative humidity is the kind of humidity that collectors must always be concerned about.

Absolute humidity is the amount of water vapor in a given volume of air. *Relative humidity*—abbreviated RH and usually expressed as a percentage—is the relationship between absolute humidity (the amount of water vapor you would find in a given volume of air if you measured it at this moment) and the maximum amount of water vapor it would take to saturate that volume of air (produce 100 percent RH) at the same temperature and air pressure. Relative humidity is usually what is meant when the word *humidity* is used alone.[2]

How they work. The higher the temperature in an enclosed space, the more water vapor the volume of air in that space can hold. Thus, when the temperature in a room drops, the air in that room is capable of holding less moisture in suspension, and the moisture present will condense on surrounding nonporous materials like metal and glass, or it will be absorbed by porous materials.

On the other hand, warming air with a low relative humidity will pick up moisture from surrounding furniture, nasal membranes, or any other moisture-containing material within the area. That is why, in winter, with hot, dry, furnace air circulating, there is a general tendency for furniture, prints, and human beings to dry out.

It may seem that dry conditions cause the most damage to materials such as wood, but over-moist conditions can also produce compression and distortion of wood and create a further extreme from the dry part of the usual seasonal cycle.

Ideal relative humidity. A relative humidity level of 55 percent represents the ideal for best protection of woodenware, leather, and parchment. If 55 percent humidity is not attainable, the acceptable range falls within not less than 45 percent and not more than 60 percent, unless the local climate is drier than that range.[3]

A dry local climate can be most beneficial to the preservation of artifacts, although some materials are likely to become embrittled, under such conditions. There is generally no need to add humidity to the air in arid areas, but one must still attempt to keep the humidity level steady; a jump in relative humidity during a rainy time could cause great damage to sensitive objects.[4]

Whatever your relative humidity is, within the 45-to-60-percent range, *the important thing is to maintain it with as little daily or seasonal fluctuation as possible.* In air with *less than 40 percent RH,* static electricity builds up; paper and some kinds of fabric stick together; removal of dust and lint becomes a bigger problem than usual; and organic materials dry out. Conversely, air holding *more than 65 percent RH* encourages mold growth.

While 55 percent RH represents the ideal, for artifacts, it is usually difficult to achieve that level in old buildings, except at great cost. In colder climates, when there is tremendous contrast between outdoor and indoor temperatures during winter months, the recommended indoor relative humidity will cause walls to sweat and ice to form on the inner side of windows in any but the best-sealed, best-insulated buildings. Condensation occurs as the warmer, moister indoor air meets and is chilled by walls and windowpanes made cold by outside air. For that reason, it may be practical, under those circumstances, to maintain a higher relative humidity *only* in specific gallery or storage areas, by means of portable humidifiers.

However, since the energy crisis has brought about greater awareness of the need to conserve energy—reflected in enormously increased costs for heating and cooling—the winter temperature of most buildings is now kept much lower than it once was. Whatever human occupants may feel under such temperature reductions, artifacts will likely benefit from the cooler buildings. For example, a relative humidity of 40 percent at 20 degrees Centigrade (68 degrees Fahrenheit) would be produced by the same *amount* of water vapor in the air as would give only 27 percent RH at 25 degrees Centigrade (72 degrees Fahrenheit).

Measuring relative humidity. The most common device for measuring relative humidity is the humidity indicator attached to temperature- and moisture-measuring devices that can be placed on desks or walls. Such sets usually contain a thermometer and a barometer, in addition to the humidity indicator. While the first two instruments may be accurate enough, the humidity device is often incorrect by 15 percent or more.

Other—and cheaper—devices of this type are cardboard humidity indicators containing cobalt salts that change color in response to changes in relative humidity. These gadgets have roughly the same questionable accuracy as the relative humidity indicators on desk or wall devices.

There are, however two instruments that are not only accurate, but are also relatively inexpensive: the wet-bulb thermometer and the sling psychrometer. With both, one takes the comparative reading between the dry and the wet thermometers, consults a sliding-chart rule, and reads off the RH percentage.

An *aspirated psychrometer*—made with a tiny fan to blow across the wet-bulb thermometer—is somewhat expensive, but it provides quick, accurate readings, without the need of whirling a sling psychrometer about.

For a continuous record of humidity levels, a *recording hygrometer* is necessary. Although it is rather expensive, this device will reveal changes in RH over night-time hours and on weekends and holidays, as well as rises and falls in RH with changing weather conditions that might otherwise not be noticed. All these measuring devices are available from instrument companies and scientific supply houses.

Devices for Controlling Humidity

If your budget includes plans for a new building or renovation for an old one, then of course an air conditioning system with all the necessary controls is the ideal arrangement for controlling temperature and humidity for your collection. It should be noted, however, that the cost and complexity of installing air conditioning in an *existing* building, particularly an old one, makes that approach impractical in many situations. Nevertheless, with all the current choices in equipment for controlling indoor climate, there may just be a system that will work in your building. Consult with an engineer before you give up the idea.

Whatever approach you choose, always be sure that you know the rating or capacity of any humidifier you may use. In general, the capacity of any uncontrolled humidifier should be low, in order to prevent too much of a good thing. By the same token, the capacity of a portable *dehumidifier* must be large enough for the task at hand, to keep RH below 65 percent.

In most instances, portable humidifiers can provide satisfactory control for RH in confined areas or even in fairly large spaces. Either evaporative humidifiers or those of the spray type can be used. Remember, however, that distilled water must be used in spray-type units—plain tap water contains dissolved mineral salts that a spray unit can deposit all over a room.

Inexpensive steam humidifiers are usually made without a control mechanism, and they can send out condensing water droplets like a small rain storm in a room that is becoming too humid.

Evaporative humidifiers become less efficient as the humidity rises, providing a natural safety device.

If the summers in your area are humid, then *dehumidifying* units can be used, and the water that they condense can be bottled and safely used for the winter humidifying units. Neither humidifiers nor dehumidifiers, however, can do their best work in rooms with a great many windows or in areas where there are a great many people moving in and out. Under those circumstances, several units would be needed. For small areas, such as closed cases, humidity control may be gained through use of silica gel or other materials conditioned to a certain humidity level and installed in a hidden part of the case.[5]

One of the most important elements to consider, in planning for humidity control, is proper maintenance of the system to be used. Any system should be monitored and checked daily, but *the portable units must be emptied of condensate or filled with humidifying water every day, including weekends and holidays.* If constant care is not given portable units, wild variations in humidity will result whenever the machines shut down.

A final note about portable units, or zoned built-in climate control: these systems can usually provide good control over a wide area, even if one unit should break down. *With large, central systems, a mechanical breakdown means the whole controlled area is affected.* Whatever your situation, be sure that problems in your system can be quickly remedied.

Air Pollution

Collectors of artifacts today must find ways to protect collections from the growing menace of atmospheric pollution, especially near industrial areas.

Smoke, steam, ash, soot, and dust puffed into the atmosphere today by our industrialized way of life carry powerful contaminants. The generation of power and heat, operation of machines for transportation, industrial processes, and the burning of solid wastes contribute noxious gases and minute particles of solid and liquid matter in increasingly dangerous concentrations.[6] In addition to being a constant danger to human life and health, these contaminants kill plants, tarnish silver, rust iron, eat away at stone buildings and statuary, and destroy increasing amounts of marine and animal wild life.

Some types of oil smoke, alone or in combination with water vapor, form sulfurous acid and sometimes "acid rain." So does the sulfur dioxide from coal smoke. These poisons also bleach paper, decay leather, erode buildings, cause metals to corrode, and are destructive to plant and aquatic life.

Hydrogen sulfide is another powerful contaminant compound often found in industrial environments. A flammable, poisonous gas with the characteristic odor of rotten eggs, hydrogen sulfide blackens white lead (formerly a common ingredient in paint); combined with moisture and ozone, this gas forms a destructive acid that attacks both organic and inorganic materials.[7]

Soot particles and dust in the atmosphere are not only gritty and dirty, in themselves, but they form nuclei for the condensation or absorption of moisture and promote increased deterioration. Dew, a weak carbonic acid solution, eats away at limestone and concrete, bleaches organic materials, forms a focusing lens for the sun's rays to destroy paint film, and speeds up oxidation of metal. Sea air contains moisture plus salts that bleach paint and organic materials and corrode metals.

Most of these chemicals work their way *inside* buildings, as well as causing problems outdoors.

Combating Air Pollution

For collections in an industrial area, there is no way to provide clean air, short of an enclosed air conditioning and filtering system. Be certain to avoid electronic precipitator filters, which are very efficient, but tend to emit ozone, a powerful oxidizer.[8] Dry filters of various kinds, including activated charcoal units, can do an excellent job, but the type and combination of filters used should be based upon expert advice. In the absence of such a system, artifacts in such areas should be stored in closed containers or protective bags.

Fabric such as unbleached muslin can be used for such protective storage. It will keep off dust and allow for some circulation of air. Polyethylene bags can also be used for storage; but one should be wary of them, because there is always the possibility of moisture condensation inside a tightly sealed polyethylene bag. If these bags *are* used, take the precaution of not sealing them completely and use an inner wrapping of paper or fabric as an additional safety measure against the possibility of moisture condensation on the inside of the plastic.

Exhibit cases should be sealed against dust and dirt; and, if possible, the air inside them should be made to circulate through a filter screen. Change or clean air conditioning or heating filters regularly. Periodically, do a thorough cleaning and vacuuming of all areas to reduce dirt before it settles on and bonds itself to collection objects. *Dusting and vacuuming should be done every day, if at all possible.* Good housekeeping—an endless chore—is still one of the most important facets of good artifact care.

Proper Lighting for Artifacts

The human eye has a tremendous range of accommodation. It can attain reasonable comfort in the full glare of sunshine, or it can adjust—automatically—to provide the keenness of vision one needs to pick a path across an unfamiliar field by starlight.

Twentieth-century technology has made brilliant artificial lighting readily available, and most of us have become so accustomed to it that we tend to expect constant high levels of illumination—even regard it as necessary. Consequently, high levels of candlepower are routinely used to illuminate the buildings where we live and work and entertain ourselves, although the human eye really does not need all that light—and may develop symptoms of fatigue when steadily subjected to too much of it.

We have also fallen into the habit of thinking that exhibitions of artifacts should be arranged under powerful, highly dramatic lighting that provides brilliant over-all illumination and strong, showy contrasts. Such high concentrations of light can not only give the viewer visual fatigue—they can be detrimental to many kinds of artifacts, as well.

The over-all light level in all buildings housing artifacts should be carefully controlled, therefore, because visible light does have damaging effects,[9] and continued exposure to it in any form—sunlight, incandescent, or fluorescent—can work permanent harm on artifacts. The damage is caused by the concentrated heat and the ultraviolet rays that those light sources produce.

Not only must the amount—or intensity—of light admitted to the building be considered, but the *duration,* or the cumulative amount of time that artifacts are exposed to light will directly relate to the damage done to sensitive objects. Several months of exposure to a very low light level may have the same effect as a couple of days' bathing in direct sunlight. Damage from light is always cumulative;[10] and it should be stressed that its effects on artifacts cannot be reversed by subsequent storage in darkness.

Therefore, proper lighting, not only from a dramatic point of view, but with regard to the safety of the artifacts involved, must be an important consideration in environmental planning for a collection.

The following materials are especially subject to damage from light:

Cellulose. Cellulose is present in wood, paper, and some textiles. It is especially sensitive to light when inks or dyes are used on the materials it helps to form.

Organic materials. Included in this category are such substances as leather, silk, wool, bone, ivory, and similar products often found in artifacts.

Paint pigments and coatings and various painting media. Natural and synthetic resins and oils are quite sensitive to light, as are the pigments used in watercolors. Virtually all *colors* are likely to fade under continued exposure to light.

Heat Build-up from Light

Heat dries and embrittles many kinds of objects. Heat damage can result from sunlight pouring in through unprotected window areas in walls that catch the sun's rays. Incandescent spotlights in unventilated display cases generate tremendous heat. High-intensity photofloods placed too close to artifacts and left burning for long periods of time while the photographer adjusts other equipment are a special hazard to oil paintings.

In some instances, heat damage can be caused by the relatively cooler-burning fluorescent fixtures. Though fluorescent tubes themselves generate little heat, the ballasts used to stabilize the current in their circuitry operate at quite warm temperatures, and if these ballasts are placed with the fluorescent tubes, inside the exhibit case, they can cause enough heat build-up inside the case to damage a good many kinds of artifacts.

Arranging exhibit case lighting that will be outside the case may be a bit complicated, at first, but that approach can simplify design of the case itself and eliminate the hazard of too much heat build-up within the case.

Whether you plan to use incandescent or fluorescent lighting in preparing exhibits and display cases, it is wise to use the lowest wattage practical for adequate illumination and to provide some ventilation at the tops of all the cases, if possible.

The Ultraviolet Light Hazard

Most light sources emit some ultraviolet light rays,[11] but both sunshine and fluorescent tubes are strong ultraviolet sources. Whether from the sun or the tube, ultraviolet light—often abbreviated to UV—combined with heat or humidity speeds up oxidation and deterioration of many organic materials, causing them to bleach and harden and, in some instances, to undergo some deformation. Too much UV fades and embrittles paper, textiles, dyes, and varnishes; it also causes discoloration and increasing insolubility in varnishes and oils. Watercolors and some oil colors fade badly under it; and objects made of wood may either darken or bleach out.

Sunlight as a UV source. Since sunlight carries the double hazard of both heat build-up and ultraviolet rays, its presence in any building housing artifacts must be carefully controlled whenever possible.

Various types of window glass made by the major glass companies will modify the amounts of heat, light, and ultraviolet energy from sunlight admitted through windows.[12] All of these types of glass are somewhat expensive, but they may be a practical solution, if display space with a southern exposure must be used.

Sheets of rigid plastic, film window shades, or film that can be stuck to window surfaces may be found in a vast array of reflecting qualities, colors, and filtering capabilities. The heavier filtering sheets may be expected to maintain their protective qualities the longest.

Simpler solutions, such as shutters, draperies, or venetian blinds, are also effective, although they bar the entry of all *visible* light, as well as that of the ultraviolet rays.

Fluorescents as a UV source. There are fluorescent tubes made that emit little or no ultraviolet energy, but they are much more expensive than the ordinary lamps that are such rich sources of UV.[13] If budget prob-

Fig. 2.1. Acrylic sheet for filtering ultraviolet light can be placed easily and inconspicuously on existing windows.

lems make these "low UV" tubes an impractical solution to the ultraviolet problem, reasonably priced plastic sleeves can be obtained to slip over any fluorescent tube and substantially reduce its ultraviolet emanations. These plastic sleeves can cost as little as a dollar and some cents for a four-foot tube, and they are made in both rigid and flexible styles. The flexible sleeve can be installed while the tubes are in place. The thicker filters are said to maintain their protective qualities for at least ten years, while those of thinner material should be checked after five years of use.

Measuring Light Levels: How Much Are You Using?

So how does one know whether the artifacts in a collection are being exposed to more light than is good for them? One measures the amount of light being used where the objects are housed.

Although measuring the light in your building may at first seem an excessively difficult, complicated process, it really is relatively simple,

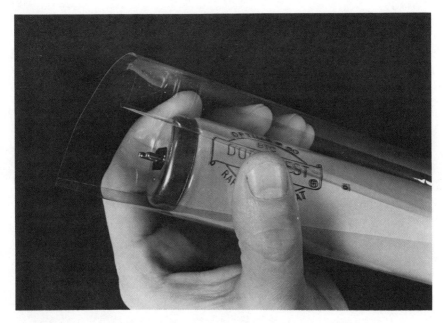

Fig. 2.2. Ultraviolet filter sleeves, either rigid or flexible, should be placed on fluorescent tubes to reduce the amount of fading, darkening, or other damage UV radiation can bring about in artifacts.

provided one has access to a photometer or a photographic light meter that is sensitive to low light levels.

Note that some inexpensive light meters have a scale that starts at about ten footcandles, which is too high for some light-sensitive materials.

Once light levels in the building have been checked, it can be a relatively simple matter to adjust them as required—perhaps the substitution of a light bulb or a fluorescent tube of lower wattage than the ones in use, or the drawings of shades or curtains at times of day when the outside light is strongest may be enough. Once the procedure for obtaining the right light level is established, measuring the light level is not something that must be repeated often. An occasional check of the situation should be enough to keep things going as they should.

Safe light levels for various artifacts. Light levels for particularly light-sensitive materials—see those listed on page 27—should not be greater than *the low range*, which is *about five to eight footcandles*.

Most durable substances in those and other groups can withstand a level of illumination of ten to fifteen footcandles; and high levels of twenty to thirty footcandles may be used around such materials as stone and metals, which light does not cause to deteriorate.

The important first step in regulating light levels is to measure the illumination, to see whether a problem exists and, if so, how serious it may be.

Light-measuring instruments and procedures. Illumination can be measured with a photometer reading directly in footcandles (or *lux*, which are about one-tenth the intensity of footcandles; ten footcandles equal one hundred lux).

One can also use the kind of ordinary light meter used by photographers. These meters will require a simple conversion table. Begin by setting the meter to a film speed of ASA 400 and a shutter speed of 1/50 of a second. By comparing the indicated f-stops or lens openings on the meter, one can obtain all the light levels needed. The table below translates f-stops into foot-candles (fc.).

f/1 = 3fc.	f/2.8 = 25fc.
f/1.4 = 6fc.	f/4 = 50fc.
f/2 = 12fc.	f/5.6 = 100fc.

Checking UV levels. Specialized meters are available to gauge the amount of ultraviolet light falling on a surface, but their high cost makes them an impractical investment for most small museums or private collectors with modest budgets. As with the measurement of footcandles, however, it does not take long, with the proper equipment, to take a reading of ultraviolet rays emitted by a light source and see whether a problem exists. You might be able to borrow a UV meter or persuade someone from a better-equipped museum or a utility company to come and measure UV levels for you. If you have unfiltered natural light or ordinary fluorescent light around artifacts, you may be certain that a substantial amount of ultraviolet energy is present. It might be wise to try to eliminate UV from obvious sources first, then measure to see whether you have accomplished that.

Staff Participation in Environmental Control

It cannot be stressed too often or too emphatically that total staff involvement is essential in maintaining an effectively controlled environment for any collection, large or small, public or private.

Staff people whose work involves frequent handling of the artifacts or routine moving about among them should be encouraged to report any evidence of change noticed in either collection objects or their environment.

It should be mentioned often, to all staff people, that properly maintained environmental control is vital to the safety of the collection, and that it is a part of everyone's responsibility.

And it may seem simplistic even to mention it, but it may be worthwhile to remind staff and volunteers, periodically, that temperature and humidity controls in buildings housing artifacts are there for the protection of the artifacts, rather than for the convenience and comfort of staff and visitors. In talking with newly hired, inexperienced personnel, stress the fact that temperature and humidity controls in all parts of the building—including offices, storerooms, and workrooms—are not to be adjusted for the personal comfort of those currently working in that area; nor should those controls be turned down or shut off after visiting hours, in well-meaning but misguided efforts to save money on electricity.

NOTES

1. *Webster's New World Dictionary,* 2nd ed., s.v. "temperature"; *Oxford American Dictionary,* s.v. "temperature"; *Webster's New International Dictionary,* 3rd ed., s.v. "temperature."
2. *Columbia Encyclopedia,* 4th ed., s.v. "humidity"; *Webster's New World Dictionary,* s.v. "humidity"; *Oxford American Dictionary,* s.v. "relative humidity."
3. Garry Thomson, *The Museum Environment,* pp. 85–89.
4. Thomson, *Museum Environment,* pp. 85–89.
5. Nathan Stolow, *Conservation Standards for Works of Art in Transit and on Exhibition,* pp. 85–88.
6. *Columbia Encyclopedia,* s.v. "air pollution."
7. Thomson, *Museum Environment,* pp. 124–154.
8. Thomson, *Museum Environment,* pp. 128–130, 142–144.
9. Thomson, *Museum Environment,* pp. 2–42.
10. Thomson, *Museum Environment,* pp. 2–42.
11. Thomson, *Museum Environment,* pp. 7–10, 163–171.
12. Pamela Kellman, "Laminated Architectural Glass: Materials for Protecting Cultural Properties."
13. Thomson, *Museum Environment,* pp. 7–10, 163–171.

SUGGESTED READING

Dersarkissian, M., and Mayda Goodberry. "Experiments with Non-Toxic Anti-Fungal Agents." *Studies in Conservation* 25 (February 1980): 28–36.

Edwards, Stephen R., et al. *Pest Control in Museums: A Status Report (1980).* Lawrence, Kansas: Association of Systematics Collections, 1981.

Guidelines for Saving Energy in Existing Buildings. Washington, D.C.: Federal Energy Administration, 1975.

Handbook of Museum Technology. New York: Research and Education Association, 1982.
A general but comprehensive survey, assembled from materials originated by the U.S. Department of the Interior.

Kellman, Pamela. "Laminated Architectural Glass: Materials for Protecting Cultural Properties." *Technology and Conservation Magazine* 5 (Fall 1980): 42–43.

The Organization of Museums: Practical Advice. Paris: The UNESCO Press, 1974.
Although written for museum workers, this book is filled with helpful suggestions for anyone dealing with large collections. Comments are backed up with examples and anecdotes from all over the world.

Stolow, Nathan. *Conservation Standards for Works of Art In Transit and on Exhibition.* Paris: United Nations Educational, Scientific and Cultural Organization, 1979.

Syracuse University Institute for Energy Research. *Energy Conservation in Museums.* Albany, N.Y.: New York State Energy Research and Development Authority, 1980.

Thomson, Garry. *The Museum Environment.* Woburn, Mass.: Butterworth, Inc., 1978.
Everything you could possibly want to know about the subject, and more.

3

Good Storage— and How To Keep It that Way

Both museum holdings and private collections may include artifacts ranging in size from those no bigger than hatpins to those as unwieldy as manure wagons, and their fragility may vary from that of delicate china figurines to that of cast-iron cannonballs. The fact that collections of artifacts are assembled in an effort to preserve them, however, means that all materials included in such collections should be given the best possible protective care and maintenance.

One element essential to such care and maintenance is a soundly equipped, well-kept storage system that provides protection and ready access to all items placed there.

Proper storage for artifacts is vital to their preservation—it should provide opportunities to guard the collection against various agents of destruction more easily than may be possible when the objects are on view. In a closed, confined space, it should be simpler to control changes in relative humidity, air pollution, vibration, light, insects and other pests, deleterious materials, and handling by humans. Not only is good storage a legal responsibility of museums—it is the cheapest, most effective technique for preserving the monetary and historical value of collections objects. Clearly, if mold growth, fading, breakage, and damage from harmful materials are not allowed to occur, expensive conservation measures for collections items may be appreciably reduced.

Unfortunately, in both museums and private collections, storage areas are often neglected, partly because they are not usually open to visitors and partly because their role in preserving a collection is often not given the high priority it should have.

A crowded, cluttered storage area can cause frustration for those who must work in it and damage to the objects housed there. A clean, uncluttered, well-organized storage area, given regular, proper maintenance, is a vital factor in the long-range survival of a historical collection.

Its function is to provide continuing, extended protection against environmental extremes, insect and animal pests, vandalism, burglary, or neglect through careless housekeeping.

It may be emphasizing the obvious, here, to mention it, but a distinction should be made—and strictly observed—between storage space for the office or workshop and that for the storage of items from the collection: sometimes budgeting may become so tight that what can begin as a bit of temporary intermixing of administrative storage with collection storage could grow into accepted practice, and that is not a good idea.

In addition to being planned to accommodate the physical dimensions of the objects it will house—whether they be hatpins or manure wagons—good storage space for artifacts should be equipped with furnishings suitable for the job and proper controls for maintaining the correct temperature, humidity, and light needed for the protection of those artifacts. And it should be kept as clean and as well-ventilated as its temperature and humidity are kept controlled—or as the budget will allow.

Portable humidifiers and dehumidifiers can often control humidity levels effectively. Either incandescent lights or fluorescents or a combination of the two can provide proper, adequate lighting for storage areas. If fluorescent lights are used, they should be shielded to lessen the danger of degradation to paper and textiles from the ultraviolet rays that they emit. Readily obtainable filters for fluorescent tubes can screen out their ultraviolet rays and eliminate that source of possible damage to stored artifacts. Plywood covers on the inner side of windows may improve security as well as help keep out damaging sunlight.

Furnishings for Storage Areas

Furnishings for storing collections of artifacts should be strong and adjustable and should include, from the beginning, a few sturdy tables on which to set objects that must be examined or sorted.

Storage equipment is of many types and materials. Among the best are steel sections that can be bolted together or assembled with special clips. Companies that sell storage equipment are listed in the yellow pages of the telephone directory, under general headings like "Materials Handling" or "Moving and Storage Equipment." Such companies stock a great variety of shelving, platforms, and bins. Most such furnishings are intended for industrial use, and they are more than adequate—they are excellent for storing historical objects; and most of them are easy to assemble in various configurations. Many large department stores also sell strong, inexpensive metal shelf units in various sizes.

When wooden framework or shelf decking is used, the wood should first be either sealed with urethane varnish or primed and painted with latex enamel. That is especially true if the wood has been poorly seasoned. Such wood may also contain fungicides, insecticides, or other materials that can be harmful to artifacts placed in contact with it.

If cabinets are being considered for storage of various items in a collection, one should assemble all the information obtainable and compare the merits of each type of cabinet that would be suitable. Determine the size and special features required in a unit that might fit your needs and ask the manufacturer whether such a cabinet is available. Manufacturers can provide just about anything a collector might need in the way of storage. Makers of laboratory furniture, including those listed in the "Suppliers" section of this book, carry museum storage cabinets.

Where fragile or unusually costly items are concerned, consider buying museum-quality storage cabinets, if money for them is at all available. Although such cabinets are expensive, they can provide security, and the storage conditions they present are hard to match. For example, textile cabinets with large, pull-out trays for flat storage and sealed doors for protection against dirt and insects might be obtainable. Other kinds of cabinets are designed to hold very heavy loads, or objects of particular shapes or sizes. If nothing else, a look at the specialized furnishings in manufacturers' catalogues could provide the germ of an idea for accomplishing the same sort of protective storage with homemade or salvaged equipment.

Proper use of storage furniture. Whatever the kind of storage equipment you use, you should eliminate from your storage area the common problems of trying to squeeze any single object into too small a space or of piling too many objects, large or small, one atop another in large, boxy spaces without enough partitions or shelves for proper separation and support. Such practices make large objects vulnerable to bending or breakage and allow small objects to become inaccessible, so that when one specific piece is needed from such a space, the one wanted is invariably at the bottom of the pile.

Fire and Water Hazards

While a fireproof storage area is ideal, if such space is available, fire hazards can still be minimized in old buildings by a few simple precautions. *DO NOT* smoke in a storage area. Do not store organic materials near heating pipes or radiators. Do not leave packing materials, cleaning rags, or oily cloths lying about. Remember also that objects such as old linens, woodenware, wax figurines, documents, and the like, are combustible, especially in the dry storage conditions of many museums. Place fire extinguishers of the proper class near storeroom exit doors and be sure that they are carefully and regularly inspected (see chapter 5, "Fire Protection").

Storage of photographic film may pose related fire-safety hazards. If you have old nitrate-based film that is starting to acquire an oily feel, you should dispose of it. Cellulose nitrate-based film not only decomposes—it can cause intense and extremely destructive fires if ignited from any source. Check carefully any stored film in your possession—you cannot afford to have such potential time bombs in your storage area; see Chapter 17, "Photographs," for more information about dealing with this problem.

Since water damage can be almost as destructive to an artifact collection as fire is, ask yourself these questions: Are vulnerable objects stored under leaky roofs or eaves? Are items stored near windows placed far enough away to escape rain damage if the windows are left open or if the glass is broken? Are overhead pipes carrying water, waste, or steam tight and in good condition? If objects are stored in the basement, are the lowest storage shelves in use well above known flood levels? Is there a sump pump in the basement? Even without flooding, does the humidity level in the basement rise above 65 percent during damp seasons? Unequivocal answers to those questions may indicate corrective measures that should be undertaken to protect your collection.

Good Housekeeping: A Preservation Essential

Regular, careful housekeeping and a general policy of making storage areas off limits to visitors can provide additional safety for collections objects in storage. However, the storage area should not suffer from. neglect simply because it is not constantly on view—that is especially important to remember when collections are housed in old buildings, where rats, mice, bats, squirrels, and insects can gain access more easily than they might in newer structures and may continue their depredations longer without being detected. Throughout all buildings housing artifacts, plain *good housekeeping* is essential to conservation procedures, and the temptation to neglect it in storage areas can result in irreparable damage to collection items. Artifacts left unattended for long intervals of time can accumulate layers of dirt and dust—and unnoticed damage from animal or insect pests. Nutrient materials—such as soap, wax, paper, glue, and excelsior—allowed to remain strewn about in storage areas are open invitations to such unwanted animal and insect visitors. Careful periodic store room checking and regular visits by a reliable pest-control service will help reduce the incidence of infestation by bug and animal pests. One cannot stress too much the necessity for keeping the storage area clean. That dull but necessary chore may not be as stimulating as working out display techniques or researching a restoration problem, but it *is* essential for the well-being of a collection.

Accessibility and Record-Keeping in Storage Areas

Artifact collections can be stored in an infinite variety of ways, depending on the size, nature, and number of the individual pieces involved. Keep in mind, however, that to be useful, objects in a collection must be readily accessible; and they must be accessible not just to a few staff members who may remember where they were put or who may be familiar with the record-keeping system for the collection. What that means is that space for storage should be planned for the best protective care of the kinds of objects that make up the collection and that a sound, workable, filing-and-finding system for those objects must be developed as a key to the location of those that remain in the collection and to the disposition of those that are no longer in your possession.[1]

Good record-keeping for collections of artifacts is essential, to keep track of your inventory; and a simplified identification-and-location file or listing is an integral part of such a system. Properly maintained, that will tell you whether your artifacts are on display or in storage, and in what area; out on loan, to whom, for how long; disposed of by sale, when, and to whom.

For articles in storage, a good simplified system of identification for objects held and well-planned storage-rack placement providing easy access to each are more practical than elaborate filing-and-finding systems that may prove cumbersome in practice. This is especially true if you employ part-time help who are not accustomed to your particular records system. To aid all staff people, both full-time and part-time, it is a good idea to post the identification-and-location list—alongside a map of the storage area—in all offices and storerooms.

A Caveat for the Curator: Beware the Artifact

A few additional words of caution should be noted, here, for the safety of the person in charge of any artifact collection. Any collection that deserves the name is likely to include some items—usually old things no longer in common use or no longer made—that may appear to be anything but dangerous. *Don't believe it:* the average historical collection usually contains any number of objects that can be lethal.

Old firearms and the accouterments that go with them come immediately to mind, but there are others, as well: old bottles and jars, old chemicals, old tools, old surgical instruments, and the time-honored "little black bags" that doctors used to carry on their rounds. Other dangerous examples include: glass "fire bomb" extinguishers that contain carbon tetrachloride; paint pigment powders that are composed of lead, mercury, or other unpleasant substances; curative water dispensers that have radioactive materials hidden inside to "revigorate" sick people.

Dust and dirt on objects or in building where you may evaluate a collection can contain moulds and spores that cause respiratory disorders. In such situations it is prudent to wear coveralls as well as eye, hand, and breathing protection (see Chapter 6, The Collections Workroom). Similar precautions should be taken when unpacking or cleaning dusty, dirty objects. Wash coveralls after each use to avoid spreading spores around. Problems can develop in obvious places, such as old farm buildings, but also less likely areas, such as a storeroom of books that were once damp and are now loaded with mould spores.

Medical artifacts. Anyone who is caring for a historical collection should be very careful about picking up broken glass, especially if the glass slivers are from the breakage of old medicine bottles or chemical bottles. The active ingredients of some old potions—potent enough, originally—may have been further distilled and intensified in strength over the years. Watch out for *all* sharp, splintery objects, and keep up your tetanus booster shots. Knives, saws, scissors, and other items from old medical kits may still be contaminated with living micro-organisms, and many of these kits still carry such active toxic substances as strychnine, opium, and morphine.

Always look for the product name usually given on any old bottle containing medicine or chemicals before you open one and begin pouring out the contents—don't find out by accident that the original fluid found in a bottle labeled "Oil of Vitriol" is the same thing as sulfuric acid, or that antique "Aqua Fortis" is still the same thing as nitric acid. If bottles have no labels, proceed carefully indeed in checking and opening each one, and be very sure to dispose of both content and container correctly. A pharmaceutical chemist can advise you about special hazards to watch for; or, if a state of emergency develops, get in touch with a medical technician at your local hospital. If such a person doesn't have the necessary information at hand, he or she can at least provide the telephone number of someone who will have it.

Safe placement in storage. In equipping your storage area, do not install shelves too high for the sort of artifacts they are to support, or it will be impossible to get objects down off them safely. In moving items from the collection into or out of the storage area, do not, ever, put any heavy or sharp-pointed object, or one round enough to roll off, on storage shelves at eye-level or above your head. Some storage shelves—the ones needed to support especially delicate or sensitive objects—should be padded, to minimize breakage; and some others should have low protective rails or "lips" to keep objects from rolling or vibrating off. Thin expanded polyethylene foam makes a handy shelf-liner for fragile objects.

Firearms and explosives. Powder flasks and powder horns in a collection may still contain black powder as potent today as it was the day it was made. And there is a good chance that many newly acquired muzzleloaders may still have live powder charges in them.

To determine whether a muzzleloader does still contain a charge, simply—and carefully—insert a thin dowel, as you would a ramrod, inside the gun barrel, to measure the depth of the bore. Next, remove the dowel and hold the measured area along the outside of the barrel. If the tip of the measure does not reach all the way to the ignition hole or nipple, then something—perhaps a live charge—is in the barrel.

Don't try to remove it, yourself—let an experienced person draw the charge, and don't fiddle with the trigger or hammer, lest you shoot a hole through a colleague.

Colleagues at military museums can often offer advice about identification of weapons and ordnance. That basic information should help you decide whether you have a real bomb on your hands.

An appalling number of so-called cannonballs—actually spherical shells—grenades, and rockets, dating from the Civil War period right up to the present, wind up in museums and private collections, still live and fused. *Do not, on any account, tinker with any of them.* If you suspect that a shell is live, *do not try to dispose of it by dropping it into the nearest body of water:* it might still be found, by someone else, and create new dangers to other people. Call your local police agencies, instead, to find out whether they have a bomb squad that can handle such problems; if they haven't, telephone the nearest military base and ask for assistance from someone there with specific ordnance training in bomb disposal. The experts may suggest that some of your objects should be disposed of, rather than defused. Don't demur; even if the object in question is one of your most highly prized souvenirs, *take their advice and dispose of it,* as an object that is dangerous to anyone within its range.

NOTES

1. Dorothy H. Dudley, Irma B. Wilkinson, and others, *Museum Registration Methods* (Washington, D.C.: American Association of Museums, 1979), pp. 187–188.

SUGGESTED READING

Daifuku, Hiroshi. "Collections, Their Care and Storage." In *The Organization of Museums: Practical Advice.* Paris: The UNESCO Press, 1974.

Dudley, Dorothy H., Irma Wilkinson Bezold, and others. "Storage and Care of Objects." In *Museum Registration Methods.* Washington, D.C.: American Association of Museums, 1979.

Dunn, Walter S. *Storing Your Collections: Problems and Solutions.* Technical Leaflet No. 5. Nashville: The American Association for State and Local History, 1970.

Johnson, E. Verner, and Joanne C. Horhan. *Museum Collection Storage.* Paris: UNESCO, 1979. The best current treatment of storage methods for a great variety of materials. Includes many simple and low-cost structures.

Lanier, Mildred B. "Storage Facilities at Colonial Williamsburg." *Museum News* 45 (February 1967): 31–33.

Rowlison, Eric B. "Rules for Handling Works of Art." *Museum News* 53 (April 1975): 10–13.

4

Planning Security
for Building and Collection

P ublic interest in collecting antiques is growing more and more popular, these days; but that enthusiasm has produced one growing side effect of great concern to serious collectors: it attracts dishonest people as well as honest ones.

More and more people strongly interested in artifacts are visiting exhibits and displays, museums and dealers, and prices for genuine antiques are steadily rising. Human acquisitiveness being what it is, any place that contains a number of items believed to be of value—and portable—becomes a likely target for burglary.

Anyone who would like to keep a collection of artifacts intact, nowadays, must therefore protect it, not only from fire and flood and unsuitable environment, but also from the increasing danger of theft, vandalism, malicious mischief, and simple accident.

With few exceptions, private collectors, dealers in artifacts, and museums alike are vulnerable in some way to the persistent attentions of the professional thief; but many collections of modest scale fall victim to the kind of common thievery that can be accomplished fairly easily by even a watchful, resolute twelve-year-old with a good pocketknife or a dime-store screwdriver.

It is difficult—and costly—to take every measure now available to defend a collection against the determined professional thief; but most collectors can do quite a bit to improve security for their artifacts by reviewing and tightening security procedures and by reducing the more conspicuous opportunities for theft. A thorough, well-planned approach to security will accomplish more than will simple reliance on the latest gadget, and all elements of protection—obvious though they may seem—should be considered.[1]

Sometimes a collection of artifacts may seem to invite vandalism or burglary through the "open" nature of some types of displays or exhibits; by faulty or inadequate building security routines, casually observed;

or, sometimes, by inadequate training in security for staff personnel.

How many unguarded exits does your building have? Are windows in it left open overnight or when the building is empty? Is there easy access to the building from a dark alley? Such questions may seem unfair, because one cannot easily change the location of an existing building, nor can one, because of fire safety regulations, keep all doors in a building locked at all times. One can, however, list a few different approaches that *are* possible—and may be more practical in one's own situation.

Buildings and Grounds

It is axiomatic that buildings and grounds where valuable things are stored should be lighted well enough at night to deny potential burglars safe hiding places from which they might force a way inside; and there are now available quite a good selection of security light fixtures and equipment to make such lighting easily possible at modest cost. A reliable electrician or your utility company can advise you about solutions to outdoor lighting problems on your property. If your building has hidden angles near rear entrances or basement windows, floodlights properly adjusted can make those places much less appealing for illegal entry. Trees and shrubbery used to landscape your site should not be so thickly planted nor so close to the building that they provide good hiding for prowlers. During periods of repair, new construction, or painting and cleaning outside the building, don't leave ladders lying about outdoors to provide burglars easy access to second-story windows. All tools and equipment used in outdoor work at the site should be put away before workmen leave, to prevent making illegal entry easier for watchful thieves looking for such an opportunity.

Locks and Keys

All doors providing access to the building itself should be equipped with good deadbolt locks, and it is wise to limit distribution of the keys to those locks, issuing them to only those staff members who must enter and leave the building on official business when the doors are locked. Keep a record of the number of keys distributed and the names of their holders. The more keys there are in circulation, the greater are the chances for one's being lost. If that should happen, you will either need to meet the expense of having your locks changed, or live with the knowledge that anyone who finds the lost key will have ready access to your building and your collection.

It is a good idea to establish a certain routine to be followed in opening and closing the building each day, setting time and procedure for checking lights, fire or smoke alarm systems, and burglar alarms—if you have those aids—and for closing and locking all windows, inner doors that require it, and all doors that lead out of the building. Each person who has a key to the building should also be given a printed checklist of the routine to follow in securing the building after working hours.

Inside the building, keys to storage areas or to cases containing items of special value should also be limited to only those who need keys for routine work with the collection. And some system of communication is needed, so that when authorized personnel move an object from its customary place in a case or in storage, that move is reported and the object's new location is listed. That information will help the next careful person who notices the object's absence from its usual place not to report it to local police as missing or stolen.

New electronic "key card" lock systems offer better and more flexible security than mechanical systems in many cases. Cards can be programmed to open doors only at certain times, or on certain days, and lost cards can be easily excluded from the system. All activities can be recorded on paper, so that all comings and goings may be reviewed. Another very useful device is a magnetic lock that can hold fire exit doors shut unless the fire alarm is activated—note that fire exits should *never* be locked with a key. Although electronic systems are generally expensive, they should definitely be given due consideration in any review of security procedures and equipment.

Displays and Exhibits

Displays and exhibits should be set up without hidden corners or areas that guards cannot easily keep in view, if such arrangement is feasible. And when particularly valued small pieces from a collection are arranged for display—especially such vulnerable objects as early lighting devices, knives, firearms, jewelry, and primitive art—they should be placed, for safety, either in a glassed-in enclosure or well beyond arm's length of an acquisitive visitor. So-called psychological barriers, such as platforms or low rails, are not, as a rule, very effective deterrents to pilferage; they seem to be recognized as restraints only by people who wouldn't dream of touching or handling valuable artifacts, anyway.

Three simple collection safeguards—often considered routine essentials—include a daily checking of gallery items; placement of identifying

Fig. 4.1. To protect them from accidents, as well as from theft or vandalism, fragile or valuable objects should be kept in locked cases.

labels under each artifact on display; and file photographs made of all objects in all displays, as they go up. Each of these procedures can be an excellent safety measure, but none of them will do much good unless it is followed regularly.

In addition to protecting displayed or stored collection pieces from theft and vandalism, careful collectors must also safeguard them from accidental damage. Objects on exhibit should be securely mounted, so that floor vibrations, breezes from nearby windows or doorways, or the jarring of sonic booms from aircraft passing overhead will not cause them to fall off their mounts.

Often, an artifact must be fastened to a wall or to some other stable support, either for its own physical security or to enhance a design effect. One should proceed with that very carefully, however, never drilling or nailing into an artifact or using "museum wax" to fasten it to its support. Such treatment can easily damage an object a great deal more than one might expect, and certainly lessens its value. The safety of the artifact is far more important than any dramatic effect attained in that way. To fasten an artifact securely—and safely—in place, shape a clamp or a bracket from wood; or bend one to fit, out of brazing rod, scrap metal, or plastic. Both metal and wooden brackets should be padded with some soft, inert material, such as polyethylene foam or tubing, to avoid possible abrasion to the artifact.

Bulky, heavy objects should never be displayed atop tall, thin pedestals, where they can be easily knocked over and possibly broken, or where they could, in falling, cause injury to anyone standing nearby. Fragile items or those that are easily knocked over should be placed behind a protective barrier or in a room corner, rather than in areas of poor visibility or heavy pedestrian traffic, such as doorways or narrow passageways.

Guards

Although there are on the market today a great many kinds of electronic sensing devices, special door locks, and sophisticated alarm systems, it remains true that nothing is more effective against burglary than an alert guard, or a guard with a well-trained dog.

Selection and training. Guards—watchmen—monitors—sentinels—caretakers—may at various times perform duties almost as varied as the titles given them; but their work will be done effectively only in proportion to the degree of care taken in their selection and their training—both the employer's responsibility. *Excellent advice on security problems is available from the Smithsonian Institution, which also provides assistance in the training of guards for museums.*

Speaking very generally about the selection of guards for a collection of artifacts, one begins, always, with the basic personal information that helps to estimate an individual's general capabilities: age, general health, educational background, special interests, special work preferences and training, earlier work experience, average length of time worked for previous employers—that sort of thing. Before interviewing a new applicant, it is helpful to remember that you will want to consider whether such a person, if employed, will be deputized and bonded. To help make that decision, learn as much as you can, in general conversation with the applicant, about his or her general outlook, attitude, responsiveness, quickness of mind. As a general rule, an individual who seems sleepy and slow-moving may be as honest and well-meaning as the day is long—but he is likely to be a bad bet as a watchman.

One should also be wary of setting up a situation in which someone living in or near a building housing artifacts is supposed to "keep an eye on things" when no one else is around. That sort of arrangement does not provide the kind of protection needed for valued objects one wants to keep.

Duties. Duties of collections guards will, of course, vary, depending on the unique requirements of each different situation. All new guards, like all other employees who will hold keys to the building, should receive a copy of your checklist for the routine of opening and closing the building daily, and someone already familiar with it should take the new guard through it on a practice run.

Again speaking very generally, one should be sure that, before going on duty, each guard knows the location of all fire exits, hoses, electric switches and panels in each building he or she is to be responsible for; that each knows also the location of all manholes, water mains, and shut-offs in the building's vicinity, as well as the location of whatever special keys or wrenches are needed for access to those utilities—and knows how to use them.

A concerned employer will also make sure that collections guards have definite positive functions to perform on a tour of duty, since the stultifying inactivity of merely sitting in one place and trying to stay awake and vigilant is enough to deactivate the most dedicated employee.

Guards on night duty, for instance, should periodically check all buildings for unlocked windows and doors, leaking pipes, water taps left running in restrooms, and—in severely cold weather—frozen radiators or evident problems developing in a central heating system. There should be routine checking of galleries and storage rooms, to be sure that all collections items remain in their accustomed places and that no visitor—unexpectedly immobilized, perhaps, by sudden illness—has been inadvertently locked in at closing time and is still in the building. Night guards should also be informed when authorized personnel will be working in the buildings or on the grounds after closing hours, and they should be provided a list of those individuals.

All guards who will be on duty in a building after the alarm system is activated should be thoroughly informed about what stands behind the locked and sensitive doors. They should be briefed on all procedures to follow, so that they will know exactly what to do in case of emergency.

Liaison with local police. An alert, well-trained security staff is an asset even the modest budget should be tailored to provide. To help your security staff protect your collection around the clock, it is important to establish and maintain a good working relationship with the local police department.

A good way to begin is to invite municipal law officers to your site for afternoon coffee and cake or a pancake breakfast, and conduct them on a tour of your building and grounds. Give each officer a map of the property, with areas of special vulnerability marked. Discuss possible solutions to such emergencies as, for example, rioting on the premises, and find out what you and your staff should do in the interval between your call to local law officers and their arrival at your building.

It is also good policy to post, beside every telephone in the building, an emergency procedures chart. Such a chart should list procedures to follow in case of fire, electrical problems, suspected theft, observed theft, personal injury, menacing person, and bomb threat. Many of those possible contingencies seem almost laughably unlikely, but such situations can arise, and it is enormously helpful to have an established written procedure, already familiar to your staff, for everyone to follow.[2]

Electronic Security and Alarm Systems

Electronic security gadgetry includes many new devices and systems, nowadays, including controls for lights and detectors for power and heating systems, automatic telephone dialers, and radio signaling and receiving systems. Electronic lock systems operated by plastic cards can be programed to allow certain people to enter a building only at preset times, and all activity can be recorded on paper. Needless to say, all this technology is difficult to sort out, and some of the devices available are very expensive. If you decide that you want a security system and know what you want it to do for you, then read the available literature about the current devices obtainable, and you should be in a position to begin dealing with sales and installation people.[3]

Although the detecting of illegal entry into your building or room— *after* the fact—is urgently important, the physical strength of your building's walls, doors, and windows can be a better deterrent than the threat of an alarm. Alarms, by themselves, will not necessarily deter an intruder who knows what he wants from your collection; but locks, doors, and windows that cannot be quickly penetrated may well dissuade a burglar from taking a chance on being caught. The imposing appearance of robustly constructed walls and entries may be one of your best security elements. Flimsy wall construction, especially in wooden buildings, may provide and even seem to invite easy access, if not properly reinforced or protected by alarm devices.

Security and alarm systems may be connected to a central guard station within your building, to a security or answering service elsewhere, or to a police station, according to one's local situation.

Remember that even complex security systems may at some time undergo mechanical failure or may not provide adequate security for your collection, for the simple but human reason that the more elaborate such systems are, the more people place complete faith in them and fail to remain alert. Even the best system can break down occasionally or can be bypassed by a resourceful professional burglar. If you do install such equipment, remember also that the more people who know about it and about where and how it is installed, the less effective it is going to be.

Some Systems Currently Available

Below are some currently available types of alarms, some of which you can install and some of which need specialized factory installation. There are many other types of devices to be found, and new types and combinations of equipment are being developed all the time. In general, two or more kinds of detectors should be combined to form an effective system, but be sure to obtain a security survey and estimates for various systems before installing anything. A quick check into the reliability of the alarm company will help ensure that they may still be around in a few months when you need service for your machines.

Audio detectors. Audio detectors can be used as check-in stations by guards. They also pick up noises in rooms not in use. These devices may be combined with a two-way public address system for museums or businesses.

Closed-circuit television (CCTV). CCTV is only as effective as the people who monitor it, and the monitoring is a very boring job. The system may be connected to a recorder, such as banks use. It requires regular maintenance for reliability.

Door switches. Electronic door switches can be turned on after the building is empty, to monitor specific areas for unscheduled entry. Many can be easily bypassed; but they may be effective if used in combination with other devices.

Micro-switches. Micro-switches can be placed under or behind museum objects. They will set off an alarm or a signal at a central panel if the object is disturbed. Wireless models are available.

Motion detectors. Many types of motion detectors are available, but those known as passive infrared detectors are considered superior. Ultrasonic and microwave units seem to be more difficult to use effectively without undue false alarms.

Photo-electric devices. These devices can be set up in a number of ways. Those using an infrared light source are more difficult for an intruder to spot.

Switches or circuits. Electronic alarm switches or circuits can be wired around doors, windows, or skylights. They can often be detected and are best used with other devices.

NOTES

1. Robert G. Tillotson, *Museum Security,* pp. 70–113.
2. Tillotson, *Museum Security,* pp. 190–192.
3. Eugene L. Fuss, "Security in Cultural Institutions," in *Technology and Conservation,* pp. 34–37; Tillotson, *Museum Security,* pp. 82–126; Lawrence J. Fennelly, *Museum, Archive and Library Security,* pp. 281–578.

SUGGESTED READING

Fennelly, Lawrence J. *Museum, Archive and Library Security.* Woburn, Mass.: Butterworth Publishers, 1983.
Contributions from security professionals in a variety of institutions, covering a large range of security information.

Fuss, Eugene L. "Security in Cultural Institutions: Advances in Electronic Protection Techniques." *Technology and Conservation Magazine* 4 (Winter 1979): 34–37.

Nauret, Patricia, and Caroline M. Black. *Fine Arts Insurance: A Handbook for Museums.* Washington, D.C.: Association of Art Museum Directors, 1979.

Phelan, Marilyn. *Museums and the Law.* Nashville: The American Association for State and Local History, 1982.
Though intended for museum professionals, this book is a valuable reference for anyone concerned with objects of historical or artistic value.

Tillotson, Robert G. *Museum Security.* Paris: International Council of Museums, 1977.
This comprehensive survey of security hardware and techniques offers an excellent background in the subject, although readers should always seek current advice about the latest devices available.

5

Fire Protection

I n the day-to-day situations involving historical materials, few things can be more serious than fire in collection areas. In addition to endangering all human and animal life present at its outbreak, fire in a collection area carries the potential for destroying irreplaceable artifacts—possibly an entire collection. As your local fire marshal or insurance agent can tell you, planning for protection against fire is an extremely important element in safeguarding your property.

The emergency procedures chart that should be posted near all telephones in the building (see chapter 4, "Guards" section) should include procedures for all staff people to follow in case of fire. Periodic fire drills should be conducted, so that all the staff may be familiar with that basic routine; even though the actual need for it may never arise, if and when fire does break out, there is no time, then, to waste—the staff should already know exactly what to do,[1] and the ranking executive officer present should see that it is done. That person should be the last one to leave the building, having seen that everyone else is out, first.

Directions to follow in case of fire might appear on the emergency chart in boldface type, set off in a "box" of heavy ruled outlines, listing basic steps to follow, in order of precedence:

---

1. **Call Fire Department:**
   Phones 123–4567 or 890–1234
2. **All staff: Alert all visitors and escort them out of the building by exit routes for your area (see map below).**
3. **All staff: If fire is too big for a single individual to put out, LEAVE THE BUILDING.**
4. **Do not re-enter building without an executive OK.**

More specific details, if needed can follow, concisely, along with a clear sketch of the building, showing the shortest way out for people in each area.

The first step, always, as soon as a fire is detected, is to *call the Fire Department, no matter how small the fire may seem.* Even if you believe that you can put the fire out before professional help arrives, CALL THE FIRE DEPARTMENT. The firemen would much rather roll up when there is no apparent need for them than to have the public put off calling for professional help until a fire gets far out of hand, becomes harder to control, and is, consequently, much more dangerous than if firemen had been summoned when it was first discovered.

Having called the Fire Department (Step 1) and got everyone out of the building (Step 2), then (Step 3), if you think that the fire is still small enough for you to put out with an extinguisher, without danger to yourself, find the nearest extinguisher suitable for the kind of fire at hand and go to work. *Do not, however, attempt to fight large fires or to rescue any collection objects; and (Step 4) having once left the building, do not go back inside until given the official all-clear.*

Some Things To Do To Prevent Fire

There is nothing mysterious or magical about fire prevention. Vigilance, proper maintenance of equipment, and good housekeeping can prevent most fires from starting.

Ask the local fire marshal, fire chief, or a qualified fireman to come to your premises for a regularly scheduled inspection of possible fire hazards at least once a year. During that period of time, normal wear and usage may have brought about defects in electrical wiring, evidence of age and wear in chimneys and heating plants, leakage in fuel oil lines, accumulations of oily rags in custodians' closets, dirty packing rooms, and similar familiar—and unsafe—situations. Since about 75 percent of all fires start in winter months, according to the National Fire Protection Association, your heating system in particular should always be checked yearly. To keep close watch for fire hazards on your premises, get a "Fire Safety Self-Inspection Form for Museums" from the National Fire Protection Association of Boston. Properly observed, this master check-list will help you see that critical areas of concern are checked for fire hazards frequently—and regularly.

Alarm Systems and Fire Drills

It is a good idea to install smoke detectors in remote areas not often visited in a building, especially if the property does not have a central fire alarm system. Individual smoke detectors are far better than no fire warning at all, but they do have one disadvantage that illustrates the soundness in considering some sort of central system: if no one hears the alarm sounded by an individual smoke detector, the device does no good at all. An alarm system can, of course, be connected in various ways to outside receivers. And it should be stressed that, to maintain their efficiency, all alarm devices should be regularly checked and tested.

In a large, complex building, fire safety regulations and procedures should be posted in each office, for all personnel, and fire drills should be conducted regularly enough for all staff members to be familiar with the procedures to follow, including the safe evacuation of all visitors. Have some staff member check the efficiency of drill procedures each time.

Legally approved exit signs should be visible at all exits where the local fire code indicates a need for them. Emergency-exit doors, fire escapes, and alternate escape routes from the building should be provided, as well as folding ladders, if such measures are considered necessary. Your local Fire Department officials can tell you the best course to follow, there.

All fire hoses in the building should be regularly checked, to be certain that they remain in good condition. Staff members should not attempt to move these hoses about or to use them, however—that job should be left to the firemen, trained in handling high-pressure hoses safely.

Liaison with Local Fire Department

Good fire-safety planning can be helped a great deal by the same kind of strong, working relationship with the local Fire Department that you will want to develop with your local police. It's an excellent idea, once or twice yearly, to invite your local Fire Department people to your site for evening coffee and cake and a conducted tour of your building, stressing the irreplaceable nature of the building's contents and explaining precautions that have been taken to protect building and collection.

The firemen can provide invaluable help in identifying specific problems and suggesting solutions in case of fire—such problems as proper handling of stored chemicals, safe power cut-off procedures, and temporary protection for objects particularly susceptible to water and smoke damage. Salvage tarpaulins should be obtained and stored throughout the building, where they may be made use of, in case of fire. On walk-through tours of the building, the firemen should be shown where these tarps are kept, so that they can put them to use, if fire should occur, to protect objects that may be salvaged or even to divert some of the accumulated run-off water, if necessary.

Fire Extinguishers: Types and Use

Everyone on the staff should know three things about every fire extinguisher in the building: its location, its class rating, and the correct way to use it.

Location. If fire should break out in a collection area, the fire extinguishers for use against it ought to be plainly visible, easy to get to, and readily made portable, so that they may be reached and put into use as quickly as possible. Although fire extinguishers are not decorative, they should not be discreetly tucked away in a closet or behind a panel, in some distant back-room corner or at the far end of a long hallway, where their potential usefulness is negated by poor accessibility. *Fire extinguishers are a vital part of your safety equipment; put them up where you can find them and use them, if you need to.*

Class ratings and use: extinguishers to fit your fire. Different types of fire extinguishers are made to fight different types of fires. An extinguisher made to put out burning paper or wood is not the type needed to put out a grease fire or one involving energized electrical equipment.

Manufacturers of fire extinguishers categorize combustible materials in three basic classes—*Class A, Class B, and Class C*—and they identify the kinds of fire extinguishers made to put out fires in these different classes of material by a corresponding *class rating* clearly marked on the casing of each extinguisher. Make yourself aware of the rating on your extinguishers and use them only for the proper class of fire.[2]

Class A extinguishers are made to put out fires burning such ordinary combustibles as paper and wood.

Class B extinguishers are made to combat fires involving flammable liquids, solvents, grease, and oil.

Class C extinguishers are for fires in which energized electrical equipment is a factor.

A fourth kind—or class—of material that can catch fire and burn includes chemicals and metals, such as magnesium, phosphorus, sodium, potassium, and Dow metal, but *this class of fire should not be fought by any amateur—it requires professional training and equipment.*

You and your staff need to know the class rating of each fire extinguisher in your building, so that, in case fire does break out, you will know which extinguisher to use as soon as you can identify the type of material that is burning.

Each staff member should also be given the experience of handling the types of extinguishers kept in your building, in practice sessions that your local fire department can help to set up and supervise. Remember that a twenty-five-pound extinguisher is good for only about one minute of flow, and don't expect miracles of any single piece of fire-fighting equipment.

Generally, Class A extinguishers are water-based and are operated by any one of a number of mechanisms. In addition to being rather heavy and unwieldy, they can cause water damage to some types of objects. If there is a choice, do not bring a potential element of destruction in to use in your collection area.

Some of the older "dry-powder" extinguishers are recommended only for Class B and Class C fires, as are carbon dioxide gas extinguishers. One type is suitable for Class A, Class B, and Class C fires, and is very efficient, compared to others or its kind; these dry-chemical extinguishers are the most commonly found sort, at present; but if you are buying, check to be sure what you are getting. All these types are clearly marked, and your fire department or insurance company or the National Fire Protection Association—at 470 Atlantic Avenue, Boston, Massachusetts 02210—can tell you where to get further information.

Points To Consider in Buying Extinguishers

Hand-held types. When you must buy new fire extinguishers, it pays to keep several factors in mind. First—don't buy extinguishers so heavy that only professional weight-lifters can pick them up; 98 percent of the handling of those extinguishers will be done by you or your staff people, and weight-lifting isn't among the job qualifications that brought all of you there.

At the opposite end of the spectrum, avoid also beer-can-sized aerosol extinguishers. In addition to their small capacity, they are so cheaply made that they are not dependable, and fire companies warn against placing any reliance on them.

Also—and especially—avoid the obsolete carbon tetrachloride type of extinguisher. Sprayed on a fire, carbon tetrachloride breaks down and forms phosgene, a poisonous gas formerly used as a military weapon.

Foam extinguishers are useful, but they cause a tremendous mess, and many collection owners prefer to replace them with more modern equipment.

And—be sure that you know the company that makes the units you buy, and keep in touch with the salesman who handles the transaction, so that you can come nearer being assured of service for your extinguishers in the future.

At present, one of the most highly recommended fire protection systems for collection areas is one halon extinguisher and one dry-chemical extinguisher that is rated for all three classes of fires—Class A, Class B, and Class C. These two units should be placed together, wherever such equipment can be reached most conveniently if needed. The halon extinguisher leaves no residue at all and is best used on Class B and Class C fires, though it is only slightly effective on Class A fires. The dry-chemical type is quite versatile and effective and could be used as a back-up for the halon extinguisher, if that one does not put out a fire immediately.

Built-in systems. An alternative to the various types of hand-held extinguishers is a "dry-sprinkler" system, with individually activated heads. The "dry-sprinkler" is a permanently installed system that does not contain water until a fire alarm is detected; at that point, only the sprinkler heads immediately in the area of the fire will open, and they will close when the fire has been put out. Although there is always obvious risk of water damage to museum objects when any sort of sprinkler system is used, the "dry-sprinkler" system might be considered in some collection areas because of its great effectiveness in stopping a fire in the early stages.

The supreme extinguishing system utilizes large tanks of halogenated gas to put out fires, but these systems are so expensive that they are usually used in small, well-contained areas only.[3]

NOTES

1. Robert G. Tillotson, *Museum Security*, pp. 190–192.

2. *Portable Fire Extinguishers 1978* (Boston: National Fire Protection Association, 1978).

3. *Installation of Sprinkler Systems, 1978* (Boston: National Fire Protection Association, 1979); *Halogenated Extinguishing Agent Systems, Halon 1301, 1977* (Boston: National Fire Protection Association, 1977); Tillotson, *Museum Security*, pp. 56–68.

SUGGESTED READING

Cohn, Bert M. "Fire Safety in Recycled Buildings: Establishing the Level of Protection Equivalent to Code Requirements." *Technology and Conservation Magazine* 5 (Summer 1980): 40–45.

Harp, Dale W. "Intumescent Paints: A Useful Component of Fire Protection Plans." *Technology and Conservation Magazine* 6 (Spring 1981): 30–31.

National Fire Protection Association. *Protection of Museum Collections.* Boston: National Fire Protection Association, 1974.

Schur, Susan E. "Fire Protection at Mount Vernon: Incorporating Modern Fire Safety Systems into an Historic Site." *Technology and Conservation Magazine:* 5 (Winter 1980): 18–25.

"A Sensing Approach Smokes out Possible Threats to Historical Structures." *Technology and Conservation Magazine* 6 (Summer 1981): 9–10, 12–13.

6

The Collections Workroom: Equipment and Use

This discussion of workroom furnishing, equipment, and procedure is addressed to people who are responsible for some basic care of artifacts in a small museum or a private collection. Often, the individual shouldering these responsibilities for a modest collection on a slender budget may not have a seasoned expert's years of experience and specialized training to draw from, and the information offered in this book is written especially for such individuals.

That being so, this is a good place to emphasize the fact that even though one may lack a good bit of the scientific training important to conservation of collections, anyone who plans to do the work can reinforce and increase his or her current knowedge about it by taking the time to study the books and journal articles listed in the bibliographies that follow each chapter of the book and by carefully and methodically following the advice given there.

Care and restraint are more important in good artifact conservation work than are specialized tools or scientific apparatus, which can be no more helpful than expensive toys if one does not know how to use them or how to interpret the results achieved. Most of the tools and supplies suggested here are relatively inexpensive and can be added to the collections workroom a few at a time, as the need for them arises—or as the budget dictates.

The most important rules in artifact conservation are these:

1. Always work only to the limits of your understanding.
2. Adopt—and follow—systematic procedures.
3. If a conservation problem is beyond your ability to solve, for the sake of the artifact, concede that, and get in touch immediately with a specialist who can help you with it.

For continuing sound advice and sustaining help from professional people experienced in the care of artistic and historical works, you might consider joining the major professional organizations, such as the American Association for State and Local History and the American Institute for Conservation.

The American Association for State and Local History (AASLH), at 708 Berry Road, Nashville, Tennessee [37204], publishes books on the collection, care, and preservation of artifacts, operation and maintenance of historic sites, and other subjects in historically related fields. Its monthly magazine *History News*—free to all dues-paying members—not only provides current news and comment from experts in these historically related fields; it carries a series of technical leaflets dealing in detail with specialized aspects of work with artifacts, historical collections, and historic sites.

The American Institute for Conservation, at 1511 K Street, N.W., Washington, D.C. [20005], is also a membership organization, made up of conservators and interested laymen. Its publications include the quarterly *AIC Newsletter* and the semiannual *Journal of the AIC*. The AIC was not established to provide do-it-yourself guides, as AASLH does, but it may often give important information about various materials and processes in current use among professional conservators that also has application in the general care of objects.

Gradually build a library of books and journals on paints, woodworking, conservation, and related subjects. These books usually run to small editions, and they are worth the price you pay for them; they will be among your most valuable tools, in the long run.

An Up-Front Reminder: Workroom Records

Before going on to specifics about workroom furnishings and equipment, we should stress, here, the necessity for and the importance of records kept on work done in your workroom. Workroom records, carefully kept, detailed, and dated, are integral to the work of caring for artifacts. *Make the time to keep full records of all conservation and repair work that is done in your workroom, no matter how obvious a given procedure may seem and no matter how crowded your schedule may be.*

Records of what has been done to an artifact are vital to further work with the object, to good preservation of collections, to your own professional integrity, and to people who will come after you. In addition to those impeccable reasons for keeping good workroom records, there is, as well, the mundane, brass-tacks fact that documents clearly stating work plan and procedure and step-by-step photographic records of the job prevent misunderstandings with insurors, donors, or clients about what has been planned or what has or has not been done to an artifact in your care. Many of us have regrettably short memories, and in the event of disputes about the condition of an object before you received it or after you began work on it, precise, accurate records and clear photographs are unassailable evidence.

One should keep in mind that one's own memory is not infallible, either; so, as you proceed on any restorative, conservation, or repair work, date and document your work, step by step, on a work sheet, to keep the record, the work plan, and your own professional reputation straight.

When you apply an adhesive, a cleaning solution, or a coating — especially if any of these are patented products — write down as exactly as you can the specific description of the material used. The person who may later be obliged to take apart a decoy duck that you have glued together may have difficulty working out a solvent for the adhesive used, if you have specified nothing more than the trade name of the product. The product may have changed formulation by that time, or it may no longer be on the market. Stating that the adhesive used was a "synthetic resin soluble in acetone" not only appears more professional, but it is considerably more helpful to your hardworking successor.

Bearing these details in mind, one should always be thinking about the advantages of *reversibility* of any material or process used in working with artifacts. In professional conservation laboratories, reversible treatments are always preferred, so that later treatment — perhaps essential repair work, hundreds of years from now — or the substitution of improved materials for worn-out parts may be made without undue difficulty.

The code of ethics of the American Institute for Conservation is an excellent guide to follow in working with artifacts. One should also bear in mind that any conservator one may employ should adhere to that code for all collections work. See "A Code of Ethics for Conservators," in *Museum News*: 58 (March/April) 1980: 27–34; and "AIC Code of Ethics and Standards of Practice," in *Furniture Care and Conservation*, by Robert F. McGiffin, Jr. (Nashville: American Association for State and Local History, 1983), pp. 179–194.

In deciding what sort of treatment an object should have, always consider the reversibility problem; and in your work notes, describe the materials you are using and the ways they may be removed. Occasionally, permanent, irreversible materials appear to be the only substances suitable for the job to be done, but their use should be undertaken only if no other materials will prove effective and the object truly requires drastic help to survive.

Again—keep step-by-step photographic records of your work, before, during, and after treatment. Excellent down-to-earth advice about both photographing the objects in your collection and photographing work in progress appears on pages 32–35 of Robert F. McGiffin's *Furniture Care and Conservation,* cited above.

The kind of camera you use may depend on your budget or your own preferences, but be sure that it is a camera capable of taking close-up views and showing detailed work clearly. A blurred box-camera shot taken three feet away is seldom helpful for record purposes. If possible, learn to develop your own negatives. The average photo processing plant does not bring out the best in negatives; and if you do have good ones, done on fine-grain film, they can be enlarged in printing to bring out whatever details you wish to show.

Among your records, you should also keep a file on whatever cameras, optical equipment, and tools you buy for the workroom, including all warranties, instruction sheets, and receipts. Such a file can save you difficulties when a piece of equipment needs repair work or new parts.

Collections Workroom Location and Furnishings

A good workroom for an artifacts collection can be visualized with any number of idealistic requirements, but probably the most important qualification, for efficient work, is that the workroom be in a quiet part of the building, away from the main line of pedestrian traffic, off limits to casual visitors, and a good distance from the staff candy machine or coffee maker. Much of the work that must be done in a collections workroom requires a good bit of uninterrupted time, strong concentration, and close attention to detail. Interruptions in such work lead to distraction from the operative line of thought about the job, and that, in turn, leads to mistakes.

Lighting

The collections workroom should have adequate natural light, and the staff should be able to open the windows that provide that light, to increase ventilation of fumes as necessary. General lighting today is usually provided by fluorescent lights throughout all areas of a building; but if your building is equipped with fluorescent fixtures, be cautious in purchasing fluorescent tubes for them. All major manufacturers of lighting equipment offer several shades of "white light," ranging in tone from icy blue or greenish to a somewhat pinkish yellow. You may wish to combine different hues, or you may decide to purchase "color-balanced" tubes, but all fluorescent tubes produce strong emissions of light rays at certain wave lengths that result in uneven color rendition.[1] One or two small table lamps with flexible shafts will be handy for producing concentrated or raking light. Such lamps can cost from about fifty dollars or so upward.

Two photoflood bulbs plus reflectors and tripod will help in photographing collections records; and an ultraviolet examining lamp will occasionally be helpful in discovering information through the fluorescence of adhesives or varnish coatings. A mercury-vapor type of lamp costs more than a hundred dollars, but less expensive fluorescent tube types are available for around thirty dollars.

The ideal workroom will have a good many electrical outlets spaced at regular intervals around the room, plus a few supplementary heavy-duty extension cords with duplex outlets attached. Be careful in placing extension cords, however; few items are as annoying and as hazardous to walking about as extension cords strewn at random on the floor in heavy-traffic work areas and walkways. All workroom outlets should be of the modern, grounded type.

Work Tables

Examination tables and work tables will be among your most important workroom tools. Until you have settled the question of work-table height, overall dimensions, and shelves, your best bet is to start with a temporary table. One can be made from a flush-level, solid-core door or a piece of three-quarter-inch plywood mounted on saw-horse trestles. Your final main work table should be free-standing, so that there is access to it from all four sides, and it should be from three to four feet wide, depending on your reach, so that it will be big enough to accommodate work with large mat boards and textiles.

If your workroom space is limited, you may also want to have your work table on rollers or casters for the most flexible use of existing space.

The area underneath the tabletop working area can be utilized for shelves, racks, and drawers for the storage of tools, paints, paper, and other supplies. Be sure to plan enough knee space, however, so that you will not be obliged to thrust your knees awkwardly out at sidesaddle position when you are seated for work at the table.

The surface of the tabletop can vary, but a tough plastic veneer or an epoxy or enamel coating may be the best choices, aside from special lab tabletops. An element in favor of coated surfaces is that they make repair to a damaged tabletop fairly easy.

In addition to the main work table, which may be used for examination of incoming artifacts, for cutting paper, for working on textiles, and for general light duties, there should be a heavier workbench and a top-quality bench vise for hammering, sawing, and general rough work. This equipment should be placed in a separate area, somewhat removed from the general working space, so that the large amounts of sawdust, filings, and dirt loosened from the impact of the heavier work will not contaminate other artifacts and materials currently in the workroom. If at all possible, this heavy-work area should be partitioned off from the rest of the workroom, and, if necessary, it should be equipped with an auxiliary ventilating fan. A large shop vacuum cleaner or a tank vacuum, to be used after every dusting, filing, or sawing operation, will also help to reduce the dirt hazard.

Examination-table gloves. A large supply of white cotton gloves should be kept on hand at the examination table. The kind of washable or disposable gloves to be found at photo supply stores should be used when handling paper, textiles, and metals, in particular, and it's also a good idea to wear them in working with other sensitive materials such as unglazed pottery. Oils and perspiration from bare hands can stain or permanently etch a variety of materials. It should be a house rule that everyone who handles objects vulnerable to such staining should use gloves and should take care to work with *clean* gloves at all times, changing to a fresh pair as the work soils them.

Workroom Sink

A sink or a washbasin with drainboards is essential for any small workroom. If your local water supply carries such impurities as sulfur, chlorine, or minerals, it will be necessary to buy a water de-ionization filter or containers of distilled water for most of the work you will need to do on artifacts. Distilling machines for pure water are also available, at considerably greater cost. If you occasionally need a large container for washing big items, and a big sink is prohibitively expensive or space-consuming, you can improvise by making a wooden box of the required size and lining it with heavy-duty polyethylene sheeting; or make a more permanent basin by lining your wooden box with fiberglass cloth cemented down and coated with polyester resin. Don't forget to provide a way to drain the water *out* of your homemade basin, once you've finished using it.

And always be very careful what you pour down the drain at a workroom sink. Left-over driblets of plaster of Paris and many kinds of fillers and adhesives can "set" and harden in drainage pipes and traps, creating blockages that can't be dislodged without incurring unplanned, unnecessary, and expensive plumbing bills.

Don't ever pour solvents down a sink drain, either. Solvents disposed of that way and left lurking in a sink trap can create a pocket of explosive fumes that is extremely dangerous. Aside from the immediate danger of fire and explosion that they can create if left lying in the sink's drainage trap, solvents that one may manage—mistakenly—to flush all the way out of the building's pipes can also kill the helpful bacteria needed to keep septic tanks or sewage systems working properly, and they can introduce noxious materials into any water system they enter. *Repeat: Never pour solvents down a sink drain—any sink drain.* Before you use a solvent, very carefully read the manufacturer's instructions for its use and its disposal and follow them exactly. And if it should happen that a new employee somehow forgets and takes a shortcut by pouring "just a little bit" of unused solvent down your workroom sink, *don't flush it down;* call a good plumber, tell him what you've got, and keep the sink off limits until the plumber gets there to take care of it.

Workroom Storage and Security

A good workroom should provide adequate storage for such diverse items as paper, chemicals, tools, and general supplies, as well as plenty of suitable room for the various artifacts that will need to be kept there from time to time. Since many of the collections artifacts are valuable, it is important that the workroom, like any other room where the objects may be stored, be secure. Be certain that doors and windows can be locked to prevent easy access from outside by thieves or vandals, and be just as certain that storeroom doors and windows are checked for security with all other access ways when the building is closed, nights and weekends.

Workroom Equipment

Equipping your workroom will be a never-ending process, but it should not be viewed as a challenge to acquire every different tool, gadget, and miracle chemical you can find. Endless numbers of catalogues and magazine articles will coax you to try treatments or buy materials that may or may not suit your needs—that may even be useless or even harmful to your particular artifacts, in the long run. Try to assess your workroom needs and capabilities very carefully—that will help you to avoid buying items that may later prove unnecessary. A vast array of unused specialty tools and rare, use-once-every-five-years nostrums will not be of much help to your collections.

Optical Devices: Binocular

A binocular magnifier that fits over the head and is manufactured in varying scales of low magnification sells for about $30. Even at that low price, the optics are relatively good; and there is the further advantage that prescription eye-glasses can be worn under these magnifiers.

A binocular—or stereo—microscope is a rather sizable investment, running to some $1,500 or more for a flexible system. Cheaper ones are available, but their optical systems are less effective than those commanding higher prices. In the long run, it may be more practical to use the inexpensive headset lenses and save your money for a first-class stereo microscope sometime in the future than to compromise and start off with a mediocre one. In addition to that, a waiting period may indicate that you do not really need such a costly device at all.

Optical Devices: Monocular

Monocular loupes can be purchased from jewelers or opticians in various magnifications. One type fits against the eye socket; other types fit over one's glasses or can be permanently attached to them. These sell for $5 to $10. Hand lenses or linen-tester lenses range from $5 to $15; or a large combination reading glass with a built-in fluorescent light source mounted on a flexible stand can be bought for about $65.

Using Magnifying Devices

For ease in working with magnifiers, use the lowest practical magnification. That way, you will have a greater depth of field—that is, the objects will not shift in and out of focus so quickly as to make your work more difficult—and you will see a wider area of the material being inspected. With higher-powered lenses, focusing is more critical; you see a smaller area, and the apparent motion of tools under the lens is greatly exaggerated.

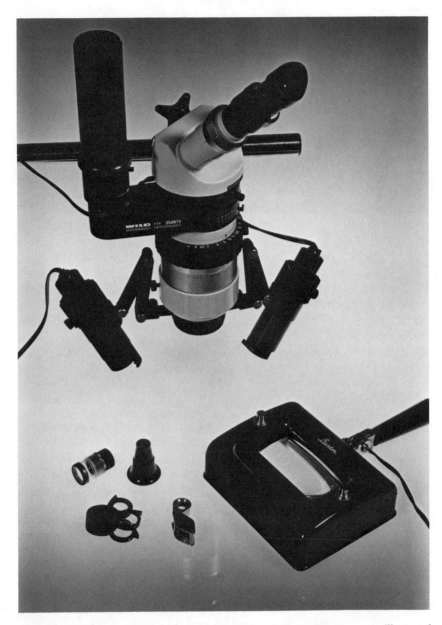

Fig. 6.1. Everyone may not need a binocular microscope, or even an illustrated magnifier; but even small, good-quality lenses can help in examining artifacts.

Working with magnifying lenses tends to make one's eyes tire rather quickly. If you are using *monocular* devices, learn to keep both eyes open, to prevent squinting and discomfort. Before looking up from an instrument, close your eyes for a few seconds as you raise your head; then focus on something at the other end of the room for a short time, before you resume your work at the lenses. These tricks will help prevent eyestrain or nausea.

The area examined through poor magnifying lenses will be fuzzy at the edges, distorted, or colored, and that will make your work difficult. You have only one pair of eyes, so it is wise always to buy and use the best lenses you can possibly afford.

Balances

Unless you are doing micro-chemical work, an inexpensive beam balance sensitive to half a gram will probably meet most of your workroom needs. You can also have these balances graduated in ounces, but the metric system is more widely used in scientific work and is far easier to deal with in calculations. The cost for beam balances usually ranges from around $50 to around $100.

Procedures for Workroom Weighing and Measuring

Combining solids with liquids. A slight digression at this point may be in order, to discuss recommended procedures in use of weighing and measuring devices to make solutions required in various percentages. When combining a solid with a liquid—mixing washing soda with water, for instance—measure, *first*, the *weight of the solid* and *add to that enough liquid to make the required amount.* To make a one-liter solution of 5 percent washing soda, for example, first weigh fifty grams of soda and put it in a graduated container; then add enough water to make one liter (one gram of solid is equal in weight to one milliliter of water). Incidentally, the terms *cc* (cubic centimeter) and *ml* (milliliter) have the same meaning, though *ml* is more commonly used at present.

Adding liquids to liquids. When adding a liquid to a liquid—combining ammonia and water, for example—measure both fluids, volume for volume. Although liquids do not all have the same specific gravity (weight per volume), the usual practice, outside of exacting analytical laboratories, is to assume that they do. Thus, to make one liter of a 5 percent solution of ammonia, add 50 milliliters (ml) of ammonia to 950 ml of water.

If you do not have metric measures, you can use the avoirdupois system, based on the assumption that a pint of liquid weighs sixteen ounces. However, it is more difficult to determine exact percentages of solutions with avoirdupois measurement, since 16 ounces divided into 100 percent gives odd fractions. Adding 1 ounce of ammonia to 15 ounces of water, for instance, gives a 6¼ percent solution. To make a one-pint solution of 5 percent ammonia, ⅘ of an ounce must be added to 15⅕ ounces of water—measurements that are a bit awkward to achieve accurately. Therefore, for those who cannot afford metric balances and graduates, at present, and may instead be using kitchen scales and pint measuring cups, the simplest method is to assume that *1 ounce of chemical plus 15 ounces of water equals a 5 percent solution; and 1½ ounces of chemical to 14½ ounces of water equals a 10 percent solution.*

Workroom Tools

Unless you are already skilled in carpentry or woodcraft, there is no need to buy a great quantity of hand tools for the sort of conservation and repair work needed for artifacts collections; in fact, obtaining tools without some knowledge, first, of what you will need to be doing, specifically, is likely to be a waste of money and may be more harmful than helpful to your workroom tool budget. The suggestions presented here emphasize the gentle approach in working with historical objects, which means that such tools as saws, drills, and sanders should be needed very infrequently. Woodworking skills can certainly be put to good use in making proper supports, shelving, storage systems, and display furnishings for the artifacts in the collection, however.

Like workroom lighting, storage space, and magnifying equipment, tools selected for the collections workroom should be of the best quality you can afford. Cheap tools are no bargain. They often will hone to a rough edge, will not stay sharp, and they may bend or break quite readily. The cost for replacements, after some little time, may very well run higher than would the original investment in good tools.

Good maintenance care for your workroom tools is essential. See that they are always cleaned after use, kept sharp, and that they fit tightly in the handles. A loose hammer head that flies off on the down-stroke is a dangerous projectile. Screwdrivers will not work properly if their straight edges are nicked, gnawed rough, and rounded by use on screw heads of the wrong size and left that way through careless maintenance. Supply your workroom tool kit with enough of a variety of sizes of screwdrivers to insure that you have one to fit any screw head without "butching" it. Trying to remove a "butched" screw is one of life's more exasperating frustrations.

Never dump good tools indiscriminately all in a heap in a tool box—such treatment is the best way known to damage them; it is ruinous for delicately honed edged tools such as chisel and plane blades. Your tools should be kept in special drawers, racks, or boards, whichever sort of space will provide safely for the tool with the least stress for it. An orderly, protective tool storage system is also good record-keeping—you can tell immediately which tools are available for use, and those that are missing can be more quickly accounted for. If certain tools are constantly being borrowed by certain individuals, suggest that those people buy a set of their own. If you lend your tools, especially drill bits and chisels, you have only yourself to blame if all your time is spent at the sharpening stone.

Danger: power tools. This cautionary note can't be repeated too many times: *Always* use power tools with special care—and leave them alone entirely if you are not familiar with their operation. An eye patch or a stump where a hand or a finger used to be does not increase your working efficiency. Spring-loaded tools are also dangerous, and it helps to remember that they can gouge artifacts quite as well as they can destroy flesh.

Workroom Safety Equipment

Throughout this section, there has been emphasis on safety when working with tools, solvents, chemicals, and electricity. In addition to those essential precautions, it is imperative to check regularly with your insurance agent, your fire and police departments, and with the representatives of manufacturers of products that you buy, to be certain that you are complying with *all* regulations as to the use and storage of equipment and machinery or the storage of inflammable materials. This is especially vital when your collection is housed in an old, historic building that may be a firetrap. Carelessness or ignorance will not absolve you from a heavy fine, cancellation of insurance, loss of collections items, nor will it excuse accidental injury to staff or visitors. In some states, general safety regulations are rather stringently defined, and a great deal depends upon the specific title given to your work area, whether it be referred to as a "shop" or a "studio" instead of a "laboratory," for instance. *Whatever* the safety regulations for your location may be, find out everything you can about them and comply with them to the letter.

Fire Extinguishers

Speaking generally, fire extinguishers in the collections workroom should be of the A-B-C type (see "Fire Extinguishers: Types and Use," in chapter 5), preferably as a back-up to the more expensive halon gas extinguisher. In areas where there are materials of the kind that present a specific hazard, however, select the extinguisher that will work best for that hazardous material. For instance, an A-B-C extinguisher or a pressurized-water type will be more effective on burning solids than will a halon or a carbon dioxide model. Remember *never* to use water around energized electrical equipment, however.

Place all extinguishers in the building so that you can get at them quickly and easily. A good location is near a doorway leading out of the area. Have each extinguisher checked periodically for pressure, and be sure that each is the product of a reputable company employing reliable sales people who can re-charge the equipment for you.

Check to be sure that you do not have any of the older, outmoded types of equipment on hand—carbon tetrachloride extinguishers can produce vapors more toxic than the fumes from a fire.

And see chapter 5 for more information about selection and use of fire extinguishers.

Safety Apparel

Various kinds of hazardous materials are standard equipment in collections work areas, and others appear there from time to time. Protective clothing to prevent injury is a must.

Gloves, aprons, and lab coats save wear and tear on one's street clothes and one's skin—and they are cheap insurance, always worth their price. Provide them—and *always use them.*

Gloves and other protective clothing are made in a variety of materials, such as polyethylene, vinyl, and neoprene, as well as rubber, so be certain to choose the type that will protect you best against the kind of material you may be working with at the time.

Safety goggles or other protection for the wearer's eyes and face should be part of the standard equipment in a collections workshop. Choose either the plastic full-face protective mask, the goggle type that fits snugly around the eyes, or the gas-proof variety, depending upon your needs. *And never work without them, whether you are pouring acid or using an electric drill.* The human eye is frightfully easy to injure—and sometimes there is no way to repair damage to it.

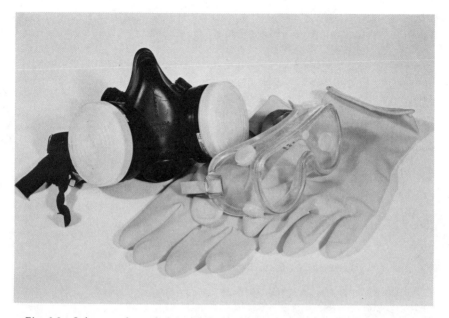

Fig. 6.2. Safety goggles and gloves of the correct material for the job are good protection from dangerous fluids and flying fragments. A respirator with the necessary filters can protect against a variety of toxic vapors, such as those of solvents or ammonia.

Workroom Garbage Cans

Workrooms serving artifacts collections should be equipped with large metal garbage cans that are OSHA-approved and especially made for the safe disposal of oily rags, solvent-soaked cotton, and vast amounts of paper. Empty workroom garbage cans daily, to avoid the building up of fumes and the possibility of fire in the refuse. Fire-retardant cans are available from shop and laboratory supply houses.

Proper Ventilation

Good ventilation for a collections workroom is not a matter for debate—there are no ifs about it: the kinds of substances required to do the work needed dictate that good ventilation is a must. When you are working with paint, solvents, chemicals, and other substances that generate assorted noxious vapors, you must have good ventilation, or serious and permanent damage can result for anyone present within that area.

If you cannot afford factory-made ventilation equipment, see a local heating contractor. A good one should be able to make for you a practical, useful fume cabinet or install serviceable exhaust hoses of large, flexible tubing. Flexible local exhaust hoses offer great adaptability in working on different kinds and sizes of objects. Always follow through on safety procedure when working around substances that require these hoses, however, and wear a respirator with a filter designed for the type of material you are working with—organic solvents, ammonia, toxic dust, or whatever.

Be certain, before you have a new ventilation system installed, that it will be big enough to draw out all the fumes likely to be generated in the area it is to serve, and be doubly certain that it is explosion-proof.

Never take a chance on working in an unventilated room; the accumulated fumes can lead to explosions, chronic illness, and even death.

Hazardous Materials and Equipment

All good workshops must store a good many different kinds of hazardous substances. Some may be poisonous; some, gaseous; some, highly inflammable; some, explosive—all of them part of the common stock in trade of a good workshop, and all of them dangerous unless properly stored and carefully handled.

Fire Hazards

Flammable materials—chemicals, paints, adhesives and solvents—in excess of immediate needs should be stored in OSHA-approved fireproof lockers; and all work areas should be posted with "No Smoking" signs that are strictly enforced, to avoid unnecessary danger of fire. The advice to comply scrupulously with all laws and insurance regulations bears repeating, here and elsewhere throughout this book. Safety regulations are made in an effort to keep down accident and injury, and compliance with them should never be halfway.

Poisonous Substances

Post a poison chart in a prominent place in your workroom, so that you and all members of your staff will know what to do or what to tell a doctor summoned in an emergency. A good chart will help you decide what precautions to take in your work, also, and which substances to avoid using altogether. Poison charts are available from laboratory sup-

Fig. 6.3. For protection against fire, flammable liquids, such as solvents, stains, and varnishes, should be stored in an approved, double-walled safety cabinet.

ply houses. One such source is Fisher Scientific, 5481 Creek Road, Cincinnati, Ohio 45242.

Along with your prominently posted chart of toxic materials should be a chart listing emergency first aid procedures. Both should be placed at eye level, in plain sight, and all staff members should be fully aware of their location and their content.

Storage for Hazardous Materials

Appropriate storage and shelving for hazardous materials must be properly planned and carefully carried out. Keep acids and alkalis well separated, for example, so that, in the event of breakage or spillage, there is less danger of a strong reaction.

If you must keep and handle a large variety of chemicals, be sure to obtain a laboratory safety manual; in addition to pointing out the specific dangers of individual chemicals and the dangers of mixing certain substances, these manuals often contain a full safety section—including quite graphic illustrations of what can happen to human eyes or flesh if one is even a little bit careless with strong chemicals. The shock value of these warnings is tremendous—and their message has helped to prevent many an accident.

In general, avoid using exotic solvents, acids, and alkalis in the collections workroom. The immediate dangers of such substances as well as their carcinogenic and other long-term effects are numerous;[2] and in most instances, other and better-known substances can be used for the job at hand, with much less danger to the user.

Electrical Circuits and Appliances

Be certain that your electrical circuits are never overloaded with more electrical appliances than is safe for the amount of current your building is wired for. If you begin to blow fuses or trip certain circuit breakers repeatedly, check with a good electrician—you may be simply overloading one or two circuits with more appliances than they can handle, or you may be developing a hazardous situation somewhere, with worn wiring or damaged insulation.

And never give cheap, light-duty appliances house room. The same should be said for electrical equipment with frayed or broken wires. Electrical fires are no fun to fight (see chapter 5, "Fire Protection").

NOTES

1. Garry Thomson, *The Museum Environment,* pp. 46–52, 157.
2. Michael McCann, *Artist Beware* (New York: Watson-Guptil, 1979); and *Manual of Hazardous Chemical Reactions* (Boston: National Fire Prevention Association, 1968).

SUGGESTED READING

"A Conservation Workroom." *Intermuseum Conservation Association Newsletter* 4:2 (1968).
      A listing of the conditions, furnishings, tools, and supplies needed for setting up an arts conservation workshop. This newsletter can be obtained from ICA in Oberlin, Ohio.

Coremans, Paul. "The Museum Laboratory"; and Bruno Molajoli, "Museum Architecture." In *The Organization of Museums: Practical Advice.* Paris: The UNESCO Press, 1974. A general survey of the functions of a museum lab, techniques employed in examining objects, and considerations for physical layout.

Organ, R. M. *Design for Scientific Conservation of Antiquities.* Washington, D.C.: Smithsonian Institution Press, 1968.

Complete and current advice on setting up a laboratory for care of artifacts. Covers physical layout, arrangement of furniture, plus a description of tools and equipment and their use. Highly detailed and specific. Although meant for large institutions, even a small museum will find much useful information. Recommended.

Source Book for Science Teaching. Paris: UNESCO, 1962.

While this book was published for teachers working in poor countries, with the expectation that they would be obliged to make scientific apparatus out of scrap material, the same situation may apply also in small museums. Thus the section on how to build balances and other lab equipment out of junk will be particularly helpful. Also included are a variety of work notes, tables of weights, and a host of other useful bits of information.

Technology and Conservation (One Emerson Place, Boston, Massachusetts 02114).

Quarterly journal featuring articles on working professional laboratories in almost every issue; may provide helpful details for setting up a small work room.

Thomson, Garry. *The Museum Environment.* Boston: Butterworths, 1978.

Extensive information about all elements of the environment and preservation; a bit technical at times, but an excellent reference on the subject.

7

Packing Artifacts for Shipment

Allowing artifacts from your collection to travel beyond your own premises—on loan, for exhibition, for repair or appraisal, or for whatever reason—means that your responsibility for their well-being will extend beyond the indoor environment that *you* control and that there will be some risk involved. Naturally, you cannot guarantee their safety, once the objects leave your sight; but there are some measures you can take to minimize the hazards that your artifacts may face in travel.

Caveat

It should be said, at the outset, that no matter how carefully one packs artifacts for shipment, travel automatically means wear and stress and a shortened life span for the objects shipped.

Changes of humidity during travel will affect especially paintings, textiles, and items made of leather and wood.

Vibration or more severe mechanical shock can dislodge from any object pieces that began the journey adhering loosely.

There is always the possibility that the entire artifact may disappear in transit—through loss of tags, misshipment, theft, or vandalism, or through the unaccountable phenomena that insurance companies and shipping firms call "acts of God."

And sometimes, when an object has reached its destination safely, it may straightaway be damaged, there, through careless handling, negligence in unpacking, improper storage, or inappropriate mounting for exhibition.

An especially hazardous time for a traveling artifact comes when it is packed for return shipment. Like many routine jobs in organizations likely to be understaffed, the repacking is often done—hurriedly—by handlers who feel less of a sense of care and responsibility for the object than does its owner-shipper; the original wrappings or padding or the shipping container that the object came in may have been discarded and replaced by simpler, less protective substitutes. *And the effects of such shipping damage may not become apparent until several months after the object has come back to your collection area.*

Pre-Shipment Preparations

What Can Be Shipped? What Can't?

Any artifact being considered for shipment away from a collection should first be carefully examined, to determine its current condition, before a decision is made to let it travel. Such examinations and decisions should be made by the individual ultimately responsible for the overall welfare of all artifacts in the collection—the organization's executive officer, owner-collector, or curator.

Since that individual must also be accountable for losses incurred by damage to collection items in transit, the executive officer should also oversee the packing, if there is no regular workroom supervisor.

Any examination of an object to decide whether shipping would be safe for it must include almost endless questions, as varied as the objects in the collection may be.

Paintings being considered for exhibit, for instance, should, instead, be scheduled for repair if, on close examination, they are found to have loose, wobbly frames, bits of broken gesso, or loose, cupping layers of paint. It may be a good idea to include in your "Packing Procedures" a note to packers to secure and/or pad unsecured wires or hangers or protruding screw eyes on the backs of framed artifacts, so that they can't mar or poke holes into objects packed next to them. Fragile pieces of sculpture with protruding or unsupported parts will also need special padding and support.

Loan requests for objects so weak, so old and time-worn, or so often patched that they cannot survive travel should, for the good of the artifact, be refused.

Certain types of artifacts—some kinds of glassware and some wooden musical instruments, for instance—are extremely sensitive to temperature or humidity changes and could break or crack or come apart in transit, simply from the stress of changes in climate. Special care must be taken in deciding whether and how to ship them.

Before textiles leave the collection, one should determine the nature of the material and its weight and method of fabrication well enough to judge whether it may travel more safely folded, rolled, or flat.

These questions and others of similar insight, depending on the nature of your collection, should be routinely considered before any object is given final clearance for shipment.

Written and Photographic Records

Because human memory is imperfect, the precise condition of artifacts that are to leave their home collection even very briefly should be fully recorded on a *shipping record sheet* before they travel; and, ideally, photographs should be made of each item, *before* it is shipped and *after* it is returned. The ideal time to make the "before" photos is at the time the object is examined and cleared for shipping; the "after" shots should be made as the item is unpacked, on its return.

Both the photographic and the written records are particularly important for objects whose materials and method of fabrication are exceptionally fragile or especially vulnerable to shock, breakage, or crushing. Even the uninstructed will be aware of the special handling needed for recognizably fragile objects; but, again, a note to packers in your instructions on procedure should point out that *some* artifacts that *look* durable enough may also need special handling. Stoneware ceramics and cast-iron artifacts, for example—heavy, hard materials—may not immediately appear to be objects that can be easily broken in shipping, but they are, in reality, quite easily fractured; and in the event of breakage, even though one *can* reconstruct the original form from the broken pieces, these supposedly sturdy materials are difficult to mend satisfactorily. Objects made of more ephemeral materials may be almost impossible to mend, even if one has all the pieces, without photographs that show the way they looked, originally. Consider, for example, an ethnographic mask made of bark cloth, cane, and badly worm-eaten softwood, returned from loan almost completely crushed. Even though all of the pieces are returned, it may well be impossible, without the aid of photographs, even to conjecture about its original appearance, with only the broken splints and crumpled bits of bark cloth as clues.

There is no such thing as having records that are too complete, especially for artifacts that will, from time to time, leave your care, even temporarily.

Photographic comparisons will also show any alteration in condition that has occurred while the artifact was traveling. For objects on loan, before-and-after photographs are excellent records. In case of damage detected on the object's return, such photographic evidence for the owner, the borrower, and the insurance company will help to iron out the problem. Before-and-after photos can also help to determine what may have gone wrong if damage should occur while you are transporting objects for your own purposes, so that greater care may be taken in subsequent shipping procedures; or perhaps they may help you come to the decision that an object is too delicate to travel at all.

Establishing Procedures and Staff Training

Packing artifacts for shipment is a time-consuming chore; and since many small collections are chronically short of staff, it often happens that the job of packing may be done, from time to time, by various members of the staff who do not work at that regularly. It is therefore essential, for the safety of the artifacts, that any organization in those circumstances provide all employees who may be assigned to packing and shipping with a set of standard packing procedures and to see that each employee is taught the correct routine before doing any packing.

From a solely practical point of view, establishing a standard, supervised set of procedures for packing and shipping your artifacts may not only be good for the artifacts; it may also be helpful if accident—or litigation—should overtake the shipment along the way: insurance companies may be less likely to charge the sender with negligence if they know that that organization has such packing and shipping safeguards.

In addition to being provided a set of standard packing procedures and training in their use, the packing and shipping employees should be provided with adequate working space and the tools, supplies, and equipment needed for the job.

The packing area. The work area for packing and shipping should be provided with movers' dollies of sufficient strength and straps and padding in sufficient quantity to move and secure collection objects safely. Materials and instructions for construction, padding, sealing, and addressing shipping crates should also be provided.

And the packing area should be kept clear of other workroom tools, materials, and debris. Maintaining this area as uncluttered space helps to minimize accidents at the starting point. Ideally, the packing area should be easily accessible to storage and display rooms and close to the outside loading area. Packers should not have to shift heavy artifacts routinely up and down stairways, maneuver them around a succession of tight corners, or co-ordinate all efforts through swinging doors.

Shipping Crates or Cases

Artifacts being packed for shipment should be completely enclosed, boxed in, with a tough, puncture-proof outer casing of some durable, protective material such as heavy plywood. Open, slat-work crates should never be used.

In preparing artifacts for shipment, use your best judgment about building the shipping crate and providing supports for it. Every artifact has unique characteristics that may require special attention in packing; look at various examples of boxes made to ship artifacts in; decide how yours must be built; then build the best box you can, and pad and pack it very carefully.[1] Remember that insurance is only a form of compensation that cannot replace lost or broken artifacts.

To keep dirt and liquids from penetrating a shipping crate and its contents, either (1) make the box of waterproof materials, or (2) coat it with waterproof paint or polyurethane, or (3) line it with waterproof paper. A layer of waterproof material, applied either inside or outside, helps to tighten a wooden box; the waterproofing can be put inside, as a lining, or, preferably, outside, in the form of a coating of oil-base paint or polyurethane varnish.

A wooden shipping case, incidentally, provides the artifact more than just protection against bumps and blows; it also lends some protection from changes in humidity. Sealing the outside of the case turns the wooden structure into a large humidity buffer. Just be sure that the case is neither too dry nor too damp when you pack the artifacts.

When the route that your artifact must travel is going to involve a great range of temperature and humidity changes, the interior of the shipping crate should be well lined with humidity-absorbing materials, to lessen the shock of such environmental changes.[2] Plastic packing materials, though they are effective as padding and, to some extent, for insulation, have no stabilizing influence on humidity. Cellulosic substances, such as paper, cardboard, and wood, can help to lessen environmental shock by absorbing or releasing moisture as the environment within the shipping box changes. In some instances, an even more effective humidity-buffering material, such as silica gel, may be needed.

The sides, top, and bottom of wooden shipping crates should be joined with glue, reinforced by screws instead of nails. Screws as fasteners provide greater safety for the artifact, both in transit and on arrival at destination: nails sometimes pull out and can drop inside the crate, where vibration or impact can cause them to be jarred into contact with the artifact; and the pounding and prying needed to drive nails in and pull them out, in sealing the crate for shipment or removing them to unpack the artifact on arrival, merely add further dangers to the objects you are trying to protect. Screws are more easily—and more accurately—inserted and removed in packing and repacking.

Shipping boxes can be reinforced with both external and internal braces, if the weight and bulk of the items being shipped justify that. External wooden braces of one-by-four lumber not only strengthen the box; they can also be used as welcome "handles" for carrying or skids on which awkward, bulky packages can be set down for temporary storage. Excessive weight or bulk should not be crowded into one single shipping crate, and on no account should one ever skimp on padding or cushioning for the artifact being shipped. Use screws or bolts as fasteners for both kinds of braces, also, if you decide to put them on your shipping crate.

Some Do's and Don'ts for Packers and Shippers

Among the firsts in packing and shipping instructions to staff should be the reminder to clear the working space before bringing in any artifact for packing. Work tables often build up a cumulative clutter of loose hand tools, knives, screwdrivers, screws, and nails, staples, or other edged or sharp-pointed items that sometimes get mixed in with packing materials, and such everyday debris can damage an artifact even before it leaves the collection. Packers should make it a rule always to see that the spot where they intend to put down the next artifact to be worked on is clear and free of litter.

Staff people should be instructed never to try to carry large, heavy, awkwardly shaped items alone, without help. Two or more people should work as a team in moving and packing such objects, for the safety of both the artifact and personnel.

And packers should be made aware that such ordinarily harmless things as fountain pens, pencils, screwdrivers, or small hand tools, often carried in pockets or attached to clothing, can dent, snag, scratch, or otherwise mar or damage artifacts. So can wrist watches, tie clips, identification badges, rings, necklaces, pendants, or lockets, and metal buckles or key rings on belts. Packers should remove all objects of this kind before picking up or beginning to pack an artifact. Aside from the risk to personal safety inherent in such usually harmless everyday items, there is the risk of damaging the artifact.

Cushioning and Securing

The ideal artifacts packing operation produces a "womb within a womb," giving the object to be shipped maximum cushioning and minimum movement within the case. A safe, established procedure for going about it can help to eliminate many potential problems.

Packing and cushioning materials should not stain, discolor, or soil the artifacts they surround, and materials that can produce chemical effects on the objects shipped should not be used.

For example, vapors from mothballs or moth crystals included in a packing box can soften and melt the asphalt center of some types of waterproof paper.

Excelsior, often used as a buffer in packing, breaks into small, messy bits and dust particles that can sift through an artifact's outer wrapping, to the surface of the artifact itself. The acetic vapor from new excelsior has been reported as the cause of corrosion in metal objects.

Colored papers, accidentally dampened, can cause stains on artifacts with porous surfaces; and inks from ordinary marking pens can bleed through paper and cause irreversible damage to enclosed objects with absorbent surfaces.

General Packing Instructions[3]

1. If the object you are packing is of a sprawling, awkward shape, or if it has projecting parts, gently pad the parts that stick out, using bolsters of acid-free tissue or similar material.

2. Next, wrap the object in a dust-cover of acid-free tissue or heavier paper, as required. Secure the wrappings with colored tape, which will help identify the package contents as an artifact—and include in the unpacking instructions on the box an alert to the recipient that the colored tape signifies an artifact. Unpacking instructions also should indicate the best way to unwrap enclosed objects so as to avoid damaging them.

3. Enclose the wrapped object in a layer of padding. For framed items or paintings, this might be a box constructed of paper-faced foam board; for other objects, a layer or two of air-cap or expanded polyethylene cushioning will suffice.

4. When placing the package in the packing case, be sure it is surrounded on all sides by at least two inches of additional cushioning. Light-weight objects may be placed loose in the box, if their padding alone will keep them in place. Heavy objects may require braces to hold

Fig. 7.1. In preparing small artifacts for shipment, gently support projecting parts and open interiors with wads or bolsters of crumpled tissue before wrapping the objects with tissue or glassine.

them in place, or braces may be needed to support different components of certain kinds of objects, such as very fragile pieces of sculpture. Pad all areas properly. Choose a cushioning material that is neither too compressible nor too stiff to support the object, while giving it protection from vibration and mechanical shock. "Ethafoam" and similar materials are well suited to the task and are chemically inert. It has been found that air-cap or "bubble-wrap" may contain unstable substances in its outer layer, and so should not be kept in long-term or direct contact with artifacts. When using air-cap, place a buffering layer of acid-free tissue between it and the artifact.

In Transit

To ensure proper care of your artifacts at destination and to alert the receiver to their presence, if small items are in the box, make a packing list for each crate, identifying all the objects enclosed in it, so that none

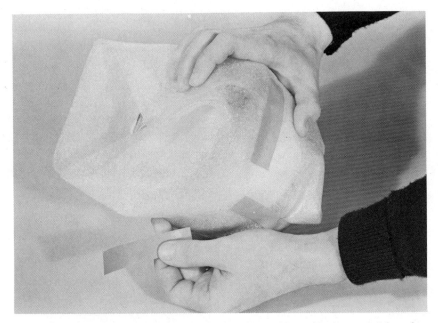

Fig. 7.2. Small objects to be shipped should be wrapped in cushioning material, such as expanded polyethylene, and fastened with colored tape for identification as an artifact and for ease in unpacking.

will be thrown away with the packing materials. Use glue to attach the packing list to the outside of the crate, near the address label and the instructions for uncrating and repacking.

Upon arrival at their destination, the shipping boxes should sit in the receiving area for at least a full day before being opened, to let the objects inside become gradually conditioned to the new environment. If a safe package is extremely cumbersome or heavy, then those on the receiving end must be forewarned, so that the object is not left sitting outside the door upon arrival. As soon as the box is actually on its way, the recipient should be advised that it is in transit and be given the approximate date on which it should arrive.

Always, for greatest safety, if it is at all possible, you yourself should transport as many of the objects you must send out as you can. The best way to do it is in a climate-controlled vehicle. Cushion the shipping box with blankets or movers' pads and strap it down, so that, in the event of a sudden stop, neither the box—nor you—will be damaged.

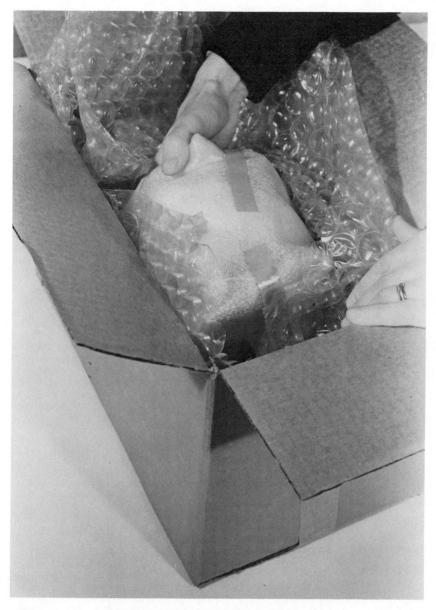

Fig. 7.3. *After it has been properly wrapped and cushioned, a small artifact should be padded on all sides with at least two inches of shock-absorbing material as it goes into the shipping container. Large or heavy items to be shipped should be placed in sturdy wooden boxes.*

NOTES

1. Caroline K. Keck, *Safeguarding Your Collection in Travel,* pp. 40–78; and Dennis V. Piechota and Greta Hansen, "The Care of Cultural Property in Transit: A Care Design for Traveling Exhibitions," pp. 32–46.

2. Nathan Stolow, *Conservation Standards for Works of Art in Transit and on Exhibition,* pp. 83–88.

3. Keck, *Safeguarding Your Collection in Travel,* pp. 40–78; Piechota and Hansen, "Care of Cultural Property in Transit," pp. 32–46.

SUGGESTED READING

Keck, Caroline K. *Safeguarding Your Collection in Travel.* Nashville: The American Association for State and Local History, 1970.

Piechota, Dennis V., and Greta Hansen. "The Care of Cultural Property in Transit: A Case Design for Traveling Exhibitions." In *Technology and Conservation* 4 (Winter 1983): 32–46.
Includes much information not readily available elsewhere: modern materials and case design, and details about handling artifacts.

Stolow, Nathan. *Conservation Standards for Works of Art in Transit and on Exhibition.* Paris: UNESCO, 1979.
The original reference on the subject, with instructions for providing extra protection for extremely valuable objects.

8

Paper: Care and Conservation

Paper—that marvelously useful substance—has been around for a very long time. Some knowledge of its development and the materials and processes used to make it may be helpful in diagnosing and dealing with some of the various problems that plague paper articles.

Conjecture about the earliest development of paper place its beginnings at about A.D. 105, in China, where it was made by mixing bark with hemp. Within the next five hundred years, knowledge of this accommodating product and of ways to make it spread across and out of China, first to Japan, and then, about 751, northward, to Samarkand, in lower Russia. Arab traders brought it from there to Egypt, about the year 900. From Egypt, it traveled eastward, up the Mediterranean, with the restless Moors, who introduced papermaking in Spain about 1150. By the late 1300s, paper was being made in Italy, France, and Germany. Bark was used to make paper in pre-Columbian Mexico and Central America, as it had been in China. By 1495, papermakers were at work in England; and early records indicate that paper was first produced in the American colonies by a William Rittenhouse, of Germantown, Pennsylvania, in 1690.[1]

Until the middle of the nineteenth century, the better-quality European and American papers were made primarily of clippings from new linen and cotton rags, although old rags, canvas sails, and pieces of rope and netting were also used; if they were washed and well processed, these scraps of used fiber could be made into stable paper. With increasing literacy and greater need for paper, however, the continuing search for substitutes to be used instead of cotton and linen rags in papermaking led, in the 1850s and 1860s, to the development of papers based on wood pulp.

Because of a general lack of understanding of their composition, the kinds of paper made from wood pulp have had an undeservedly bad reputation for deteriorating.

Paper is basically a compacted mass of cellulose fibers; and the *source* of the cellulose—whether linen, cotton, jute, hemp, manila rope, sugar cane, straw, bamboo, hardwood, soft wood, or other fibers—is not so important as is the *processing* of the raw material.

Depending on the kind of processing they receive, papers made with a wood-pulp base may vary in quality from flimsy, short-lived newsprint to durable ledger papers suitable for archival work and record storage.

Raw wood contains cellulose, hemi-cellulose, and lignin, in addition to various tannins, gums, oils, and resins called *extractives*. In ordinary mechanical pulp—or groundwood—which is used to make newsprint, tissues, paper towels, and builders' wallboard, the wood is simply ground up and mixed with water, and all its natural components remain in the mix. This gives a higher yield (more pulp per amount of raw material) than does chemically treated wood pulp and results in an inexpensive product.

Although lignin acts as a binder and strengthener in wood, it is also photoreactive, and paper made from groundwood pulp can become weak, brittle, and short-lived.

Wood pulp can be treated chemically, however, to become a stable material. *Semi-chemical* pulp, made from hardwood that has been treated before being ground, has a lower lignin content than groundwood pulp, and products made of semi-chemical pulp can vary in quality from coarse cardboard to white paper of reasonably good quality.

Chemical pulp for making paper is made by boiling wood chips under pressure with any one of three basic chemicals that make the lignin and the extractives soluble, so that they can be more readily leached out, leaving mostly cellulose fiber. The three basic chemicals used are soda, sulfite, and sulfate. There are advantages to processes using any one of the three in making pulp, depending on such factors as the kind of wood available to begin with, the percentage of yield necessary, the quality of the great amounts of water needed for processing, or the properties required in the paper to be made. Since no one method will give every kind of paper, fibers from various processes are often combined to produce the kind of paper wanted. The processing can be varied as needed, to produce such different kinds of paper as grocery bags and wrapping paper, cigarette papers, wallpaper, and fine stationery.

Everyday Hazards
and Some Corrective Measures

The problems that can befall objects made of paper may be as varied as the objects themselves. An astonishing number of harmful things can occur. Many such mishaps are fairly routine and can be averted or made less injurious by elementary precautions or preventative measures. The discussions that follow deal with some minor and some major mishaps and offer suggestions that may be helpful.

Such everyday things as light, ordinary paper fasteners, candle wax, oil, grease, scotch tape, mold, water—and human handlers—all can be harmful to paper artifacts, unless care and proper precautions are exercised.

Light. Prolonged exposure to light, especially sunlight and fluorescent light—both rich in ultraviolet radiation—can cause rapid fading in inks and colors applied to paper, as well as embrittlement of the paper itself. *Any* strong light source may cause paper products to fade, even if the light source is properly fitted with ultraviolet filters.[2]

Yet, the total absence of light, combined with high humidity, is an open invitation for mold to begin growing on paper products, and light—properly handled—is a major curative for destroying such mold growth on paper. "Proper Lighting for Artifacts," in chapter 2, has a good many helpful things to say on this topic.

Paper fasteners and backings. Ordinary paper clips, staples, and pins can cause rust stains, holes, and scratches in paper articles. Matboards with groundwood pulp centers or backings made of cheap cardboard or wood cause stains, acid migration to the print, and embrittlement of the paper they touch.

Soot, dirt, and stain removal. Soot and dirt cause primary surface disfigurement, and can act as focal points for abrasion. "Air Pollution" in chapter 2 has sidelights on this; so does "Good Housekeeping: A Preservation Essential," in chapter 3.

A powdered eraser such as Opaline or Scum-X will remove most freshly fallen dust, soot, and dirt from the surface of a paper artifact. Such cleaning materials should be used only on hard-surface papers, however, and then only on the reverse side, in the margins, or in any large, blank parts of the design area. When using these powdered eraser pads, pierce the fabric of the pad and pour the erasing substance directly on the paper. Gently rub the powder over the surface, with an impeccably clean finger or a soft brush, treating small areas at a time, to pick up dirt; then, carefully brush away the residue.

Artists' soft vinyl or kneaded erasers may be used to remove dirt or smudges on the margins or the reverse side of a paper document. Proceed very slowly, to avoid tearing or abrading the paper.

Candle wax. If, on some especially formal or festive occasion, lighted candles are set about the collections area, there is the possibility of their dripping hot candle wax onto a paper document or artifact. Once cool, the wax should be gently scraped from the surface it adheres to. Any remaining stain from the wax can usually be removed with a cotton swab dipped in mineral spirits or paint thinner, while the paper being treated rests on a clean white blotter.

Oil and grease. Even minute splotches of oil and grease can be ruinous to paper artifacts. When such an accident happens, try to remove the oily traces by rolling a cotton swab soaked in acetone gently over the soiled area. Always be cautious in using solvents.

Stains. Although water baths for paper objects may remove many types of stains, the risks to the object are too great to recommend the water bath as a general stain treatment. The paper itself, and any coatings, inks, or colors involved may well suffer irreversible damage from improper cleaning in water. Even the type of water to use for the process is questionable, since tap water may introduce new agents of deterioration, and distilled water may remove stabilizing substances in the paper structure.[3] *Do not attempt to bleach out spots and stains on paper artifacts.* Spot bleaching and overall bleaching should be done by professional paper conservators only. An unsuccessful bleaching job may, at best, leave rings or "tide-lines" around the treated area. At worst, the result could be a bleached-out design area on a stark white, chemically weakened, degraded paper.

Pastes, adhesives, and tapes. Most, if not all, commerical pastes are acidic and cause deterioration of paper; rubber cements cause permanent stains; pressure-sensitive tapes—scotch tape, for example—cause permanent stains; and their use on paper objects is strongly discouraged.

Although pressure-sensitive tapes that have been applied to paper articles—however wrongly—may weaken and fall off with age, the residue from their adhesive inevitably remains on the paper. Dark-brown staining from it may already have occurred by the time undiscovered old tape begins to fall away, and, by that time, if the paper itself is affected, there is usually no help for it.

Sometimes the tape stain may be reduced with the removal of the adhesive, achieved by applying a mixture of one part acetone (highly flammable), three parts ethyl alcohol, and three parts toluene. Proper precautions should be taken when using this solution, which is toxic and very flammable. The solvent mixture should be sparingly applied, with a cotton swab, to soften and remove adhesive residues.

Attempts to remove tape adhesive stains carry the danger of harming some paints and some colors, or of creating "tide-lines" on the paper

Fig. 8.1. Pressure-sensitive tape caused the permanent stains plainly evident along the edges of this watercolor on paper. Although the tape and adhesive were removed by a conservator, the tape stains had already permeated the paper, and irreversible damage had been done.

when solvents are used. One should, therefore, test the substance to be used on a small, inconspicuous spot before proceeding.

Occasionally, a hair dryer can be used to warm the tape or the adhesive residue so that it can be gently scraped off and cleaned up with a vinyl eraser.

More Potent Threats

Foxing and Mold Growth

Foxing is a form of brown, spotty staining of paper, generally associated with negligence in the care of the object at some time in its existence. Foxing seems to be caused either by chemical reactions involving fungi and iron salts in the paper, or by a different chain of events concerned with decomposition of the cellulose and action of fungi in a damp environment. If it is detected early, further foxing on objects in the collection may be prevented, through proper care and improved environment; but reducing the *evidence* of foxing or removing foxing stains is a job for a paper conservator. Dark spots caused by foxing may be very persistent, requiring the use of various cleaning, washing, or even bleaching techniques to achieve any improvement. Again, this is a job for the expert.

If mold growth is detected on *dry* paper, brush off the mold with a soft camel's-hair brush or a photographer's blow-brush, except on art works done in charcoal or pastel—the rush of the air generated by the blow-brush can blow color particles off works done in these chalklike media. After the mold is brushed off, expose the paper to an hour of sunlight or ultraviolet light and circulating air, to kill the mold.

To give mold less of a chance to start, be sure that your storage area has adequate ventilation and less than 55 percent relative humidity. Paper documents may also be sterilized with fumes from thymol or ortho-phenyl phenol crystals, a procedure that can be carried out in a simply made, air-tight box. Over a period of several days, the paper can be subjected to repeated exposure to the fumes, killing the mold and its spores.[4]

Insects and Rodents

Check the storage area frequently for evidence of insect and rodent infestation, and keep the area clean and well ventilated. (See chapter 3, "Storage," especially the section on good housekeeping.)

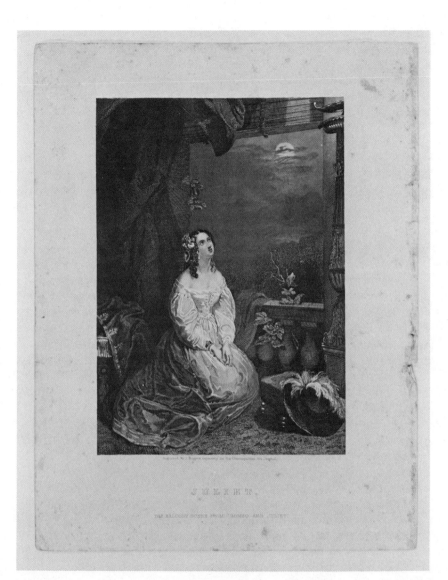

Fig. 8.2. The brownish spots known as foxing *appear all too frequently in old paper. A conservator's help is needed even to attempt to reduce or eliminate the stains.*

Silverfish, bookworms, crickets, flies, rats, and mice not only cause dirt and disorder; allowed to proliferate unchecked, they can damage and eventually destroy book covers, bindings, paper, and associated adhesives, all of which are among their favorite edibles.

To combat insect pests found in a cabinet, closet, or small room, use paradichlorobenzene moth crystals or insecticide strips containing DDVP.[5] Naphthalene moth flakes are not effective *except as a deterrent* to insects, and sprays may prove harmful to the objects you are trying to save. For massive insect infestations, the services of a professional exterminator may be needed. First, obtain the exterminator's recommendation for treating the problem, and then check the suitability of the treatment, yourself, before contracting to have the job done.[6]

Avoiding or Counteracting Excessive Moisture

Excessive moisture—dampness—high humidity—wetness—or just plain water—too much of it is not good for things made of paper. And with almost any paper object, any real moisture can often be too much. Paper articles exposed to high humidity or too much wetness can develop weakened adhesives, water stains, blurred inks and paints, mold growth, or a change in paper dimensions. Too much moisture can cause things made of paper to *cockle* or *buckle*—that is, wrinkle, pucker, begin to look "blistered," or warp, bulge, or undergo surface changes from flat to rippled.

If wetness in or on paper is combined with abrasion, localized pulping of the paper can result. In addition to that, wet paper objects piled together, one atop another, may "felt," or physically lock together, so that the separate sheets meld into a single mass.

Dampness should be kept out of all collections areas, storage, and workrooms. Paper objects with coated or enamel finishes are especially vulnerable to a damp environment, which can make them stick together. Insect infestation is generally more likely to occur in damp areas, also.

Extremely high or extremely low levels of humidity, heat, and light can cause rapid oxidation in paper, leading to brittleness, deterioration of cellulose content, and the fading of applied inks and colors. Fluctuations in *relative humidity* levels are also stressful to paper artifacts, and they should be kept from exposure to it. A steadily maintained relative humidity of about 40 percent to 50 percent is considered ideal for paper, and if you can maintain the relative humidity of your collections area within those limits, your artifacts will be the better for it. Mold growth is likely to occur—on any organic material, not just paper—when relative humidity runs over 65 percent.

Water-soaked papers. Water damage can occur in collections areas for many reasons, and it always causes problems. If you have a number of documents that have been water-soaked—whatever the reason—your first step toward salvaging them should be to consult a paper conservator or the conservation center nearest you.

If you are unable to get help or advice close at hand, often the best thing to do to prevent rapid deterioration of the soaked papers is to freeze them, since mold growth is an immediate danger, especially if the soaked pages are moved from the wet area into a warmer atmosphere.

To prepare soaked documents for freezing, place sheets of silicone-release paper or waxed paper between soaked pages, especially in dealing with coated paper. If the wet papers are large—and bulky—your best bet for freezing them may be a local frozen-food plant or a frozen-food locker. Take them there in a refrigerated truck, if you can arrange for the use of one. Until transportation for freezing can be set up, separate the documents into bundles and wrap each bundle in freezer paper. The usual temperatures used for quick-freezing foods—often as cold as minus-40 degrees Fahrenheit—are too cold for wet paper documents, which are less susceptible to damage from the cold if they can be frozen—and, later, stored—at temperatures ranging between 10 degrees F. to 20 degrees F.[7] *Always obtain expert advice before defrosting any frozen paper object.*

Most wet paper items may be dried between layers of clean white blotters, without any weights on top; or they may be placed on top of blotters to air-dry. Resist the temptation to hasten the drying process by using an electric iron on your documents; ironing will often change the character of the paper for the worse, and any original impressions in the document, such as a plate mark, will be obliterated.[8]

If it's impossible to arrange for freezing water-soaked papers, the next best thing to do is keep them away from warmth and begin the drying process as soon as possible.

Creases, Folds, and Tearing

Carelessness in handling and storing paper objects can cause such *preventable* physical damage as creases, torn places, and fold lines, as well as providing fresh sites for attack by mirco-organisms. Anyone working with paper has the opportunity to cause great damage very easily—and unintentionally.

To recondition paper that has been too long rolled, folded, or creased: first, carefully remove any pins, staples, or clips attached to it and throw them away. Then put the paper in a *humidity chamber*.

The humidity chamber need be nothing fancier than a large reasonably air-tight box, with a fiberglass screen fitted securely inside, at the top, to hold the paper, and, at the bottom, a shallow, waterproof tray. To make it work, put about half an inch of cold water into the bottom tray; put the paper above it, on the fiberglass screen; and close the box. After the paper has been in the chamber long enough to pick up enough humidity to become limp and flat, take it out and place it between several sheets of white tissue paper and four clean white blotters, under a weighted piece of plate glass or thick Plexiglas. Flattening the paper with an electric iron is *not* a good idea—it can cause adverse changes in the structure and appearance of the paper. *Don't do it.*

And—don't leave the paper in the humidity chamber for more than half a day, or mold growth can be expected.

For localized treatment, apply a 50 percent solution of alcohol in water (testing for solubility, first) to the fold line or the crease with a soft brush, and flatten the problem area, using small pieces of tissue and blotting paper, glass, and a small weight. Do not expect all papers to flatten out completely; some items acquire distortions so ineradicable that they cannot be eliminated entirely.

Mending torn paper. Paper can be torn accidentally, with lightning speed and no effort at all. Great care must be taken at all times in handling it; and because it is so easily damaged, one should know how to go about making minor repairs to the torn places.

To repair a ragged tear in a paper document, be sure that the edges are carefully aligned in their original positions as the rest of the paper is kept lying flat. A thin needle probe can be used to line up the edges and tease out the fibers of the paper a bit, so that they overlap one another slightly. On the reverse side of the tear, apply a patch of thin Japanese tissue, brushed with "dry" wheat starch paste.[9] Place pieces of tissue paper and clean, acid-free, or white blotting paper above and below the repair; then press the area lightly under a small glass plate with a weight on top. Change the tissue and blotter "splints" after a minute or so; and then change them every ten minutes for about a half hour, to ensure that nothing sticks to the repaired area. The mend should be inconspicuous, with no cockling.

To repair tears in heavy papers, use proportionately heavier Japanese tissue for reinforcing. Adhesive for the process should be made of wheat and rice starch only, made expressly for that purpose; no readymade

Fig. 8.3. A relaxing chamber for rolled or creased paper may be made by suspending a mounted plastic screen in a large tray above a small amount of water in the tray bottom. A glass cover over the top permits monitoring of conditions inside.

adhesives or special tapes have yet been proven safe to use on valuable papers. Although the paste must be carefully cooked, it is the only nondestructive, reversible adhesive that can be recommended at present for simple torn-paper repairs. If any of this paste is left over, after the repair work is done, store it in an air-tight container, with a cotton ball soaked in a saturated solution of thymol in ethanol taped to the inside of the lid, and the paste will keep and be usable for several months.

Proper storage. Store paper documents and prints flat, rather than upright, and put them in acid-free and lignin-free boxes or cases, to keep the edges from becoming frayed, torn, or bent. Paper items in storage should be matted or interleaved with acid-free board or buffered paper for the best protection.[10]

Photographs should not be stored near any buffered or alkaline papers, boards, or boxes. (See chapter 17, "Photographs," for their care and storage.)

All storage areas should be kept clean and well ventilated, and they should be inspected frequently for evidence of insect or rodent infestation.

Matting, Mounting, Framing,
and Encapsulation

Check your collection of old framed watercolors and prints, to see how many have wooden backings—and note how many of those bear the imprint of the knots and the wood grain visible through the back of the paper. Some of that deterioration is heightened by air pollution coming through gaps in the frame backing, into contact with the paper. Not only are these types of stains almost impossible to remove, but they also cause embrittlement of the paper. When this sort of marring is found, replace all wood and suspect cardboard with acid-free cardboard mats and backings—and do it soon.

If a wooden backing board is considered an important or distinctive part of the artifact, a polyester film barrier may be used between it and the paper with its archival backing.

Backing and matting boards must be made of acid-free and buffered cardboard stock, of "museum" or "conservation" quality. Cheap mat board and brown corrugated cardboard are too acidic for the good of worthwhile paper artifacts. When purchasing mat board, check to see that what you have bought is, in fact, acid-free. A test kit to determine these properties is a helpful tool. Test kits for checking the amounts of acidity, groundwood, and alum present in wood-based products are available from Professional Picture Framers' Association, 5633 South Laburnum Avenue, Richmond, Virginia 23231.

Although acid-free mat board of chemical wood pulp is an acceptable material to use, the surface appearance, strength, and density of all-rag boards may be preferable. Some colored archival mat boards are on the market, and although some colors were not considered safe to use next to valuable papers and photographs, these mat boards are being improved constantly. Check a reliable, up-to-date source before using any colored mat boards, or put a white, acid-free mat next to the document, with a colored mat on top of that.

Hinges for the paper support should be made of Japanese tissue, its thickness dependent upon the weight of the document it is to hold. No prepared tapes of any sort should be used; even so-called "archival" tapes are not recommended for use on valuable papers. The hinge paste must be prepared from either wheat or rice starch, as described above. It bears repeating, here, that pressure-sensitive tapes, rubber cement, dry-mounting tissue, and other adhesives may cause staining on paper articles, and they are usually difficult to remove.

The glass and the backing used for a framed paper artifact should be

Fig. 8.4. *Good protection for paper is afforded by hinging to an acid-free backing and mat. Matted items may be framed or placed in storage boxes or drawers.*

sealed, to prevent dust or contaminated air from entering the frame. Many methods of assembly are possible, depending upon the type of mat needed, and other factors.[11]

Do not mount a print, a drawing, or a watercolor directly against glass; instead, use a mat or some other separating strip, sufficiently thick to keep the paper from touching the glazing. If this is not done, and if condensation forms on the inside of the glass, the print may become spotted with mold or cockled, or it may even stick to the glass.

For prints and maps up to about a size of two-by-three feet, single-strength glass is usually sufficient for glazing. For larger sizes, double-strength glass is needed. A specially coated glass has been developed for its non-glare properties and is considered safe to use on works of art. The invisible colorless coating of this non-glare glass is relatively durable and will not, of itself, cause problems. "Denglas" is an expensive but useful glazing material, since it eliminates most surface reflection.[12]

More expensive than glass, acrylic plastic sheet (Plexiglas, etc.) may be preferred to glass, in some instances, because it is light and shatterproof. Acrylic plastic glazing is also available in ultraviolet-filtering formulations, which are useful, but even more expensive. *A warning note: Beware of using Plexiglas on works of art done in charcoal or pastel, because the plastic can acquire an electrostatic charge, enabling it to pull particles of the medium off the surface of the paper.* The outmoded "frosted" non-glare glass has similar properties, so keep it also away from your valuable paper items.

When shipping framed prints or paintings with glass in the frame, cover the glass with a hatchwork of masking tape, to prevent it from moving around, in the event of breakage. *Do not, however, let the tape lap over onto the frame,* since the adhesive that holds the tape on is capable of lifting up bits of the frame's finish. When the object arrives at its destination, the tape should be taken off within a matter of days, or it can become very difficult to remove.

Another method of protecting paper artifacts is to encapsulate them in polyester film. The process of encapsulation is relatively safe and simple. Encapsulation consists simply of enclosing a sheet of paper within an envelope made up of two sheets of transparent polyester film—such as Mylar, Melinex, etc.—closed at the edges with 3M-brand No. 415 double-sided tape. The tape should not touch the paper: a gap of half an inch between the paper edge and the tape is advisable. This procedure offers a great protection, even against rough handling, and it is easily reversible. The materials for encapsulating papers are easily purchased, and even pre-cut and taped or heat-sealed kits are available.

It should be noted that encapsulation does nothing magical to "pre-

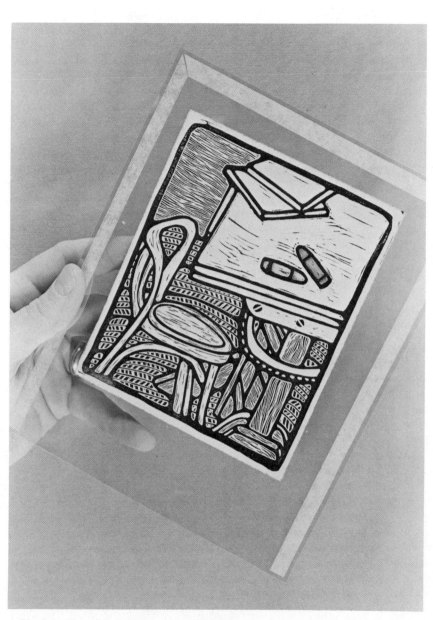

Fig. 8.5. *The polyester film envelope shown above could be closed on the fourth side, for complete encapsulation of the paper inside. This technique protects the object, but does not preclude other treatment that may be needed before the document is enclosed.*

serve" papers, other than protect them from handling and, to some extent, from short-term environmental hazards.

Some papers may require acid neutralization before encapsulation.[13] The neutralization of acids in paper, and the subsequent addition of an alkaline reserve, are steps that should be carried out by a professional conservator.

Note that special matting and encapsulation will give little protection to paper if the important first steps of humidity and temperature control and good housekeeping are ignored. In addition, nonreversible processes of lamination or encapsulation should be avoided, or permanent damage to the paper object may be the result.

NOTES

1. *Columbia Encyclopedia*, 4th ed., s.v. "paper."

2. Garry Thomson, *Museum Environment*, pp. 15–27.

3. Lucia C. Tang and Norwell N. M. Jones, "Effects of Wash Water Quality on the Aging Characteristics of Paper," *Journal of the American Institute for Conservation* (Spring 1979).

4. *Thymol and o-Phenyl Phenol: Safe Work Practices* (New York: Center for Occupational Hazards, 1984).

5. It should be noted that, at the time of this revision, moth crystals containing PDB (paradichlorobenzene) have not been registered for use in public buildings (Stephen R. Edwards, et al., *Pest Control in Museums*, p. A–23).

6. Stephen R. Edwards, et al. *Pest Control in Museums*.

7. Kenneth W. Duckett, *Modern Manuscripts: A Practical Manual for Their Management, Care and Use*, pp. 110–111.

8. Peter Waters, *Procedure for Salvage of Water-Damaged Library Materials*.

9. Clapp, *Curatorial Care of Paper*, pp. 92–94; Merrily A. Smith, *Matting and Hinging Works of Art on Paper*, pp. 30–31.

10. Clapp, *Curatorial Care of Paper*, pp. 85–87.

11. Smith, *Matting and Hinging Paper*, pp. 1–22.

12. The manufacturer of Denglas is: Denton Vacuum, Inc., 8 Springdale Road, Cherry Hill, New Jersey 08003.

13. *Polyester Film Encapsulation*, Library of Congress, pp. 5–7.

SUGGESTED READING

Arney, J. S., et al. "The Influence of Deacidification on the Deterioration of Paper." *Journal of the American Institute for Conservation* 19 (Fall 1979): 34–41.

Baker, John P., and Marguerite C. Soroka, editors. *Library Conservation*. Stroudsburg, Pa.: Dowden, Hutchinson, & Ross, Inc., 1978.

Carey, Kathryn M. "Preservation of Colonial Court Records: Treating a Vast Collection of Historic Documents." *Technology and Conservation Magazine* 6 (Spring 1981): 42–45.

Clapp, Anne F. *Curatorial Care of Works of Art on Paper*. Oberlin, Ohio: Intermuseum Conservation Association, 1978.

Cohn, Majorie B., editor. "Wallpaper Conservation: A Special Issue." *Journal of the American Institute for Conservation* 20 (Fall 1980 and Spring 1981): 49–151.

Cunha, George Martin, and Dorothy Grant Cunha. *Conservation of Library Materials*. Metuchen, N. J.: The Scarecrow Press, Inc., 1971.

Dolloff, Francis W., and Roy L. Perkinson. *How To Care for Works of Art on Paper*. Boston: Museum of Fine Arts, 1971.

Duckett, Kenneth W. *Modern Manuscripts: A Practical Manual for Their Management, Care, and Use*. Nashville: The American Association for State and Local History, 1975.

Edwards, Stephen R., et al. *Pest Control in Museums: A Status Report (1980)*. Lawrence, Kansas: Association of Systematics Collections, 1981.

Frangiamore, Catherine L. *Rescuing Historic Wallpaper: Identification, Preservation, Restoration*. Technical Leaflet No. 76. Nashville: The American Association for State and Local History, 1974.

Graminski, E. L.; E. J. Parks; and E. E. Toth. *The Effects of Temperature and Moisture on the Accelerated Aging of Paper*. Washington, D.C.: U.S. National Bureau of Standards, 1978.

Hunter, Dard. *Hand Made Paper and Its Water Marks: A Bibliography*. New York: Burt Franklin, 1967.

Hunter, Dard. *Papermaking: The History and Technique of an Ancient Craft*. New York: Dover Publications, 1978.

Louden, Louise. *Paper Conservation and Restoration*. Appleton, Wisconsin: Institute of Paper Chemistry, 1978.

Polyester Film Encapsulation. Washington, D.C.: Library of Congress, 1980.

Smith, Merrily A. *Matting and Hinging of Works of Art on Paper*. Washington, D.C.: Library of Congress, 1981.
A very helpful, basic how-to-do-it guide.

Tang, Lucia C., and Norvell N. M. Jones. "The Effects of Wash Water Quality on the Aging Characterstics of Paper." *Journal of the American Institute for Conservation* 18 (Spring 1979): 61–81.

Thomson, Garry. *The Museum Environment*. Boston: Butterworths, 1978.
An excellent reference, this comprehensive treatment can overwhelm one with details if taken in large doses.

Trinkhaus-Randall, Gregor. *Effects of the Environment on Paper: A Review of Recent Literature*. Technical Leaflet No. 128. Nashville: The American Association for State and Local History, 1980.

Waters, Peter. *Procedures for Salvage of Water-Damaged Library Materials*. Washington, D.C.: Library of Congress, 1979.
A good reference to have on hand; if you wait to purchase it until you need it, it will be too late.

Zigrosser, Carol, and Christa M. Gaehde. *A Guide to the Collecting and Care of Original Prints*. New York: Crown Publishers, 1976.

9

Conservation
of Wooden Objects

Problems in caring for wooden artifacts revolve around two main questions: *Did the original craftsman understand his material and work with it intelligently?* And: *Has the object been maintained in a suitable environment?*

If the first question must be answered negatively, there is not much that one can do, after the fact, to compensate for original mishandling.

In answering the second question, one must keep in mind the basic definition of *suitable environment*, which means not only properly maintained levels of temperature and humidity, kept free of fluctuation, but also protection from damage by fungi, insects, fire, water, and vandalism.

The work of the owner of wooden objects, then, must be concerned chiefly with the implications of the second question—a properly maintained environment, the need to provide one conducive to long-term protection, and the need to determine whether treatment may be needed to compensate for the effects of any previous lack of care.

A brief comment on wood and its characteristic tendencies may be helpful.

A living tree may contain up to twice its dry weight in the form of free water, which is carried upward through tubelike, vascular bundles of "conduits" in the tree trunk to the branches above, carrying dissolved nutrient minerals. When a tree is cut down, it gradually loses this free-flowing nutrient-bearing water, but it still contains residual moisture within its cell walls. When the moisture content of the wood in a cut-down tree finally reaches a level of equilibrium with its local environment, the wood is considered to be seasoned.

As cut wood seasons, the loss of cell-wall moisture causes a shrinkage that is greatest in the tangential direction, less in the radial direction, and least apparent along its length. Most traditional lumbermen and craftsmen understood this, and—consequently—sawed or split timbers, planks, and clapboards on a true radius, or perpendicular to the growth rings. Since the natural fiber of the wood was followed, in cleaving, this technique resulted in pieces of lumber that had little tendency to cup or warp. The modern parallel-sawing technique, which does not take wood grain structure into account, utilizes most of the wood in a tree trunk; but except for a few center slices, modern boards, as they dry, tend to warp more severely in proportion to the distance from the center of their original location in the log.

How Temperature and Humidity Levels Affect Wood

Because even seasoned wood responds to varying humidity levels by undergoing dimensional changes, it is futile to attempt to close cracks or to flatten warped pieces of wood by force. The use of weights, clamps, or glue may be temporarily successful in correcting these problems, but if the stresses that caused the warping or cracking are still in the piece, they will manifest themselves somewhere else, creating what may be an even worse problem.

One major cause of damage to wooden objects is moving them suddenly from one environmental climate to another, subjecting the piece to a series of abrupt changes in temperature and humidity en route. It is little wonder that objects that travel come back with popped veneer, flaking gesso, cracks, or loose parts: wood that has reached a working equilibrium in its own environment will react whenever it is subjected to sudden temperature or humidity changes—creating stress for the wood and distress for its owner. *It is important to remember that wood is damaged by changing environmental conditions—it is not just dryness or dampness that causes problems.* Thorough discussion of the problems compounded by changing environmental conditions may be found in R. Bruce Hoadley's *Understanding Wood*, pages 67–105.

Antique wooden objects often display problems of shrinkage that even a good craftsman might not have foreseen. After a piece of furniture has undergone a period of having to adjust to fluctuating levels of relative humidity—some rather extreme, perhaps—shrinkage may cause its joints or its trim to loosen, and wide boards that are restrained from any movement may crack or split. Wooden buckets and barrels, intended for usage that will keep them fully moistened and swelled, can, in disuse, dry out and shrink to the extent that their hoops will fall off and their staves will no longer form a complete, water-tight circle.

Damage to wood is not all caused by simple shrinkage, however, and simple shrinkage can be reversed and corrected somewhat as humidity

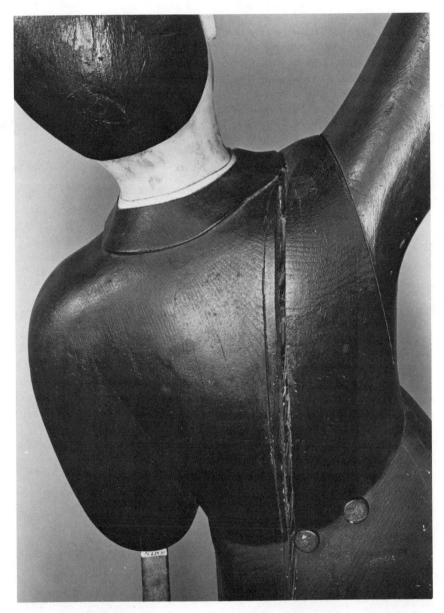

Fig. 9.1. *Cracking down the grain of the wooden sculpture above may have been unavoidable. The work was carved from a section of a tree trunk, and the natural relief for the stress of drying was for the wood to crack apart. It is possible that a controlled environment could have prevented this problem.*

around the wood increases. What *can* seriously damage wood is fluctuating humidity, causing a piece of wood to be compressed or pulled apart if, in response to the humidity changes, the piece is restrained in some way—as an axe handle is, tightly compressed in an axe head, or like a wooden panel tightly fastened within a frame. When much antique furniture was made, the relative humidity of its environment generally remained close to 60 percent, even in the winter, because, in those days, there was no central heating. Putting such antique furniture, conditioned to a humidity level of 60 percent, into a modern building, where the relative humidity drops to 30 percent or less in winter, will put the furniture into a harsh cycle of expansion and contraction that may cause permanent damage. It should be noted that wood will continue to respond to humidity fluctuations forever, although—if it is damaged— it may not assume its original dimensions again.

A relative humidity level of 50 percent to 55 percent is considered ideal for wood, though many collectors and small museums cannot afford the equipment to maintain that level constantly. Obviously, a native environment that is very dry can be excellent for the preservation of wood and other organic materials. In arid regions, there is no need to try to establish and maintain a higher humidity, but, as in any other area, it *is* necessary to try to avoid *rapid changes* in the humidity level; and if it is at all possible, one should maintain a constant, unvarying humidity level, during both wet and dry seasons.

Still, many old wooden pieces that obviously never enjoyed the luxury of a consistent humidity level have come down to us almost miraculously intact.

What is almost as important as the constant relative humidity level is *a slow and limited change* of humidity, through the seasons, rather than abrupt changes. When a wooden object is put into a building where the air conditioning is intended only for human comfort—that is, where the air conditioning is turned on in the morning and turned off at night— the object suffers *more* than if it were stored in a barn.

Under conditions of extreme dryness and heat, such as those present in uninsulated attics in summer or overheated buildings in winter, wood will still survive—but it will shrink, crack, or check, and its glued joints will fail. With the coming of the current world energy crisis and the rising costs of heating and cooling, it is interesting to the conservator to notice that however chilly *we* may feel, the cooler buildings we now maintain in winter have had fewer ill effects upon wooden objects than the warmer building temperatures so many of us have grown accustomed to, in recent years.

Fig. 9.2. *The front board of the slant-front desk above is restrained from any movement by the battens on each end. The wood cracked, because cyclical expansion and contraction built up great stress that could not be released by other means.*

Sometimes, maintaining the stability of wood is simply a matter of common sense: for example, wooden objects should not be placed in an area where rapid or uneven heating and cooling will be certain to occur, such as near an outside door, a fireplace, or a heater, in direct sunlight, or next to a heating or cooling vent. The radical and frequent changes in temperature that occur in these areas will almost certainly cause cracking or warping of any wood placed nearby.

Strong light can bleach wood and fade the organic dyes used to stain some wooden pieces.

And adverse changes in wood may develop, *in spite of good care,* under some circumstances. A good example is that of an oil painting made on a wooden panel; such a work of art is likely to warp to a convex front, because the drying out of the unpainted back side of the wood is going to be done much faster than the gradual drying of the paint-covered front surface. The shrinkage of the unpainted back surface of the wood pulls the panel around into a curve.

These kinds of changes in wooden objects may be slowed or may even be stopped, but they cannot be reversed: some of the cells of the wood are compressed when warping and other dimensional changes occur, so that the dimensions of the wood are changed. Attempts to correct the situation only put stress on the new "set" of the wood.[1]

Wood stored in damp, airless basements is open to attack by fungus growths that can cause dry rot in the wood itself and an accompanying breakdown of the finish and the glue. Wood subjected to continual wetting, with little circulation of the air around it, will rot in only a few years—which is why many mortised joints, parts of pilings, and ships' hulls "between wind and water" are areas of constant trouble. Paint, oil, or varnish alone are not cures for the problem of persistent wetting— only adequate air circulation helps. A practical demonstration of that can be seen in surviving seventeenth- and early eighteenth-century houses constructed of unpainted wood but built to allow adequate air circulation to all parts.

In short, to preserve wood, maintain adequate ventilation with little or no change in humidity level. Portable humidifiers and dehumidifiers can prevent a myriad of irreversible problems (see chapter 2, "Controlling Collection Environment). Moving wooden objects quickly from one environment to another is very risky, and should be avoided whenever possible. The shock of going, in winter, from a warm building into an ice-cold van and, in summer, from an air-conditioned storage space out into 90-degree temperatures, or—in any season—from sheltered areas

Fig. 9.3. Paintings on wood panels often assume a convex curve because changes in the moisture content of the back surface of the wood occur much faster than those on the front, which is protected by the paint layer. Compression of the wood near the back surface causes the curving, which is usually considered permanent.

out into windy, rainy weather may be enough to inflict serious damage on any wooden object.

How To Treat Warping and Splitting in Wood

As discussed above, warping and splitting in wood can be caused by the way a tree trunk is sawn into boards. There are other causes, as well. Assuming that a wooden object has been well made, originally, other elements may lead to structural problems.

A variety of remedies have been tried: steaming and clamping the piece, painting or waxing the underside or the back side, using nails or screws to attach wooden or metal restraining clamps or reinforcing strips to the wood; or making a series of parallel saw cuts on one side of the wood, to relieve the stress.

Some of these attempted remedies may work—sometimes; most of them are tricky or hit-or-miss or even dangerous to the wooden object;

and none is guaranteed. For the most part, it is better to leave a piece of warped, split wood as is, than to gamble on damaging it futher in trying to fix it.

And, in such situations, beware of the amateur restorer; if a perfect-looking piece is what is really wanted, it's best to buy a slick reproduction; if you want a damaged piece of wood properly treated, entrust it to a qualified conservator.

Another "cure" widely touted for warping or cracking wood is the liberal use of "nourishing oil." This "cure-all" may be a commercially made or a home-made product, concocted of such nondrying oils as olive oil or lemon oil, and/or a slow-dryer such as raw linseed oil, with some kind of wax—or waxes—added. Such mixtures do nothing to replace the lost moisture in damaged wood, and so provide no corrective effect for any sort of structural problem. Any finish or dressing for wood must be regarded as primarily cosmetic, rather than remedial to ills of the basic material itself.

Ridding Wood of Insects and Fungi

Small animal pests, insects, and fungi are persistent sources of damage to unprotected wood. As mentioned in the "Good Housekeeping" section of chapter 3 (which see), collections housed in old buildings and in storage areas that are not well maintained are places where these enemies to wood congregate most often and do their dirty work best. Good housekeeping is a must.

Sometimes, however, even despite diligence and watchfulness, insects, fungi, and rot may attack wooden artifacts. Once discovered, they must be got rid of, and effective treatments for that must sometimes be stringent.

Before discussing various methods of treatment, it must be stressed here, that *all insecticides, fungicides, and fumigating materials are toxic*, some of them extremely so. Just one whiff of hydrogen cyanide gas (HCN), for instance, can be fatal to human life. Many of the phenol compounds can cause death by being absorbed through the skin. Although most of the lethal substances that can serve as fumigants are no longer available on the open market, those that are contain a variety of toxic materials and possible carcinogens. Very few insecticides are considered safe to use any more, and the list is shrinking.[2]

Good artifacts are worth protecting, true; *but even more so is human life.* Before resorting indiscriminately to dips, sprays, or gases to rid your collections of insects or fungi, be sure that you *know the properties of the materials you are handling. If you are not certain of them, hire a professional pest control service and research the method they suggest before any work is done.* Remember, too, when handling artifacts that have been treated in the past, that many powdered insecticides, such as arsenic or DDT, are residual. *Wear gloves when handling such objects.*

Insect Fumigants

Cyanide gas, methyl bromide, or carbon disulfide have been used on mixed materials that cannot be safely or easily penetrated by powders or liquids. Another gas mixture—Vikane (sulfuryl fluoride)—has been considered an acceptable risk for fumigation. Ethylene oxide mixed with an inert gas is currently used in many museum fumigation chambers, though the safety of doing so is being questioned; investigation indicates that this gas is more dangerous than was previously thought. Pest control operator may no longer be permitted to use methyl bromide to fumigate objects inside a polyethylene tent, as was common in the recent past.

Insecticide strips containing DDVP (2, 2-dichlorovinyl dimethyl phosphate) or moth crystals of paradichlorobenzene may be about all one may use with any safety on collections objects. The object to be treated may be placed in an airtight container or tented over with a polyethylene sheet on a frame, so that the plastic does not touch the object. Hang either an insecticide strip or a cloth bag of moth crystals above the wooden object, and check the wood's surface after one day. If the finish has become milky-looking or sticky, take it out of the polyethylene tent and let it dry in a dust-free area for several days. Otherwise, continue the exposure for about a week; let the piece stand for about two weeks, and then repeat the treatment, to kill any newly hatched insects. Since the moth crystals require a temperature of about ninety degrees to vaporize effectively, an insecticide strip may be the most convenient first choice for this treatment. At present, moth crystals containing PDB (paradichlorobenzene) are not registered for use in public buildings, though the impregnated strips are. Keep up to date with notices from the Environmental Protection Agency or the Association of Systematics Collections for news on pesticides.[3]

The most effective fumigation of wood or any other organic material must be done in a vacuum chamber, to ensure that the fumigant is drawn into the object as effectively as possible, and then drawn out again, after treatment. The current leading fumigants are Vikane, ethylene oxide and methyl bromide. Ethylene oxide and methyl bromide are suspected of being carcinogenic, and all three fumigants are *extremely* toxic. It now appears that no lethal gases should be used outside of a properly built and monitored chamber, with air sampling, record keeping, and other safety provisions as prescribed by OSHA.

Combination Insecticides and Fungicides

It should be noted that liquid preservative materials for wood should be applied to bare-wood items only and that they are generally intended for gross, outdoor objects or structural elements. These materials are often based on chlorinated phenols in a petroleum solvent or aqueous mixtures of metallic salts like zinc or copper. They serve the dual function of preserving wood against such fungi as dry rot and of killing insects at any stage of the insect life cycle. These preservatives are residual, give long-lasting protection, and may be dipped, sprayed, or painted on.

Creosote is a relatively effective, but outmoded, wood preservative; it stains wood a black color, leaves an oily residue, and irritates human tissue. Creosote should not be used on historic materials.

Petroleum solvents with pentachlorophenol or copper naphthenate may be obtained in different solvent grades. The better "water-white" grade does not stain, dries quickly, and can be painted over. Be sure to test the piece to be treated, however, to be certain that the solvent will not damage the object's surface appearance or patina. Again, it should be noted that *these preservatives are all toxic,* and they can be absorbed through the skin; always wear neoprene gloves when using the solvent solutions. In addition, be aware that the solvents are quite flammable. Complex objects, such as those composed of several materials or those having painted, varnished, or gilt surfaces, should not be treated except by expert conservators.

Counteracting Rot and Insect Damage

Cleanliness, ventilation, and periodic inspection are the best ways to prevent rot and insect damage to wooden objects. Preservative materials should be used before trouble starts, in general construction or rough, outdoor objects. Wooden joints, water-line areas and underground areas of wooden structures in particular should be carefully saturated with preservative. End-grain wood pieces are also especially vulnerable, because moisture is easily drawn into the vascular bundles in the wood, penetrating well into the interior, beyond the surface. Drip caps and flashings should be used as needed, to keep water from settling behind boards and walls of buildings or from soaking into vertical, upright pieces like sign posts or totem poles.

Dead-air areas especially should be provided with improved ventilation, to keep them from furnishing a favorable environment for fungi. Once dry rot has started, not only the infected wood, but the area around it must be removed, to ensure the safety of the rest of the piece. Major surgery on a valuable object is not only expensive; it also removes irreplaceable original material. For that reason, particularly in marine environments, preventive maintenance is the only practical answer.

There are wax baths and resins that can be used to infuse wet, rotten, or weak wood, killing harmful organisms and returning to the wood fibers some mechanical strength and dimensional stability. Some of these treatments are expensive, time-consuming, and complex, and some require specialized equipment. Because many organic materials that turn up in archaeological or marine sites are already deteriorating, however, and must be salvaged for scholarly purposes, it is well to be aware that such techniques for consolidation exist. Archaeological artifacts of any material, and especially those made of organic materials and ferrous metals, may be almost shadows of their original structures when unearthed. The complications and the care that must be exercised in handling them are staggering.[4] Decisions about which materials to use and where to find the expertise to do so correctly can be obtained only from conservators who have the proper training and experience in archaeological or related areas of conservation. Archaeological conservators have been able to consolidate organic materials so weak that they have to be excavated with the surrounding soil intact. Remember that expert knowledge and help is available; there is no need to risk damage to valuable objects by subjecting them to amateur treatment.

Treating Waterlogged Wood

Of first priority in working with waterlogged wooden objects is the job of preventing the wood from drying out before appropriate treatment for it can be devised. While you are considering the problem of removing the water by drying processes that will not cause cracking, twisting, or shrinkage in the wood itself, you must keep that soaked wood wet!

There are various ways to go about removing the water gradually. That may involve special drying processes or the replacement of the water by an impregnating material that will strengthen the wood and give it dimensional stability.

A number of factors bear on the condition of wet wood, such as whether the wood was buried in mud, in salt water, in fresh water, in an acid bog, or in alkaline soil; whether it has mineralized or been in contact with certain metals; whether it contains metal fasteners or hardware; whether it has a surface coating or decoration that must be saved; whether there has been extensive leaching of cellulose; what species of wood it is and what its porosity is. Given the widely varying possibilities these differing influences indicate, it is evident that no two pieces of waterlogged wood will react in the same way to any given treatment. Also, the choice of which treatment to use is complex, especially as new information is published frequently on the successes and failures of new and old methods in laboratories all over the world. To be stringently truthful, *there is no simple cure for badly deteriorated wood.* Some basic procedures currently in use include these:

Freeze-drying. In freeze-drying, the wooden object is frozen, placed in a vacuum chamber, and the ice in its cells is removed by sublimation. Freeze-drying is much used in working with biological specimens. It is expensive and complex, especially when used in combination with other methods.

Slow-drying. In slow-drying, wooden objects in reasonably sound condition are covered with wet sand and wet sacks and are then gradually dried out over a long period of weeks and months. The object's surface may have a final finish coat of some synthetic resin. This treatment is used mostly for large objects, such as dugout canoes.

Polyethylene glycols. Polyethylene glycols (often abbreviated P.E.G.) are water-soluble waxes with a variety of melting points, and they can be used, in water baths, to replace the water in a sodden piece of wood. Starting with weak solutions, the amount of wax and the temperature are increased gradually until the water in the wood is gone. This process may take months, or even years. Some of these waxes are sensitive to high humidity, and some require complex controls to be used successfully. P.E.G. will also soften painted surfaces. After treatment with P.E.G., wood ends up being very dark and very heavy. Nevertheless, P.E.G. treatment is currently considered by many conservators to be the most effective treatment for waterlogged wood.

Waxes, resins, and wax-resin mixtures. Treatments with waxes, resins, and wax-resin mixtures have been used on wet and dry weakened wood; and they are often used in combination with other procedures, such as "solvent drying," or first replacing the water with a solvent in which bulking and impregnating resins can be dissolved. Although there are difficulties in any given method, all are continuously being tested and refined.

Working with Dry, Weak Wood

In addition to some of the methods mentioned above, there are now products commercially available that have been made especially for consolidating wood previously damaged by rot or insect attack. Some of these products are intended for use in historic structures, and some are for marine use; in general, however, most such materials are difficult to use and are not reversible if problems should arise. For their specific uses, these products serve important functions, but they should not be considered cure-alls for use on more delicate or complex objects.

Cleaning Wooden Artifacts

The first problem to consider in cleaning wood is the point at which dirt ends and historical significance begins. One might eliminate changes obviously made by previous collectors, if such changes do not really pertain to the history of the piece; and, of course, disfiguring dirt should be removed. Keep in mind that, in surface cleaning, as in other maintenance processes, one should go only so far as is essential for the preservation of the object.

Before doing anything more than surface cleaning, carefully go over all accessible areas of the object with a vacuum cleaner, using the soft brush (or dusting) attachment. In working with furniture that is upholstered or that has loose marquetry or veneer, avoid sucking into the vacuum dust bag any fragile bits of the furniture surface by holding, between the vacuum brush and the furniture, a small piece of plastic screen taped along its edges to keep it from scratching the furniture surface. *Do not* vacuum any piece with obviously fragile fabric or with flaking paint on the surface.

For further surface cleaning, avoid old remedies containing oil of any kind. First, use a sponge slightly dampened with distilled water to remove grime—if initial testing with this method shows that it will create no problems.

A subsequent step would be to go over the piece with a clean sponge dampened in a mixture of one gallon of water and one teaspoon of a cleaner containing trisodium phosphate—something such as Soilax; *but always read the label on any cleaning product you plan to use, before using it*. To prevent problems that might result from use of this solution, such as paint loss, do not use the trisodium phosphate solution on broken paint films on good pieces. Do not wet the surface any more than necessary; and, with a clean, damp sponge, be sure to remove all traces of any detergent used. Ultraviolet light will reveal any detergent that has not been properly removed.

The strongest acceptable cleaners are benzine (*not benzene*) or mineral spirits, although these solvents may dissolve and remove the old finish. It is important to be sure, at the outset, what it is that you wish to remove. A little surface dirt is usually easy to remove, but it is all too easy to go too far and harm an irreplaceable antique finish. Above all, never clean or otherwise treat a *painted* wooden object; that is a complex job for a conservator.

"Nourishing" a Wooden Finish

Avoid the erroneous notion that wood or its finishes require "feeding" regularly. That term—*feeding*—derives from certain traditional treatments utilizing tung oil, lemon oil, or linseed oil, and it seems to find credence today among people who are beguiled into thinking that they should want to keep their wooden objects as "happy" as little furry pets. The oil used in the highly touted "feeding" solutions is usually slow to dry, and so attracts dust to any surface it is applied to. Wood does not absorb such oil into its cell walls, so there is no additional protection against environmental conditions. Although the "feeding" oil may spruce up the appearance of the wood for a while, it darkens with age and also—finally—penetrates the wood, making later removal difficult and often damaging the original surface.

The notion that oils are "natural" treatments does not take into account the inherent problems created by using such materials. All finishing materials were once based upon natural oils and resins, and they all had properties that made them suitable for some uses and not for others. Many such products are still useful today, but none are all-purpose remedies.

Refinishing Wood

When a wooden object is refinished improperly, the history etched into its surface by usage is erased forever. Stripping down and refinishing old pieces of furniture for fun, profit, or self-instruction may be great sport—*if the pieces are your own.* One does not, however, have the right to play games with furniture or polychrome figures belonging to a museum. That prohibition extends not only to museum staff or volunteers, but to local furniture restorers or other craftsmen, also. Such technicians might do a good-looking job of stripping and repainting, but

Fig. 9.4. Complex objects such as this lacquered box must be handled with extra care. In this particular instance, the object shown might be considered a painting on a wooden support, definitely requiring professional treatment.

when the piece is returned from their hands, it will have lost some of its validity as a document of the past. Removing layers of overpaint and salvaging what is left of the original finish calls for a professional conservator who has had years of training and who understands the chemistry of the solvents and oils involved. Many alcohols and petroleum-based solvents can ruin varnish or paint layers if their gelling, leaching, swell-

Fig. 9.5. The finish on this clock case is an excellent example of a coating applied to an incompatible base. The surface is now coated with hardened beads of resin, although the layer underneath does not appear to be in bad condition.

ing, or solvent action is not well understood. In addition, there are real health hazards posed by the casual use of these solvents. All of the foregoing advice may sound discouraging to the novice, and so it should: refinishing *is* complex—and, usually, it is unethical, as well, where antiques are involved.

Paint-strippers made from an alkali base—most notoriously, lye— have not only all the foregoing disadvantages, but, in addition, they cause wood fibers to deteriorate and permanently change the color of some hardwoods. Your best job in caring for wooden objects can be done by staying within the limits of your capability and understanding.

Since damage, disfigurement, or complete destruction of an original finish can occur, over the years, through simple usage of any wooden object, it must be admitted that refinishing is sometimes desirable. It should be stressed, however, that, in such instances, the needed refinishing should be undertaken only by a skilled and experienced conservator. The main precautions are to avoid stripping away the surface of the wood itself and to choose a new finish in keeping with the object in question. A bit of research in books and journals dedicated to fine woodworking will reveal the numerous finishes available and the benefits and problems of each.[5] It should be noted that old-fashioned-looking results can be obtained only by using care and true knowledge of materials and methods—applied with large amounts of hand labor. Note that museum pieces are often refinished with easily reversible coatings, while household items might require a finish of greater durability.

Repairing Wooden Objects

Loose Joints

Before you begin work on a piece of wooden furniture with loose joints—or before beginning any sort of repair work, as a matter of truth—*consider for a moment whether the repair you have in mind is essential to the survival of the object*. If it isn't, then leave well enough alone.

Assuming that something *must* be done about the aging joints in a piece of old wooden furniture, and that gluing is needed, be sure that all old glue is thoroughly scraped off the surfaces that are to be re-joined: new glue does not stick well to old glue.

The looseness or snugness of the joint, *before* you work on it, may help determine what sort of adhesive you should use in repairing it, but the one glue primarily recommended for use on old and valuable objects is *liquid hide glue*. Liquid hide glue is the best strong, reversible glue for many purposes; and, in fact, it is probably the adhesive originally used on genuinely old objects.

To keep from damaging the surface when you clamp together the parts to be joined in the repaired area, place a small piece of acrylic plastic between the wood and the jaw of the clamp. The plastic will pad and protect the wood; and it will pop loose, later on, if a little glue should seep out of the repair onto it and cause it to stick, temporarily.

If the wooden joints were not originally glued, but were held together by wedges or were force-fitted, it may be possible to tighten them by using a swelling agent, though these materials are not suggested for fine or valuable pieces. There are alcoholic solutions of glycols that seem to do an effective job of swelling the wood, and they are readily available in hardware stores; but be sure that the liquid does not seep out onto a painted surface, if you use any of them, since they soften some paints.

Dents, Scratches, and Nicks

Sometimes, a depression caused by crushing or denting a wooden surface can be made to swell enough—by using steam on it—to rise back up to its original level. The usual method is to put a few layers of wet rag over the depressed area and apply to it the tip of a hot iron or an electric soldering gun one or more times. Keep the pad of wet fabric as close to the size of the dent as possible, since the steam will probably blanch the varnish on the surrounding surface, which then may need additional treatment.

Scratches and nicks in wood can usually be filled in cosmetically. Heated stick-shellec smoothed into the void is the traditional remedy, but this is a difficult process for the novice. There are any number of colored putty sticks and wax crayons on the market; and although they are not so strong and hard as shellac, they will do an adequate covering job, and they are easily reversible, later on. These materials are available at most hardware stores and lumber yards.

Alligatored and Checked Finishes

Quite common on old buggies and old piano tops, checked or alligatored finishes are the result of either improper drying of the original paint layers or of simple breakdown due to age. There are any number of proprietary and homemade solutions for filling in or rejuvenating such a defective finish. Any of these materials is a questionable answer, at best, and no true solution to the problem. At this point, you must decide whether you will live with the marred surface as is, or have the piece refinished, which will be a major undertaking and one that may eliminate historical value in the surface of the object. Your best bet is to consult a knowledgeable conservator.

Treating Fogginess, Milkiness, Rings

Fogginess, milkiness, and rings on wooden surfaces are usually caused by excess moisture. The treatment for them depends on the material used for the finish and the degree to which moisture has penetrated the finish. If such blemishes appear on a shellac surface, a rag dampened slightly with alcohol and gently wiped across the damaged spots will usually even out the marks; or a thin solution of one part white shellac to five parts alcohol may be tried.

A varnish or oil finish may be compounded of a variety of drying oils and resins, so the answers, in those instances, will be empirical. Try rubbing the area with a rag dampened with alcohol, but don't continue that for very long, or the surface may soften. Or a fine abrasive such as 4/0 (0000) pumice or rottenstone, in a vehicle such as cooking oil, may do the trick; but the results are *not* guaranteed. Proceeding slowly and testing methods carefully will prevent further injury to the finish and may perhaps reveal the correct answer to the problem.

Protective Waxes

For light, protective layers over finished wooden surfaces, you may use good commerical paste waxes made of beeswax, carnauba, or candelilla wax. Butcher's Bowling Alley Wax is one such product; also available are formulations of microcrystalline wax, such as Renaissance wax. It should be noted that the latter produces a soft coating that smears easily. The important thing is to put the wax on in thin layers and buff the surface thoroughly, between layers, with a woolen cloth or a chamois or sheepskin. Do not use liquid self-polishing waxes, as some of them impart a milky surface to some finishes, and many of them contain silicones, which may penetrate the wood, making later cleaning or finishing extremely difficult, if not impossible.

Some commerical dust-attracting liquids, such as Endust, may be used, but that should be done as sparingly as possible, and *then* such products should be put only on the dust rag, or they will form a sticky surface on the wood. Waxing may be done once or twice a year, but it should not be a weekly practice, or a gummy, sticky surface may be the result. *Dusting with a clean rag is the best regular care for wood.*

NOTES

1. Garry Thomson, *Museum Environment*, pp. 208–210.
2. Stephen R. Edwards, et al., *Pest Control in Museums*, pp. 1–A-30.
3. Edwards, *Pest Control*, pp. A-1–A-30.
4. Ivor Noel Hume, *Martin's Hundred* (New York: Alfred A. Knopf, 1982), pp. 157–166, 176–180.
5. Robert D. Mussey, "Old Finishes: What Put the Shine on Furniture's Golden Age"; Arthur D. Newell, "Finishing Materials: What You Always Wanted to Know."

SUGGESTED READING

Angst, Walter. "A Case for Scientific Furniture Conservation." *Museum News* 56 (July–August 1978): 24–28.

Angst, Walter. "Repair of a Side Chair with a Perforated Plywood Seat." *Journal of the American Institute for Conservation* 19 (Spring 1980): 75–88.

Barclay, R., R. Eames, and A. Todd. *The Care of Wooden Objects*. Ottawa: Canadian Conservation Institute, 1980.

Barkman, L. *The Preservation of the Wasa*. Stockholm: State Marine History Museum, 1956.
A general description of the treatment, materials, and equipment of the Swedish wooden warship.

"A Blast at the Past . . . Endangering Wood Species." *Technology and Conservation Magazine* 5 (Fall 1980): 5–6.

Cravens, DuVal. "Soil Fumigants: Advances in Protecting Wood From Decay." *Technology and Conservation Magazine* 2 (Winter 1977): 22–26.

Edwards, Stephen R., et al. *Pest Control in Museums: A Status Report (1980)*. Lawrence, Kansas: Association of Systematics Collections, 1981.

Hoadley, R. Bruce. *Understanding Wood*. Newtown, Connecticut: Taunton Press, 1980.
An excellent comprehensive reference about the nature of wood and the ways in which it responds to its surroundings.

Marsh, Moreton. *The Easy Expert in Collecting and Restoring American Antiques*. Philadelphia: J. B. Lippincott Company, 1959.
The title is misleading, and one should not expect to become an expert easily. The author does recommend a light hand in any repair work and offers helpful comments about materials.

McGiffin, Robert. *Furniture Care and Conservation*. Nashville: The American Association for State and Local History, 1983.
Excellent, comprehensive reference for the care of wooden objects.

Merrill, William. *Wood Deterioration: Causes, Detection, and Prevention*. Technical Leaflet 77. Nashville: American Association for State and Local History, 1974.
This publication provides the basic introduction to the care of wood and describes some of the problems one will encounter.

Mussey, Robert D. "Old Finishes: What Put the Shine on Furniture's Golden Age." *Fine Woodworking*, No. 33 (March–April 1982): 71–74.

Newell, Arthur D. "Finishing Materials." *Fine Woodworking*, No. 17 (July–August 1979): 72–75.
Excellent description of modern wood finishes, their peculiarities and performance.

Nicholas, Darrel D. *Wood Deterioration and Its Prevention by Preservative Treatments*. 2 vols. Syracuse, N.Y.: Syracuse University Press, 1973.

Peltz, Perri, and Monona Rossol. *Safe Pest Control Procedures for Museum Collections*. New York: Center for Occupational Hazards, 1983.

Phillips, Morgan W. "Consolidation of Porous Materials: Problems and Possibilities of Acrylic Resin Techniques." *Technology and Conservation Magazine* 4 (Winter 1979): 42–46.

Plenderleith, H. J. and A. E. A. Werner. "Wood." In *The Conservation of Antiquities and Works of Art: Treatment, Repair, and Restoration*. New York: Oxford University Press, 1971.
This reference is not intended for amateur conservators, but it does show the complicated nature of problems in preservation. It should be noted that some procedures and materials are considered out of date.

Rosenquist, Anna. "The Stabilizing of Wood Found in the Viking Ship of Oseberg." *Studies in Conservation* 4 (1959).
Techniques in the conservation of wood; methods that have worked and not worked over a long period of time.

10
Skin and Leather Artifacts

The skins of animals, more than any other organic material used for making artifacts and wearing apparel, are so adversely affected by excessive heat, moisture, and micro-organisms that there is frequently nothing of their original nature and characteristics left when they are subjected to such extremes. When items made of skin have come to such a pass, even the best conservator or protein chemist may be unable to solve the problems that have developed.

Properties of Animal Skins

Animal skin is composed of three layers: the cuticle, or epidermis; the soft grain layer, containing skin pigmentation, sweat glands, and hair follicles; and the corium, or basic skin, containing the fiber bundles.

Because the skin of a live animal is composed of almost 60 percent water, it is flexible, and the fiber bundles of the inner layer overlap and slide over one another. After the death of its animal owner, a skin removed from its host dries out and becomes stiff and inflexible.

The first step in processing a flayed skin, no matter how that skin is to be subsequently used, is to scrape all fat and flesh off it. If the fat is left on, the skin will rapidly deteriorate or become "fat-burned" and full of weak spots. Any flesh left on forms a perfect culture medium for all sorts of mirco-organisms; and in the presence of moisture, the raw skin is soon reduced to a putrefied, stinking mess. Skin flesh and fat are usually removed by a combination of scraping with a blunt iron knife, plus rubbing with an absorbent, such as heated corn meal, bran, sawdust, or various kinds of soil.

Once the fat and flesh are removed from a skin, a great variety of processing methods may then be applied to it. The cultural group that produced a skin artifact, the period of time from which such an object dates, and the ultimate use of the processed skin are all considerations in determining which of several conservation methods might best be used on the piece.

To understand how to treat artifacts made from animal skins and to know what the limitations of treatment for them are, it is first necessary to know something about the traditional ways in which skins are prepared for use. To avoid using the wrong treatment on an object made of skin, one should be able to distinguish a *tawed skin*—one tanned with minerals, primarily alum and salt—from a *buckskin*—tanned by the Indians' chamois method, in which pelts were treated with the fat, livers, and brains of animals and then hung to dry. A "regenerative" process applicable to a Siberian shaman's bag might be disastrous if applied to parchment. Thus, proper artifact identification is especially crucial to the care of leather goods. The reader is referred to the bibliographic sources at the end of this chapter for an essential working knowledge of leather processing. Avoid the temptation to treat all leathers with dressings in the hope that you will improve their condition. Unwarranted treatment often does more harm than good, such as providing moisture and nutrients for mould growth that had not existed before the treatment.

Primary Care of Skin and Leather Goods

Since leather objects that have become hardened by excess heat, powdered by acidic industrial and automotive fumes, or made to deteriorate by moisture-loving bacteria cannot be returned to their original condition, *the most important element in conserving leather goods is primary care*. The specific practical advice below, if followed, will prolong the life of leather artifacts.

1. Give all leather objects adequate ventilation and proper humidity. A relative humidity level of 50 percent to 55 percent is considered ideal. Below that level, leather tends to dry out; and at much above 55 percent relative humidity, there is danger that mildew and other unattractive bacteria will go to work staining, eroding, and eventually consuming the leather.

2. Avoid extreme heat in areas where leather objects are stored. Heat not only dries out the leather, but it may also harden or permanently embrittle it. Keep leather objects away from radiators, heat registers, and hot pipes. Do not display leather goods in strong light, which not only damages leather by heating, but by subjecting it to ultraviolet rays and even visible components of light that cause leather to deteriorate.

3. Especially avoid subjecting leather goods to the disastrous combination of heat and excessive moisture. A continuous drip from a leaky steam pipe will not only cause parchment to cockle and leather to harden, but it will turn objects of rawhide into hide glue. Once such damage is done, the process cannot be reversed by any miracle potion known.

4. Keep leather goods away from water. Objects of soaked leather may shrink, cockle, and lose their shape or flexibility, depending on their original processing. Sodden furs may lose their hair, and putrefactive organisms will have a chance to go to work. If accident should subject items from your collection of leather artifacts to this sort of damage, remember that any drying should be gradual and should not be accompanied by heat, lest the problem be compounded.

5. Do your best to keep industrial or automotive fumes and the gases from combustion of sulfur, coke, and coal from getting to prized leather objects. These substances can combine with minute particles of iron in leather to form destructive sulfuric acid, the action of which results in a nonreversible powdering of the leather known as *red rot*. This condition is a result of the breaking down of the fibrous structure of leather— partially or completely. Moisture can also aid in the formation of destructive acids from airborne pollutants. It may be necessary to resort to tightly sealed cases for your leather goods to minimize the trouble; or, for collections containing a large number of leather objects, one may want to consider installing air conditioning. Whether used as free-standing units or integrated with the air conditioning system, filters for the air should usually be the activated charcoal variety, rather than the impressive-sounding electrostatic precipitator. The electrostatic type cleans the air efficiently, but it also produces ozone, which is destructive to all sorts of sensitive materials, including leather.[1]

6. Protect leather objects from moths, beetles, rats, and mice. Remember that many leather items represent potentially nutritious protein; and a mouse is just as happy to chew on Admiral Peary's mukluk or the cover of the Gutenberg Bible as on one of your own worn-out old shoes.

Clean, tight storage plus careful spraying in cracks and crevices of the storeroom with a standard insecticide will minimize the threat of insect damage. Paradichlorobenzene crystals (moth flakes) may also be used, if the storage container is tight enough to exclude moths and other insects and to retain the PDB vapors; and if the temperature in the container is warm enough (90 degrees) for the flakes gradually to evaporate to form a fumigating gas. The flakes must be in concentrations strong enough to be noticeable and somewhat irritating to human sensibilities in order to be effective. This applies to protection for wool, leather, and furs. PDB treatment should not be done on a prolonged basis. Note also that PDB is not permitted for use in public buildings, and is properly used in sealed cabinets only. An alternative fumigant is the type of impregnated strip containing 2,2-dichlorovinyl dimethyl phosphate. Either material should be tested for a short period of time, to be sure how exposure to it may affect each object. If any softening or change in surface finish or decoration of the leather occurs, that object should be removed from the treatment area and allowed to air dry for several days, and an alternative insecticide should be found. Finally, it should be remembered that *all insecticides are toxic* and that touching the substances that activate them or inhaling the fumes that they cause can be dangerous.[2]

7. Do not varnish or grease leather that has not been treated that way in the past, and do not try to restore old colors to leather items that may have faded. First, it is likely that any treatment made now, without absolute proof that the material requires it, will do much more harm than good and will certainly be highly noticeable. In the case of coloring materials, there is little chance that one could replicate the exact materials and the precise technique of the original procedure. Disfigurement and possibly damage to the object can often result.

8. Gentle physical handling of leather objects will help to keep them in good condition. For example, items that have been shaped to hold a set form, such as purses, bags, and clothing, should be gently stuffed with acid-free tissue or polyester fiber-fill—the type found in most fabric stores—whether on display or in storage. Leather objects should not be folded or stacked, in storage; tearing from the resultant stress or deformation of shape is the likely consequence. Keep iron and copper alloys away from leather, since these metals cause staining and rotting in leather goods. Metals that *must* be near or attached to leather objects should be properly coated to prevent damaging reactions. Avoid using paint, tape, or adhesive labels on leather, since their tenacious grip often cannot be released without damage to the skin of which the artifact is made.

Mold and Mildew

Growth of mold and mildew is encouraged on leather by high humidity, high temperature, and lack of ventilation. Brush off as much of such fungal growth as possible and expose the item it grew on to sunshine and fresh air for a few hours. If the item is of tanned leather, it can usually be cleaned with saddle soap before sunning.

Objects made of leather and skin may be fumigated by placing them in a closed cabinet for at least forty-eight hours, together with a dish containing thymol crystals or ortho-phenyl phenol. The crystals are set in a dish over a mild heat source—say, a forty-watt light bulb—close enough so that the steady, mild heat will cause the crystals to evaporate and create a fumigating gas. This treatment will kill the micro-organisms present, but will not offer lasting protection for the artifact. It is suggested that parchment and vellum should not be exposed to thymol vapors. Before treating any material, be sure you know what you have in hand and read carefully about the process of disinfection.[3]

Although certain mold inhibitors may be used on some types of leather, real prevention of fungal growth is better and safer than quantities of curative treatments. One or more portable dehumidifiers will help to solve mold problems, and their cost can be well justified by considering the alternative—which is certain deterioration of the leather objects affected.

Dry or Stiff Normal Leather

During a useful life, it should be expected that many objects—such as boots, saddlebags, baggage, cartridge holders, belts, and harnesses— will have been exposed to the normal attrition of average wear and tear, alternative wetting and drying, and the like. Many such items may be in basically sound condition, needing only lubrication and suppling to make them acceptable for display. It should be emphasized that *only certain kinds of leather should be treated with lubricants*, and in each instance the character of the leather and the choice of dressing should be carefully considered. Generally, neat's-foot oil and other oils are too messy to use, unless they have been used on the object before, as might have been done with harnesses, for example. Care must be taken with light-colored leathers to avoid dark staining through inappropriate treatment. And, of course, some items that are not true leather may well be ruined by the application of *any* fluid. *Such materials include tawed skins, vellum, parchment, and rawhide*. The following suggestions may be of help in many instances, but there *are* problems, such as severe damage or deterioration of the material; or perhaps one must deal with an unidentified material, which requires expert handling. If the suggested readings at the end of this chapter do not provide a clear answer, try to find a professional conservator who can furnish further advice.

Corrective Measures for Leather Goods

While many conditions that affect leather goods are irreversible, there are some corrective measures that can be applied. Bear in mind, however, the necessity for proper identification of the type of leather to be worked on; then, *test the treatment before proceeding*. Be sure to keep in mind that leather dressings usually do very little to improve the condition of leather; *their effect is often a cosmetic improvement only.* Dressings can also provide a medium for mold growth, so use them sparingly, if you are sure they are needed at all.

In general, leathers made before 1800 are easily identifiable as to original processing, while it may be difficult to be sure about the nature of later leather without scientific analysis to ascertain types and combinations of tannage. While such aids may not be practical, it should be borne in mind that deciding how to treat a specific leather object may be a very complex problem. Before starting any of the treatments given below, remove as much dirt as possible from the object to be treated by gently brushing it or using the brush attachment of the vacuum cleaner, shielding the object with a plastic screen.

Untanned hide or skin. Untanned hide or skin includes parchment and vellum, which are thin and fragile; and rawhide, which is very thick and tough. The most damaging element to any of these substances is moisture, which can cause decomposition or a disastrous deterioration into gelatin. Dryness, on the other hand, will cause materials in this category to shrink and stiffen. There is little one can do by way of treatment that will not cause damage to artifacts in this classification.

Oil-tanned leather. The "chamois" or "doeskin" leathers in this grouping do not seem to suffer from red rot, so the usual problem encountered with them is ingrained dirt. A powdered eraser material may be applied and rubbed into the surface, then brushed off. Chamois leather may be cleaned with a potassium oleate soap and then treated with a solution of 10 percent neat's-foot oil in methyl chloroform. *CAUTION:* Although methyl chloroform (also called trichloroethane) is not one of the most dangerous solvents, it can have serious side effects if it is used without safeguards. Sensible precautions, such as the use of proper gloves, goggles, adequate ventilation, and a respirator, should be practiced when using any strong solvent.[4]

Mineral-tanned leather. Mineral-tanned leathers include tawed skins, which are not true leather. These substances are particularly attractive to silverfish and other insect pests, but perhaps their greatest potential source of trouble is the fact that the tawing process is reversible. The mineral substances in the skin are easily removed with water, leaving a skin that is susceptible to rapid deterioration. Tawed and chrome-tanned materials should be cleaned with a granular, powdered-eraser substance, and no further treatment should then be attempted.

Molded hide items. Shaped objects such as jugs, buckets, helmets, and boxes that are made of leather or hides are processed to be very hard and to keep their original shapes. That property of their construction can make repairing such items relatively easy, if they are broken; the pieces can be simply glued together with a suitable adhesive, such as a resin-emulsion white glue made for the purpose and available from conservation supply houses. Note, however, that resin-emulsion white glue may become irreversible as it ages, so repairs with it should not be undertaken without careful consideration of the possible consequences. To treat the leather after removal of loose surface dirt, apply—sparingly—some LNO dressing, a solution of 40/60 lanolin and neat's-foot oil; follow that with a protective coating of microcrystalline wax. Although leather dressings can be made up rather easily, one will save time and effort by ordering pre-mixed solutions. The conservation supply houses listed under "Suppliers" can provide several types of leather dressings with different properties; the formula mentioned here is generally quite useful, but may not be the best for all circumstances.

Leather over wood. Great difficulties may often be encountered when working with complex objects made of more than one substance, because the characteristics of more than one material must be considered and treatments that might cause damage to any of the materials present must be avoided. Boxes and cases made of leather over wood can develop problems of stability if woodworms are present; if there is evidence of active wood destruction in any object you are working with, deal with it as suggested in chapter 9. Do not use water when treating antique objects of this type, because there is a possibility that water-soluble glues were used in their construction. When repairs are completed, a light application of LNO dressing, followed by microcrystalline wax, may be helpful to the outer layer of leather.

Leather bookbindings. Leather bookbindings made during the period of 1850 to 1900 are especially susceptible to damage from red rot. This condition can be caused in various ways: the action of residual sulfuric acid that remains in the leather after processing is one way; red rot can also be caused or hastened by the presence of sulfur dioxide in polluted air.

Red rot deterioration begins with a pinkish tone on the flesh side of the leather, but since that portion is usually glued to a piece of board, the condition may go undetected in the early stages. The rot gradually becomes a darker red and appears next on the grain side of the leather, as it actually destroys the fibrous structure of the materials. Leather becomes more and more powdery as the rot progresses, and scientific opinion is that it cannot be reversed or arrested. A potassium lactate buffer solution—that can be bought ready-made from conservation materials suppliers—can be applied to leather bookbindings to slow this

Fig. 10.1. Stiff leather objects, such as fire buckets and helmets, are not intended to be softened up by any sort of treatment. Sometimes they can be glued together when broken, but one should be especially careful not to harm surface decoration; paint or gilt on such objects may come off very easily.

rot, in instances where the leather is still in reasonably good condition. If red rot is far advanced, potassium lactate will do nothing to help, and there is no general agreement that it really helps a great deal, under any circumstances. LNO dressing may be carefully and sparingly applied to rot-stricken bindings, but one must be particularly cautious in applying it around the edges of the leather, near papers or other materials that may become stained by the leather dressing. After applying the LNO dressing, if the book is strong enough, spread it open a bit, stand it on end, and leave it that way overnight. On the following morning, rub off any excess dressing, to prevent staining. Extra care should be taken when cleaning areas of bookbindings where gold leaf of other decoration has been applied to the surface. Moisture in particular will encourage decorative materials such as gold leaf to peal off the leather. If surfaces treated with LNO dressing remain tacky after a day or two, an application of microcrystalline wax should provide a smoother, harder proctective surface layer. Since there is a good chance one could harm the paper or binding, and little chance that the condition of the leather can be improved, the application of dressings to bookbindings is discouraged by many conservators.

Sole Leather. Purposely processed to be made quite stiff, sole leather should be cleaned with saddle soap and a minimum amount of water, followed by an application of microcrystalline wax when the surface is dry.

Shoes and boots. Dress shoes and boots should be cleaned with saddle soap, using very little water unless the leather is old and must be manipulated to straighten it. A wetter saddle soap mixture *might* soften the shoe enough to be manipulated, but the leather might be too fragile, too old, or too stiff to be moved at all. When dry, the surface of the leather may be buffed softly or further protected with microcrystalline wax. Old work boots will often be stiffer and show more signs of neglect than dress boots—and they also require more effort to soften. If boots are still stiff after treatment with saddle soap, a second stage will be necessary: rub in one or more applications of LNO dressing and flex the leather continually until it reaches the desired softness. The boots or shoes should then be tightly stuffed with acid-free tissue overnight, to minimize wrinkles and the common tendency of footwear to turn up at the toes. Bear in mind that this treatment will not always produce the miraculous results one may hope for.

Patent Leather. Patent leather—the shiny finish sometimes put on leather—can be extremely difficult to treat if there is any damage or disfigurement on the surface. The usual dressings for leather are apt to

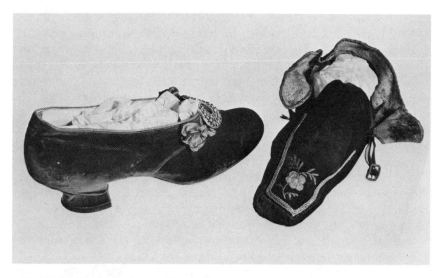

Fig. 10.2. Shoes—and virtually all objects made of flexible leather—should be gently stuffed with acid-free tissue to maintain shape.

cause problems with a patent leather finish, so the best approach is simply to brush loose dirt off it—and call a conservator for advice if you have a patent leather item that needs treatment.

Shaved or split cattle hides. Wallets, satchels, upholstery, and military items are sometimes made of hides that have been shaved or split. That kind of leather may be used with the grain side out or with the suede or velvet surface showing. On grain surfaces, LNO dressing may be used lightly, or microcrystalline wax may be applied. Oily stains can be removed from matte finish leathers with methyl chloroform (trichloroethane), but be always aware, in using this solvent, that it is potent and that it can produce serious side effects if it is used without safeguards. Do not use waxes or oils on matte leathers. Repairs to these materials, as to most leathers, are extremely difficult to do well, and are generally not worth amateurish attempts. Items of grain leather showing signs of age are best treated with LNO dressing.

Harnesses. Generally, work harnesses and traces have been traditionally treated with neat's-foot oil, and that treatment may be continued. It is, however, rather messy. After being oiled and allowed to stand overnight, the harness should be wiped with a dry cloth to remove the excess oil. The harness should then be stored in such a way that it does not stain walls or surrounding objects. A cleaner treatment, and one more in keeping with that used for many other types of leather, is LNO dressing, applied in much the same way as neat's-foot oil.

Russet leather. Russet—or light brown—leather harnessing was kept "for show" for carriage horses or favorite mounts used by the more affluent in city driving or on Sunday rides, in the days before the automotive age. Any equipment made of russet leather should be kept as close to its original color as possible. Avoid heavy oils like castor oil or neat's-foot oil and begin cleaning this handsome material with saddle soap. If the leather appears to be in very good condition, micro-crystalline wax may be used on the surface. Before using LNO dressing on russet leather items that are showing their age, test the dressing in an inconspicuous spot to determine whether its use will darken the leather. Since one of the primary attributes of russet harness is its color, it would be pointless to apply a treatment that would turn it dark brown.

Goatskin, sheepskin, calfskin, and pigskin. Among the kinds of animal skins commonly used to make wearing apparel and accessories, saddle soap may be used best as a cleansing agent on pigskin. The pigskin should then be treated with LNO dressing or microcrystalline wax.

All tanned skins may be protected from red rot with potassium lactate buffer solution and later given an application of LNO dressing or micro-crystalline wax. Note, however, that *all* light-colored skins should be tested before proceeding with LNO dressing, as the dressing may some-times darken the leather color.

Many objects made of skin present their own peculiar problems, some of which can be anticipated: Victorian gloves, for instance, may be made of *tawed* skin, and so should not be treated with any of the materials mentioned for other skins.

Skin—or leather—bookbindings may be cleaned with a barely damp sponge and neutral soap, then "rinsed" several times with a different clean, barely damp sponge—but it must be remembered that this is a great way to remove gilding, and it should be avoided wherever gold-lettering or gold decoration is present. For use on ungilded objects that can be safely sponged off, the neutral soaps good for this can often be obtained from suppliers of institutional cleaning materials, though the packages are usually rather large. Do not use standard laundry soap of any kind, but check with conservation supply houses.

Reptile leathers and skins of fish. Alligator leather often develops red rot; but any sort of treatment for it is made more difficult by the fact that the treatment has little effect if applied from the scale side. Potassium lactate solution, which may slow the rot, may be applied on the skin side, if that side is accessible. Scale surface treatment is obviously a protective and cosmetic job only; a light application of microcrystalline wax may be used.

Snakeskin is usually a tawed material, and therefore should not come in contact with any moist substances. Microcrystalline wax will help to protect and give a pleasing appearance to the scale side of snakeskin objects.

The skins of fish commonly used to make decorative objects are generally the skins of either sharks or rays, and these substances are usually not a true leather; microcrystalline wax may be safely used on the outside surfaces of this kind of skin.

Fur skins. Since most traditional methods of dressing fur involved the use of emulsions—notably animal brain tissue—the same methods may be used for most ethnological specimens. The skin should be slightly dampened on the flesh side, to relax it, if necessary. Allow about ten minutes for the moisture to penetrate, then follow with LNO dressing. If you have a fur garment that is a product of modern civilization, it is best handled by a furrier. For one thing, fur coats or fur garments usually have a lining; also, they are often made of skins of small animals and are, consequently, much more fragile than the fur garments made and worn by Indians, Eskimos, or Lapps. Don't be disappointed if there is some hair loss from ethnological specimens. The original methods of processing by many native groups make some loss of hair almost inevitable as the skin ages.

*   *   *   *

Some problems in the care and treatment of leather have no solution, as is true with care and treatment of wood and of all organic materials—simply because deterioration has already gone too far before a solution is looked for. It therefore bears re-emphasis, here, that *the conservation of all organic materials is achieved basically through proper care and storage*, rather than in the conservation laboratory. Long life for collections objects is the concern of every curator, collector, and dealer.

NOTES

1. Garry Thomson, *The Museum Environment* (Boston: Butterworths, 1978), pp. 142–144, 241–246.

2. Stephen R. Edwards, et al., *Pest Control in Museums: A Status Report (1980)*, pp. A-1–A-30.

3. *Thymol and o-Phenyl Phenol: Safe Work Practices* (New York: Center for Occupational Hazards, 1984).

4. Michael McCann, *Artist Beware* (New York: Watson-Guptil, 1979).

SUGGESTED READING

Davis, Charles Thomas. *The Manufacture of Leather: Being a Description of All the Processes* . . . Philadelphia: H. C. Baird & Co., 1885.
Background in the tools and techniques, with mounted samples.

DeWitt, Donald L. *Leather Bookbindings: Preservation Techniques.* Technical Leaflet No. 98. Nashville: The American Association for State and Local History, 1977.

Edwards, Stephen R., et al. *Pest Control in Museums: A Status Report (1980).* Lawrence, Kansas: Association of Systematics Collections, 1981.

Farnham, Albert Burton. *Home Training and Leather-Making Guide.* Columbus, Ohio: A. R. Harding, 1950.

Horton, Carolyn. *Cleaning and Preserving Bindings and Related Materials.* Chicago: American Library Association, 1979.

Middleton, Bernard C. *The Restoration of Leather Bindings.* Chicago: American Library Association, 1972.

Mucci, Paul. *Paper and Leather Conservation: A Manual.* College Park, Maryland: Mid-Atlantic Regional Archives Conference, 1978.

Peltz, Perri, and Monona Rossol. *Safe Pest Control Procedures for Museum Collections.* New York: Center for Occupational Hazards, 1983.
One of many inexpensive but up-to-date data sheets from this source; highly recommended.

Plenderleith, H. J., and A. E. A. Werner. "Animal Skin and Skin Products . . . Parchment." In *The Conservation of Antiquities and Works of Art: Treatment, Repair, and Restoration.* New York: Oxford University Press, 1971.
A conservator's guide, though slightly outmoded; good examples of problems, but not instructions for the amateur.

Reed, R. *Ancient Skins, Parchments, and Leathers.* New York: Seminar Press, 1972.
An excellent text covering the nature of skin, processing methods, examination, testing, and care.

Waterer, John W. *A Guide to the Conservation of Objects Made Wholly or in Part of Leather.* London: G. Bell & Sons, 1973.

11

Metal Objects:
Care and Conservation

A number of metals used today—iron, copper, tin, lead, gold, and silver, among them—were also known and used by the ancients. Research indicates that copper may possibly be the oldest known metal, and that gold may possibly have been the first put to human use.[1]

Gold and silver have been known from prehistoric times. Early man made ornaments and decorative items of both and believed that gold held magical powers. Successive generations worldwide have used both metals to produce decorative, commemorative, ecclesiastical, and ceremonial objects in almost endless variety.[2]

From all indications, gold, silver, and copper were all being made into ornaments and amulets as early as the Neolithic period—about 8000 B.C. in Asia and about 6000 B.C. throughout Europe, Egypt, India, and China.[3]

Iron and lead are also, with copper, among the oldest known metals. Beads made of meteoric iron—evidently shaped by rubbing, as were stone tools—were worn in Egypt as early as 4000 B.C. Ornaments and ceremonial weapons made of smelted iron became common from about 1900 B.C. to 1400 B.C. The oldest known iron object shaped by hammering is a dagger made before 1350 B.C. and believed to be of Hittite workmanship.[4]

Lead, known and used by the ancient Egyptians and Babylonians, was shaped into pipes by Roman builders, who also used it for solder. Lead was one of the first metals mined in North America, where it was much sought after for making shot.[5]

Copper in a "free" condition—uncombined chemically with surrounding sand or rock and therefore relatively easy to obtain for use—was probably mined in the Tigris-Euphrates valley as early as the fifth century B.C. Both copper and tin and their usefulness in making alloys have been known since the Bronze Age, from about 3500 B.C., when metals came into extensive use for making tools and weapons and great advances took place in metalworking as techniques were developed for making bronze sculpture.[6]

Brass, an alloy of copper and zinc produced since imperial Roman times, is closely associated in art with bronze, an alloy of copper and tin. Pewter, an alloy of tin with varying amounts of other metals, was early used in the Far East. Some pieces of Roman pewter are still in existence; and from the Middle Ages onward, England was a pewter center. At various times, pewter, tin, and lead have all been used in industrial and art metalwork.[7]

Early decorative metalwork may have centered around gold, silver, and copper because all three of these metals might be found in a "free" condition; all three are among the softer metals, relatively easily shaped or made into sheets by beating or hammering; they can be readily drawn into long, thin strands; and all three can be polished to a bright finish, making them superb materials for experimentation by early artisans and craftsmen.

As a result, jewelry, decorative objects, ceremonial vessels, and statuary of gold and silver have appeared in almost every stage of civilization; and early metalsmiths attained highly developed and marvelously sophisticated metalworking techniques: drawing, spinning, hammering, and casting, as methods of shaping metals; and chasing, damascening, embossing, enameling, filigree, gilding, inlay, niello, openwork, and repousse, as decorative processes.[8]

General Properties of Metals

As chemical elements, metals share, in varying degrees, the following capacities and characteristics.

Metals can conduct heat and electricity; can be mixed with each other in specified amounts to form various metal alloys for specific purposes; can lose electrons and form positive ions, basic oxides, and hydroxides. Each metal has a recognizable metallic luster. Each has a definite melting point. Each has, to some degree, the qualities of hardness, tensile strength, density, ductility (the potential for being drawn into long, thin strands and made into wire), and malleability (the potential for being rolled, hammered, or beaten into sheets or shapes).[9]

And—on being exposed to moist air, many metals react chemically by beginning to corrode. Iron is perhaps the metal most highly susceptible to corrosion; and gold, which is chemically inactive, is the only one that is not affected by moisture, oxygen, or ordinary acids—although it *is* affected adversely by the halogens. Tin is less sensitive to moisture and more resistant to corrosion than many metals and is often used as a coating over iron, steel, copper, and other metals to prevent their rusting. "Tin" cans are made of thin sheets of iron or steel coated with tin to prevent the rusting of the basic metals. Freshly cut lead loses its luster and darkens on exposure to moist air, as an oxide film forms over the exposed areas. Once formed, the film protects the lead from further oxidation. Exposure to moist air causes copper to form a greenish surface film, which protects it from further corrosion. Aluminum and zinc do not appear to react to moist air, but both do: the newly exposed metal areas begin to film over almost at once with a thin, oxide coating. Like the film that forms on lead exposed to air, this coating protects the metal and stops further corrosion. Aluminum and zinc oxide films are so near the color of the metals themselves that they are not noticeable. Like gold, silver is not chemically active and does not oxidize in air; but it does react to airborne compounds such as sulfur dioxide and hydrogen sulfide, and it tarnishes when exposed to air in which they are present.[10]

The following pages deal with some of the problems that can arise in the care of objects made of iron, copper (and some of its alloys), tin, pewter, lead, gold, and silver.

Iron (Ferrous) Objects

Rusting, or oxidation on being exposed to moist air, is the Number One enemy of iron, especially when the process is augmented by the presence in the air of various salts—which appear, with others, as constituents of acid rain, road salts, sea water, sea air, and human perspiration.

Overtreatment of the metal is iron's Number Two enemy.

Although unprotected iron kept in constant contact with water, acids, or chlorides will corrode quickly, corrosion normally proceeds slowly. A good rule of thumb is: unless you know what you are doing and unless you are certain that you want to remove the surface layer of a corroding iron artifact, leave the object alone.

Some points that should be considered before one begins work on a corroded piece of ironwork include these: was the original surface shiny—or not? While a look of dusty decay and neglect is usually to be deplored, it is even more appalling to a collector or curator to see displays of iron work tools, utensils, and firearms that have been ground and polished to a bright metal finish that they never had during their useful life. Many gunlocks and gun barrels, for instance, were given a

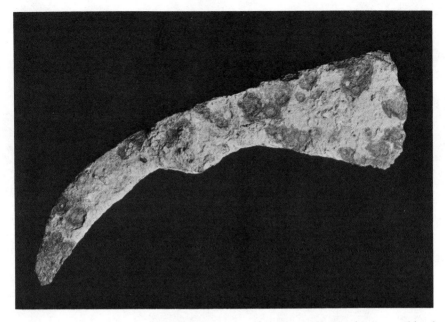

Fig. 11.1. Any object that has reached the state of erosion evident in this iron tool head should be carefully examined before any attempt is made to clean it. If the iron underneath is fairly stable, removal of surface dirt may be all that is necessary.

blue, brown, or case-hardened finish during their manufacture; and removal of any or all of these thin finish layers lessens the objects' historical and market values. Many forge-made tools still retain their dark oxide scale, the result of prolonged heating over a charcoal fire. This dark scale is part of the documentation of the object and often helps to distinguish an early piece from a modern reproduction that has been darkened with flat black paint. Aside from their aesthetic or documentary value, these dark patinas also form a stable protective coating, unlike the active corrosion represented by yellow, red, or brown rust.

Atmospheric and Environmental Protection

Ferrous objects in good condition should be safeguarded from high humidity, marine air, corrosive salts, industrial vapors, acid conditions, and fingerprints. Eliminating these various environmental hazards is not always an easy matter, but it is by far the best way to protect objects made of iron: one removes the problem, rather than having to fight it constantly on all fronts.

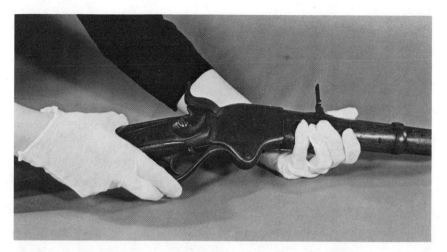

Fig. 11.2. Clean white cotton gloves should be worn when handling iron or steel objects. Even clean hands will deposit oils and perspiration, causing rust and corrosion of the metal.

To protect ferrous metals against corrosion from too much moisture, a relative humidity of 40 percent is helpful, although a constant level of 50 percent relative humidity is acceptable. The latter may also be desirable if one is caring for objects made of iron plus other materials, such as tools made of iron and wood or toleware made of a sheet-iron base covered with tin and painted.

Cleaning the air to remove pollutants in the collections area can be more complicated, but often portable dehumidifiers and air filters can accomplish that task effectively.

Best of all—and most expensive, as well—would be to install an air conditioning system that will provide a suitable and stable atmosphere automatically.

Silica gel, available from scientific supply houses, may be used to protect iron and steel objects in closed containers when total air conditioning cannot be provided. *The container must be airtight.* It can be anything from a plastic bag to an elaborate storage or exhibit case, so long as it *is* airtight. The silica gel is "conditioned" to the desired relative humidity before it is put into the container and closed in. Once enclosed, it helps to buffer humidity changes. As a rough rule of thumb, the amount of silica gel used should be equal to about half the weight of the object with which it is to be enclosed. Prepackaged or loose silica gel may be used; it can be hidden, on display, by fabric or screening.

Fig. 11.3. Objects such as toleware add complications to the care of the ferrous metal; here, there is a tin coating over the sheet-iron base, and there is a paint layer over the tin. Seek expert help.

If a clean environment with low humidity cannot be provided, then some type of protective coating for the artifact may be useful. Before applying any coating, be sure that the one you have chosen is the best one for use for the circumstances—and remember that no protective coating gives a permanent guarantee against deterioration of an iron artifact.

Once the decision to apply a protective coating is made and the appropriate coating is selected, the object to receive it must be cleaned, to remove from it any moisture, dirt, rust, or grease that may be on its surface. Vacuuming or brushing the object will remove loose dirt, and wiping it with acetone will clean the surface of oil and grease. Removal of rust that may already be present may be a more complicated process—to be discussed below.

Surface Coatings

Clear, hard coatings. Boiled linseed oil or oil-resin varnishes have long been used as a waterproofing agent for various artifacts; but it has been discovered that moisture can penetrate such coatings and that the protection is more apparent than real. The oils also cause corrosion of the metal and become difficult to remove, with age. At present, there are a number of dips and sprays formulated from synthetic resins that give better protection than the traditional oils and varnishes; but even these new coatings are effective only if they can be applied so that the metal surface is sealed in without a break and if no moisture or salts are trapped beneath the surface. These coatings are usually rather shiny, which may give a meretricious appearance to some objects.

Wax coatings. Wax coatings offer less mechanical protection than synthetic resins do; on the other hand, however, wax coatings have no objectionable shine, and they are generally much easier to apply or to remove than resins are, should removal be necessary. One can use the traditional waxes, like candelilla, carnauba, or beeswax; but it would be simpler to be consistent and use microcrystalline wax on your iron artifacts and other materials where a wax coating is needed. For objects with very rough or intricate surfaces, application of the wax may be simplified by warming the object slightly until the wax flows easily when applied, coating the object while it is warm and wiping off the excess as it cools to room temperature. A standard cookstove oven can be used for this process—*but for all-metal items only.* When wax coatings build up in layers, some kinds of waxes lose their transparency and cause an unnatural appearance on pitted iron or rough castings. Test the wax before applying it to a large area. Microcrystalline wax under the trade name of Renaissance Wax is available from conservation supply houses and perhaps other sources. Although it is quite expensive, a little of it goes a long way, and one or two tins should last for a considerable time.

Heavy oil and grease coatings. Traditionally, heavy coatings of oil or grease have usually been used for objects that are to be stored for long periods of time or under adverse climatic conditions. These coatings are generally too messy for practical use in working with small collections; but if they will serve a useful purpose, gun grease, penetrating oil, petroleum jelly, or a mixture of penetrating oil and petroleum jelly will perform well. Clearly, this ponderous kind of protection should be applied to objects that are to be placed in storage only, and a complete cleaning and degreasing will be needed before the objects so treated can be inspected or displayed.

Silicone spray. A combination of invisible protective coat and lubricant used for many purposes is silicone spray. A light-bodied fluid, this spray-on liquid can get into threads, interstices, and generally hard-to-reach places. It clings tightly, resists handling and high temperatures, and does not change the appearance of objects on which it is used. The substance that carries it feels like a grade of mineral spirits and can be rubbed off easily with a cloth, leaving the silicone behind in the pores of the metal. *It is wise to remember that silicone will also penetrate wood easily, and its presence will interfere with any subsequent treatment of any surfaces to which it is applied.* If a silicone protectant is used on ferrous metals, do not allow it to come in contact with wooden parts of the object. Because the silicone is difficult, if not impossible, to remove, even from metals, it should not be used on fine or important pieces. Silicones cannot be recommended for general use, especially on museum collections.

Heavy coatings and paint. While heavy coatings and paint are usually too thick or otherwise aesthetically objectionable for use on small items, they are sometimes an alternative answer for bulky, unwieldy objects such as cast-iron cannons, grill work, chains, anchors, and rough castings or forged objects that will be subjected to environmental extremes. Some brands of paint and thick metal coatings are said to be successfully applied over rusted or damp metal, but it must be emphasized that, for best results, any metal to be coated in this way should first be thoroughly dry and free from scale, loose rust, and chloride salts.

Calcium plumbate and the traditional red lead are two effective metal primers, although these and other paints containing lead are becoming difficult to obtain. *It should be noted that, since working with lead paints can be dangerous to human health, other types of primers would be preferable.*

Zinc chromate is another good primer available in various formulations from most hardware stores. Note, however, that special primers may be required for metal-coated iron, especially galvanized pieces. Tough epoxy-resin paints formulated for boating are available from most marine supply houses, although inlanders may have difficulty locating them, and neophytes may have trouble applying them properly. These epoxy paints must be mixed and applied carefully, so be sure to read the directions before using them. Also, keep in mind that, although epoxies may be tough, they may also allow moisture or salts to reach the metal surface through small cracks that can develop in the coating; and the removal of epoxy paint for repair or re-coating can be virtually impossible, especially on corroded iron layers.

If your collection includes old carriages, farm machinery, wagons, or steam-powered machines—most of which were painted a variety of colors on the body or running gear—consider the rust-inhibiting paints available at hardware stores. These paints are relatively inexpensive, and they come in a variety of colors. Do not purchase them in spray-can form, however, if you can avoid it; not only are they more expensive that way, but the rather heavy oils and pigments in them are forever clogging the spraying mechanism, no matter how careful one is about shaking the can and keeping the nozzle clean. Needless to say, before painting any artifacts, it is important to be absolutely certain about the original colors and design. If there is no clue to the original color left on the object itself, then it will be necessary to try researching in catalogues and getting in touch with the appropriate type of museum for information. Painting should not be thoughtlessly undertaken merely to "cheer up" historical objects.

Tannate coatings. An old trappers' trick that has been recommended as a protective measure for some kinds of iron artifacts is to boil or scrub lightly rusted objects in a solution of water and tannic acid. This forms a stable coating of iron tannate. The proportions and boiling time are empirical, rather than specific. This treatment is best reserved for the types of objects for which it may be appropriate, such as trapping gear and rough tools.

In general, chemical surface treatments such as coating collections objects with tannic acid or using bluing on gun barrels should not be carried out on historical objects unless it can be determined that the treatment was used previously. Though there is divergence of opinon on the subject, the best treatment is often the least treatment.

Cleaning Rusted Iron

Light rust. Light rust can be removed by rubbing the corroded metal with fine bronze wool and using mineral spirits, if desired. The process will remove rust, but will not remove bluing or other patinas. Very fine wet-or-dry abrasive paper, with a 400 grit, has been used with oil to clean and polish metal, but that treatment will also remove any patina present—and will take off some of the metal, as well. *Such powerful abrasives—even though they are fine grades—are not recommended for use on historical objects.*

Once an iron object has been cleaned of rust, dirt, and other accretions, its surface is vulnerable to the formation of new rust and corrosion, and it should be given a protective coating *immediately.* Cleaned artifacts should not be allowed to sit about unprotected, even for a few hours.

Fig. 11.4. The pitting of this drawknife blade began through rusting, but was greatly aggravated when the blade was cleaned with an acidic solution.

Strong acids. Solutions using strong acids, such as sulfuric acid or nitric acid, are often used as pickling agents to remove rust and scale from iron objects. *Their use on historical materials should never be attempted, however, since pitting of the metal surface is an inevitable result, and disfigurement of fine detail is likely.* Also, if all traces of such acids are not carefully washed off the metal, they will cause renewed rusting and damage to the surface.

Commercial rust removers. Commercial rust removers are generally quite potent, and when heated or used in concentration, most of them can affect one's eyes, nose, and throat, as do strong acids. In addition, when commercial rust removers are used, even in the recommended dilutions, one must periodically check the action of the solution on the object being treated. At worst, use of commercial rust removers carries the same danger as the use of strong acids—they may remove rust, but they may also cause extensive pitting of the metal surface, and it appears that virtually all chemical rust removers do cause fine pitting or etching. Phosphoric acid formulations seem to be about the least damaging of the chemical rust removers. Whether to use a stringent cleaning treatment that is certain to damage an artifact, even though its strong action may be needed, is only one of many hard decisions curators or collectors must sometimes make. It is clear, however, that curators or collectors who follow us, in future years, cannot complain about objects that have been cleaned gently and then stabilized with an appropriate protective coating. On the other hand, once etching or overcleaning of an item has been done, it can never be undone.

Electrochemical and electrolytic methods. Reduction of corrosion on iron objects by electrochemical and electrolytic methods has been done very effectively, but each procedure has major drawbacks. Electrochemical reduction requires the use of quantities of rather expensive materials and regeneration of them by treatment with powerful acids. This procedure is definitely not recommended for any amateur. Electrolytic reduction is potentially a gentle cleaning method, but it is surrounded by pitfalls. The choices of metals for the anode plates and the ingredients for the bath, both acidic and alkaline, are many and varied. The procedure itself can produce unpleasant and surprising results if the operator is not expert at it; one simple error could cause metal byproducts to be plated on the surface of the cleaned artifact.[11]

Mechanical do's and don'ts. Rust encrustation on iron can also be removed a bit at a time (working with small squares measuring about one-sixteenth of an inch) by carefully picking it off, manually, with a dental pick. Be sure to hold the pick at right angles to the work, rather than at a slant, in order to attain adequate pressure and control. The location of the pick near the edge of the rust crust may also help the work proceed efficiently. Used in this way, *these tools exert tremendous force: always wear safety glasses when using them.* And be sure—before you begin this laborious process—that there is coherent metal under the rust, or you may wind up with a bench full of rust particles and no object. That sad result is a definite possibility with materials from an archaeological site. Before beginning to chip off the rust, test the object with a magnet; if the magnet exerts no pull on the metal, then the artifact is rust all the way through. Only a qualified conservator of archaeological objects should tackle the ticklish job of consolidating completely rusted items. With luck, the expert can reinforce deteriorated metal a bit at a time, so that the form and some of the strength of the original object may be saved. It is all too easy to try this procedure on a trial-and-error basis and wind up with nothing more than some rusty-looking dirt.

On no account should one try to knock rust off a valued iron object with a hammer or any other forceful tool; *and do not use a blowtorch!* A torch may pop off loose surface rust particles, but it may also cause other deposits to fuse and become even more difficult to remove. Do not use power grinding wheels or wire wheels to clean rusty surfaces. These tools may remove rust, but they will also remove original material and leave scars in the metal, damaging the piece permanently. Not only is it difficult to reduce or remove scars produced by these treatments, but in undertaking such strong approaches, one too often makes changes in the original object, blurring edges and inscriptions and destroying what one has intended to preserve.

In general, to remove rust from any artifact, the rule is to use an abrasive softer than the material being treated. Therefore, the finest steel wool is sometimes safe to use—always test, to be sure—as are bristle or nylon brushes. However, glass fiber or steel brushes, coarse abrasives, and steel tools can be expected to damage metal surfaces. Working with miniature picks may be an effective cleaning technique, but it must be done with the greatest of care, to avoid scratching the underlying metal. The use of miniature rotary wheels has been the object of some controversy, but if the wheels are less than one inch in diameter and made of the softer materials mentioned above, they can be used—*with caution*.

Severely Rusted Objects

Rusted iron objects that do not respond to the pull of a magnet require special care to keep them intact. Not only are there the physical problems of strength of the deteriorated material, but chemical changes in the metal and the minerals now within its structure may break it apart, even if it is under no mechanical stress. Though there are some traditional treatments for such objects, the scientific advances of recent years have made these risky and unacceptable for objects of historical or artistic value.

When an artifact is brought up from an undersea site, it is often difficult to discern, within the masses of mud, coral, and corrosion, how much of the enclosed core is still coherent metal. The extent of corrosion depends on a number of factors: the length of time the object has been submerged, the temperature and salinity of the water surrounding it, the degree to which the object has become covered with mud or marine growth, or the extent to which it has been in close association with other metals, resulting in electrochemical activity that may protect one metal and corrode another. Because of this range of contributing factors, the chemistry of conserving submerged iron objects is quite complex; and the answers for preserving an iron cannon dug up from a freshwater lake will not necessarily work for an iron cannon taken from the Bay of

Fundy or the Florida Keys. Proper salvage techniques for such objects pose more problems than those for dry-land artifacts, because of the chloride content of the water and because there is, in working with iron objects long submerged in wet surroundings, a greater danger of destroying evidence and outlines as one attempts to remove accumulated calcareous growths and layers of corrosion. Allowing the marine artifact to dry can cause extremely rapid corrosion of any remaining metal and possibly even cracking of the object. Wet-site artifacts may be kept wet until they can be treated by an expert.[12]

Copper and Copper Alloys

Copper and its alloys—gunmetal, bronze, bell metal, brass, German or nickel silver, paktong, and others—are relatively stable materials when given proper care. However, pollutants in the air and chlorides from sea water or other sources can cause corrosion problems. In addition to that, most commercial and traditional copper cleaners cause more problems than they solve.

Cleaning Cuprous Objects

Before one uncorks the brass polish, the finish and patina of any object made of copper or a copper alloy should be examined closely and carefully considered. Some nineteenth-century bronzes were darkened with chemicals at the time they were made, to give them an antique look that was popular then—and still is, today, to some extent. Some brass cavalry bugles and military candle-lanterns were made with a dark finish and a matte, almost pitted-looking surface that would not reflect sunlight, and more modern military items have been treated in similar ways. Scientific and navigational instruments were often given a clear varnish or a dark, bituminous "japanned" finish, to protect them against weathering. And, of course, certain classes of artifacts and art objects have acquired a stable patina that is generally considered aesthetically desirable. Such artifacts may include items as diverse as eighteenth-century cannon, Chinese figures, or Etruscan bowls. It can be argued that when such objects were new, they were meant to look shiny; but since connoisseurs consider the patina important, one should be aware of that body of opinion.

These comments are intended in the same way as the words of caution about "brightening" iron and steel: *do not be hasty in deciding to clean any metal object down to the bare metal.* Original surfaces and subsequent chemical alterations that are of interest to the research historian and the scientist may be lost forever. Improper treatment can have great effect upon the artistic, historical, and even monetary value of any artifact.

Simple Oxidation of Copper Artifacts

Characterized by a dull reddish or brownish film, simple oxidation on objects of copper, brass, or bronze usually responds to simple polishes that contain fine whiting, or precipitated chalk. Commercial polishes are prone to changes in formulation without notice, so positive recommendations for their use are impossible. In addition, some of the paste cleaners and dips on the market as copper brighteners are markedly acidic or contain chlorides, which will eventually start new corrosion on cuprous objects. Never use abrasive papers or steel wool on copper: they are far too abrasive. Even bronze wool, available for marine use, may abrade copper surfaces. Avoid, too, the old cliche-treatment of salt and lemon juice—or vinegar—as a cleaner, as the chlorides in the salt will simply complicate future cleaning and cause more corrosion. The problems in using acidic, alkaline, or salty copper cleaners do not always stem from immediate damage to the metal. Very strong acids or alkalis will pit the metal surface, but weaker solutions may leave behind traces on the copper when the cleaning and polishing are completed. Small deposits of these chemicals on the surface or interstices may well cause corrosion after a short time.

Since proprietary copper polishes in liquid form cannot be recommended, do not use them on your historical objects. There are alternatives. Always begin by cleaning the object of grime, oil, and scum; alcohol, mineral spirits, and detergent solutions may be needed. Remember, "you cannot polish dirt."

One alternative for polishing is to use a metal cleaner produced in the form of cotton wadding, with petroleum solvents and fine abrasives added to it. It is very tidy to use, but it is best to test it yourself before using it extensively.

Homemade brass-and-copper polish is easy to concoct, by combining two parts denatured alcohol, two parts distilled water, and enough precipitated chalk to make a thick paste. Precipitated chalk can be purchased from a dental supply store, if not available from a jewelry store. Be sure not to use any *more* harsh abrasive than whiting; *less* abrasive materials such as rottenstone, jewelers' rouge, talc, or diatomaceous earth could be substituted. The proportions for this homemade polish are not critical; a bit less water could be used, if desired.

Bear in mind that polishing nonferrous metals removes a small amount of the metal each time it is performed. For that reason, it is best to avoid constant cleaning of metal collections objects if some of the causes of corrosion can be controlled. Some people may enjoy seeing household brass or copper gleaming, and may assiduously polish it every week, but for historical objects, that continual abrasion is too much.

Exposed brass or bronze or copper objects may be cleaned with less likelihood of erosion with alcohol applied with a swab, to remove skin oils and perspiration, which have corrosive properties. The metal will gradually assume a dull surface color, which may be polished off eventually, or left alone.

When cleaning copper objects, it is essential to remove all of the old polish that almost inevitably accumulates in cracks, undercuts of carvings or castings, along interstices, and behind escutcheon plates. These residues often contain ammonia and show the greenish hue of copper corrosion. Use a swab dampened in water to remove all traces of old cleaner. If stronger persuasion than water on a swab is required, use water on a soft brush or a softwood splinter, followed by complete rinsing with distilled water. Because of the damage they can cause, chemical cleaning polishes, especially those containing ammonia, should not be used.

Heavy Oxidation on Copper

If corrosion on a copper artifact is so extensive that there is doubt as to whether there is coherent metal underneath, do not attempt to clean the object; under those circumstances, the job is best left to an expert.

If polish will not remove a dull film, sometimes stripping solutions may be employed—but first it must be emphasized that *an object should not be immersed in the cleaning solution if it is made of two or more diverse metals.* In such situations, there is a good possibility of setting up electrochemical reactions between the different metals, with consequent undesirable side effects. For the same reason, plated objects should not be immersed in a stripping solution, lest the plating be stripped off. Before using a chemical bath on any metal object, check to see whether the object has handles or finials of different metal, a weighted base, a lining of other material, or even seams or patches that have been soldered. Many objects simply do not lend themselves to the technique of stripping.

A 5 percent solution of citric acid (one ounce per pint of water) will clean copper of either dull film or corrosion. Lift the item out of the solution occasionally and rub it with a dampened rag to which has been applied a dab of rottenstone. That will speed up the chemical action and will permit frequent checking to be certain that the metal is not being "scalded" or over-cleaned. When you remove the object from the bath, rinse it in water to which about 5 percent of washing soda has been added. This will help to neutralize any remaining acid. Then wash thoroughly in at least four changes of distilled water and dry. If final washing is not complete, the action of the residual chemicals will quickly corrode the object, possibly worse than if it had not been treated.

Confronting Special Problems of Copper Objects

Chloride salts. Copper-based items that have acquired chloride salts from having been under the sea or in certain types of soil show a tendency to pick up moisture from the air. Unless the object is kept quite dry, or is treated by specialized chemical processes, it will break down. These specialized treatments, however, may also result in the removal of stable or desirable patina if incorrectly done and are therefore not recommended for use by the novice. For the safety of a valuable collection, it is best to have a conservation survey done, anyway, so that all problems may be identified.

Calcareous (limy) deposits. Calcareous deposits may be found on copper objects retrieved from both land excavations and under-water sites. While acids have been used to dissolve such deposits, a 10 percent solution (1½ ounces per pint of water) of sodium hexametaphosphate (water softener for laundering; check the box for ingredients) in water will soften limy crusts with less danger of destroying the patina of the copper piece. *Calgon* is the trade name of one type of sodium hexametaphosphate available commercially. Be sure to obtain the ordinary, plain material, which is free of detergents, perfume, and other additives. The same substance may be obtained from scientific supply houses. If a heated solution of sodium hexametaphosphate is used, however, or if the object is allowed to soak longer than necessary to soften the crusts, some of the copper patina may be lost, as well, so be careful to check this sort of work periodically. As soon as the solution loosens the deposits, gently scrub them off, being sure not to abrade the metal underneath. Thoroughly rinse the object in at least four changes of distilled water.

Applying Protective Finishes

Lacquer has been the traditional protective coating for brass and copper, because of its toughness and durability. However, lacquer may change the luster of the piece; and, of course, once a lacquer coating is scratched, the oxidation starts all over again, and the old lacquer must be removed to re-polish the piece. Theoretically, lacquer thinner should strip off the old lacquer, but in practice it often takes vast amounts of it to accomplish that; otherwise, it merely thins the old lacquer down, instead of removing it. In addition, lacquer thinner is toxic and highly flammable.

Fortunately, there are alternatives to lacquer as protection for the metal, once the old coating has been removed. The simplest is an application of microcrystalline wax, which offers relatively slight protection, but is easily removable with solvents such as mineral spirits. The wax also dulls the shine of copper and brass just a bit, but that effect may not be altogether objectionable.

Another alternative is a synthetic lacquer formulated especially for use on copper and brass; it is easily removable with mild solvents, and is advertised as having tarnish-preventive properties, as well. It should protect surfaces well, without the enormous difficulties encountered with ordinary lacquer. *Incralac* is the trade name of one type of synthetic lacquer available from conservation materials suppliers. The protective properties of the material are quite good, but there is not normally a need to polish and coat copper items as a mass treatment.

Storage and Display

Avoid placing copper, brass, or bronze objects in contact with materials containing chlorides or sulfur compounds and protect them from air in which those pollutants may be present. An airtight display case or a wrapping of acid-free tissue and a polyethylene bag will help prevent further damage. Always wear clean white cotton gloves to handle copper objects.

Tin, Pewter, and Lead

Tin

Tin is one of several metals that are allotropic—that is, it can occur in two or more forms that differ in molecular structure. At temperatures *above* 13.2 degrees Centigrade, tin maintains the familiar metal form most often seen; but subjected to temperatures *below* 13.2 degrees Centigrade, pure tin often disintegrates into a grey powder commonly called *tin pest* or *tin disease*.[13] There is no known way to reclaim tin to which this happens.

In its more familiar solid state, tin is often mistakenly thought of as an ephemeral, easily rusted material, because of the general misleading word-association of *tin* with the term *tin cans*. As mentioned early in this chapter, tin cans and tinware are, basically, sheet-iron protected by a microscopically thin layer of tin, and it is the iron that corrodes, after the thin tin layer has been worn or scratched away.

Tin *can* be corroded, by prolonged exposure to combinations of air and moisture and some acids, but it is, on the whole, quite stable. For example, bars of tin that were taken up after having laid for a hundred years in the holds of sunken Confederate raiders off the coast of North Carolina were, for the most part, relatively uncorroded.

Because of its rarity and its cost, the tin used on cooking utensils now to make the relatively heavy inner coatings on pots and pans appears only on the better-grade, higher-priced copper and brass cookware.

While tin *is* stable, it is also soft, and a collector or curator wishing to brighten tinware or tin objects should use only the finest polishes, such as those recommended for silver. Since cleaning or polishing of any metal wears away its surface very slightly, industrious, regular rubbing of tin artifacts can produce detrimental effects in a rather short time.

Pewter

Known and used since the days of ancient Rome, pewter is an alloy—or a number of alloys—made basically of tin to which varying amounts of other metals, chiefly antimony and copper, are added to impart qualities desirable for making different products.

Copper and antimony add hardness—antimony adds whiteness, as well—and produce an alloy that will hold sharp impressions in casting. Bismuth and zinc are also sometimes added; and although lead and all its compounds are poisonous, lead—in greater or lesser amounts—was often found in old or traditional pewter. Lead makes pewter more malleable, turns it a darker, bluish color, and, since it is poisonous, adds the element of danger to human life if the alloy is used to make tableware or water pipes and the amount of lead in it is more than even slightly moderate. A large proportion of lead would be harmless in pewter alloys used for making such things as candlesticks or organ pipes, but it would be quite dangerous if pewter from that batch were used to make containers for holding food and drink.

Tin ore was sometimes contaminated with traces of lead as it was mined, so that pewter made from some lots of tin ore would show some lead content as a natural result. Occasionally, however, a heavy lead content in traditional pewter may well have occurred through intent— and basic dishonesty—on the part of devious pewterers, who sometimes extended the amount of metal they were making by intentionally adding to the melting pot that was supposed to contain "pure" pewter some objects known to contain lead.

Traditional pewter with a high lead content was a cheaper and generally less desirable metal than pure pewter and was known variously as *ley metal* (20 percent lead) and *pipe metal* (40 percent lead). Sometimes a knowledge of some of the more common traditional and obsolete terms for mixtures of pewter can be helpful in identifying historical objects. For more on this, see pages 3–116 of *Old Pewter, Brass, Copper, and Sheffield Plate*, by N. Hudson Moore.[14]

The cheaper pewter alloys had their uses, but the making of high-quality wares was not one of them. The term *black pewter* was applied to those items displaying the characteristic dark corrosion of lead.

Depending on such variables as the lead-tin ratio in the original alloy, the environment in which old pewter ware was kept and the uses to which it was put, a present-day collection of traditional pewter may include pieces ranging from those with a pleasant patina to those that are pitted wrecks.

Britannia metal, a silvery-white alloy of tin with antimony, copper, and sometimes bismuth and zinc, is almost a mirror twin to pewter. The two are very similar in appearance, and both were used extensively to make tableware. One distinguishing difference is that Britannia metal is harder than pewter.[14]

Proper care for pewter objects. Pewterware, like objects made of tin and lead, should be kept in a stable environment, free of atmospheric pollutants; a relative humidity level kept at between 40 percent to 50 percent is best for pewter, since higher levels tend to aggravate corrosion problems. On display, avoid putting pewter objects near materials that contain sulfur compounds, particularly adhesives and some varieties of felt. For their protection in storage, wrap pewter objects in acid-free tissue and enclose them in polyethylene bags.

General care of pewter begins with careful handling. Clean cotton gloves should be worn in working with or moving it. Since pewter bends very easily, it should be treated as a very fragile material. Pewter objects should not be heated, either, or disfigurement and damage could well result.

Major dents, gouges, and bent places in the metal may often be repaired, but the process is not so simple as it might appear; a do-it-yourselfer can, with appalling ease, produce still further damage, or even break a bent object in half. Many jewelers are able to straighten out dented pewter safely, but be sure to go to someone whose integrity and expertise you can trust.

Cleaning pewter. The grey patina of old pewter is acceptable—even desirable—to many collectors. It is a stable outer layer of the metal, and it serves as a sign of age, as well. Although pewter objects were sometimes considered substitutes for silver items when they were produced and may, perhaps, have been kept as shiny as silver when they were new, the decision to clean off the patina of age on pewter is up to the individual.

One should bear in mind that cleaning pewter is not only a laborious task, but one that removes a small amount of the metal surface each time it is done.

Dull pewter can be polished by using very fine abrasives like rottenstone or jewelers' rouge mixed in a carrier like mineral oil or alcohol. If the metal does not respond to this treatment, do not try harsh abrasives or steel or bronze wool, since pewter is even softer than any of the copper-based alloys.

Because the appropriate cleaners for pewter have a very gentle action, one must be prepared to expend a lot of hand labor to make a pewter piece bright again. For that reason, test your cleaning in an inconspicuous spot to see whether you will wish to take on the task of polishing the entire piece.

All-purpose metal polishes or harsher abrasive mixtures can very easily scratch the surface of a pewter object. If there is a question about any polish, test it on a small area of the bottom of the piece and examine the results with a magnifying glass. If a discernible new pattern of scratches appears, find a more gentle cleaning method.

Although there are electrochemical reduction methods that will remove certain types of heavy corrosion from metals, their use sometimes produces a clean surface at the expense of a loss of smoothness; they may also blur lines, inscriptions, and stampmarks, as well—all effects that lower the value of an artifact both aesthetically and historically.

The acids or alkalis used to clean pewter commercially are inimical to the metal if their action is not thoroughly understood and if the residues are not completely removed after washing. Do not be in a hurry to have this sort of commercial cleaning done; have major cleaning done only by a conservator of objects who understands and can control the process.

Occasionally, deterioration in pewter is caused by the condition known as *tin pest*, discussed with tin, above. The condition is a form of physical alteration of the molecular structure in pewter, as it is in tin— which is, of course, the basic metal used to make pewter; and in pewter, it causes a powdery, crystalline condition sometimes confused with corrosion. Tin pest in pewter, like tin pest in tin, is said to be the result of prolonged exposure to intense cold; and nothing can be done to bring back pewter affected by it.

Before attempting to clean heavily corroded pewter, do read the articles listed in the suggested readings, and if at all possible, at least have a conservator examine the object and provide a statement of condition.

Lead

While lead is as shiny as tin when it is freshly cast or cut, in a short time it acquires a characteristic stable dark grey patina.

Lead is, however, quite sensitive to any acid vapors, or to acid and moisture. For this reason, lead objects that have been in industrial atmospheres, handled by sweaty hands, or exhibited in old-fashioned oak wood cases—which retain large concentrations of oak's characteristic tannic acid—will soon acquire a powdery white surface, evidence of unstable lead carbonate or lead formate.

The best way to avoid this condition is to prevent it—keep lead objects free from an acid environment. There *are* procedures for cleaning and stabilizing corroded lead; but all of the safe methods are rather complicated. If you have a number of lead pieces in bad condition, your best course will be to find an expert with experience in treating such objects. A report on the condition of your collection will at least suggest what might be done next.

Gold, Silver, and Silvery-looking Materials

Gold

Gold in its pure state is a stable material without corrosion problems. As noted earlier in this chapter, pure gold, being chemically inactive, is the only metal not affected by moisture, oxygen, or acids, although it does react to the halogens. Aqua regia, a mixture of nitric and hydro-chloric acids that liberates chlorine, is so named for its ability to dissolve gold, the "king" of metals.[15] Since gold is a very soft metal, however, it is often alloyed with copper, silver, or other metals to lend it hardness, and some gold alloys will therefore tarnish if they are exposed to chloride salts or sulfur compounds.

Objects made of gold alloys should be protected from atmosphere contaminated by sulfur compounds in much the same way as objects made of silver (see below). In storage, such protection for them can be arranged by wrapping them in soft, acid-free tissue and placing them in airtight polyethylene bags. On display, the best protection for gold-alloy items is an airtight display case with strips of anti-tarnish cloth placed inconspicuously inside. To protect them from the chloride salts in human perspiration, wear clean white cotton gloves to handle any gold alloy object.

Objects of gold alloy can be polished with precipitated chalk or jew-elers' rouge and alcohol, but they should not be polished and rubbed any more frequently than absolutely necessary, or fine detail work on the surface will be worn away.

Gold is extremely ductile and is the most malleable of all metals,[16] which means that special care must be exercised in handling any item made of pure gold: it may be easily scratched, gouged, or bent.

Since gold can be beaten into extremely thin sheets, the gold layer on gilt or gold-leafed objects is usually very thin; and in addition to the need for very careful handling because of that, there is often some difficulty in determining what may be directly beneath this thin gold layer. On furniture and picture frames, wood or gesso is often the underlying support. Not only could the thin gold layer be worn away quickly by zealous cleaning, but the underlying material might also be damaged by alcohol or water in a polish.

If you are not absolutely certain whether an object is solid gold or a gold alloy, take it to a conservator for analysis and advice. The treatment of complex objects is not something to be undertaken by an amateur.

Silver

Environmental enemies of silver. Like gold, silver is considered one of the "noble" metals; and although silver is not chemically active and does not oxidize in air, it *is* quite susceptible to tarnishing from minute amounts of sulfur compounds or chloride salts in the atmosphere or the immediate environment.

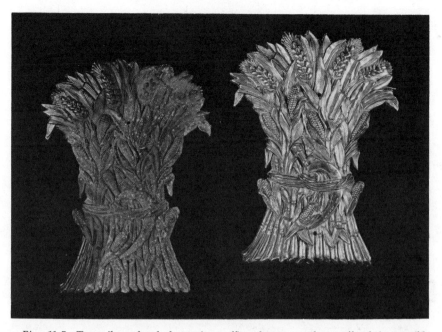

Fig. 11.5. Two silver-plated decorative coffin plates: one has suffered irreversible damage from a corrosive atmosphere, and the other has been kept in a clean environment.

Most people are unhappily aware of what happens when silver comes in contact with the chloride salts present in the perspiration of a human hand or the sulfur contained in coal gas, industrial environments, rubber items, and egg yolks. Less well known—but quite as harmful to silver—is the sulfur frequently present in household synthetic detergents, which may also contain phosphorous compounds that cause particularly stubborn stains on silver surfaces. Latex paints formerly contained rubber and sulfur compounds, inimical to silver, though most modern paints are now made with stable synthetic resins. It is simple to find out whether a latex paint will make silver tarnish: test a paint sample in a plastic bag with a silver token to see what happens.

These common environmental hazards that cause tarnishing in silver necessitate frequent cleaning and polishing of silver artifacts. Yet, frequent cleaning and polishing—even with the finest, least abrasive polishes—leads to loss of surface detail through the constant wearing away of this soft metal. With silver plate, too much polishing results in eventual exposure of the base metal. Therefore, since silver *is* so soft and

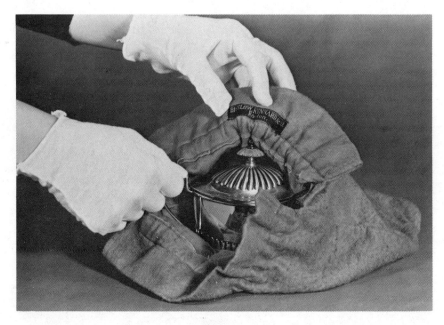

Fig. 11.6 Clean cotton gloves are essential for handling silver and other metals. Always wear them, to avoid causing corrosion and tarnish.

so easily worn by excessive polishing and handling, anyone who values silver artifacts should provide for them a sympathetic environment that will keep tarnishing to a minimum.

Protecting silver objects. Safeguarding silver from sulfurous atmosphere and materials is obviously the best form of protection for it. One method of achieving that, in storage areas, is to wrap the silver in soft tissue, cushioning it against outside air. Acid-free tissue is recommended, because of its stable nature. The tissue-wrapped artifact can then be placed in a cloth bag made for silver storage, or it can be put into an airtight polyethylene bag, which will help a great deal more.

The best protection recommended for silver, either in storage or on exhibit, is the use of paper anti-tarnish strips. The metallic substances in these materials readily absorb sulfur compounds before they can have much effect on the silver. Do not allow anti-tarnish strips to touch the silver, however; and change them periodically, or they will redeposit, on the metal they are there to protect, the sulfur they attract. Jewelry stores should be able to provide anti-tarnish strips for silver protection. On exhibit, silver might also be coated with various sprays, but these sub-

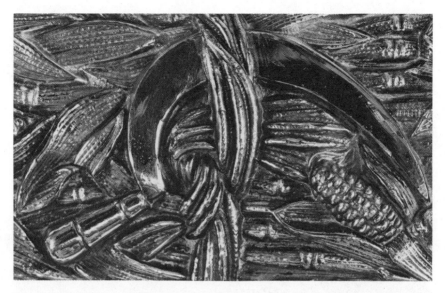

Fig. 11.7. Detail of well-preserved silver surface.

Fig. 11.8. Detail of an object similar to the one shown in Fig. 11.7, except that this one has undergone extreme corrosion, and probably has very little silver remaining under the surface.

Fig. 11.9. Cloth storage bags for silver objects may offer some help against tarnish, but a polyethylene plastic bag will be more efficient in preventing contact of the metal with airborne pollutants.

stances can change the appearance of the metal somewhat and eventually will lead to a tiresome stripping and cleaning chore in the future. An alternative is to display the silver in a relatively airtight case, with anti-tarnish paper inconspicuously placed inside.

Cleaning silver. A frequently recommended electrochemical method for cleaning silver is to soak it in a solution of one ounce of washing soda to one pint of distilled water in an old aluminum pan. If an aluminum pan is not available, one can use a glass or ceramic pan, with a sheet or two of crumpled aluminum foil put in the bottom. The silver article is immersed in the water-soda solution until clean, then rinsed off in distilled water and wiped dry with a soft cloth. *This method of cleaning silver artifacts should not be tried with plated ware, because it involves the possibility of stripping off the plate.* In addition to that hazard, silver being cleaned by this method sometimes develops a hazy surface, requiring further polishing to finish the job.

The use of dip cleaners for silver objects is not recommended, under any circumstances. Commercial varieties generally clean through the action of

Fig. 11.10. Silver on display should be placed in a case, primarily for security reasons; but if the case is tight, it also helps keep polluted air away from the metal and so will slow tarnishing. Tarnish-preventive cloth or paper strips may be placed inconspicuously in the case for further protection.

acids, which can harm the surface of a silver object directly—and immediately—or they can remain in hard-to-reach nooks and crevices of an artifact, to corrode the metal gradually. A homemade dip cleaner that was formerly recommended contains thiourea, a suspected carcinogen. *No silver dip solution should be considered safe.*

Polishes. You can make an inexpensive silver polish by mixing a paste of precipitated chalk and denatured alcohol. Although many American commercial manufacturers of silver polish now put out a product with a tarnish inhibitor, these commercial polishes are too abrasive to be recommended.

Special problems with silver objects. Urban water often contains chlorine, which, in addition to purifying the water, also has a tendency to cause metal corrosion. Deep-seated corrosion from chlorides or sulfides or the depositing of copper salts on the surfaces of silver pieces frequently occurs in excavations and underwater sites. In some instances, it is desirable to get rid of encrustations formed in that way; and in some instances, parts of them represent patinas that should be saved. These are such specialized problems that they are not dealt with at length here, but the reading list includes several articles that explain a small part of the difficulties in such complex situations.

Ambiguous, Silvery-looking Materials

During the nineteenth and early twentieth centuries, new combinations of metal alloys and new methods of coating and plating metals were developed. While objects made of these newly developed materials are of little interest to the archaeologist—terrestrial or marine—many historical agencies and collectors have, in their collections, nickel-plated stoves, tinned sheet-iron wares, galvanized items, hollow castings, loving cups, firemen's speaking trumpets, and a variety of other things made of some kind of silvery-looking metal.

A good rule of thumb in treating such objects is to *avoid using any chemical cleaners on plated or hot-dipped items to prevent the possibility of separating the layers.* Only the finest polishes should be used on these "hybrid" finishes, because of the danger of wearing off the thin plating. Sheet-iron objects, coated with a thin layer of tin or zinc that may have worn off in spots, should be protected from humidity, as the basic metal—iron—is particularly vulnerable to rust pits. Any such rusted areas should be cleaned mechanically with the greatest possible care and immediately thereafter coated with microcrystalline wax, to keep out moisture. Use a dental pick or some other fine-pointed tool to do this kind of cleaning, and work under a good magnifier to avoid scratching the uncorroded area.

Many of the silvery-looking art objects and inscribed trophies made around the turn of the century may be of German silver, of a variety of base metals, or of silver plate. Some will brighten up nicely with silver polish—and some will be hopeless. If silver polish will not do the job, leave the object alone, as stronger treatments or abrasives for that sort of surface will only lead to disaster.

Many of the hollow castings so popular in late Victorian and early Edwardian times are made of zinc. To preserve these objects, *avoid any chemical cleaning.* Many of them have been given a coat of greenish or dark brown paint, to imitate the effect of a bronze patina; but turning the casting upside down will usually reveal the characteristic bluish-white crystalline look of zinc, on the under side. If parts of these objects are broken off, use a good adhesive (see the appendix), rather than any hot-solder method to try to mend them.

NOTES

1. *Columbia Encyclopedia*, 4th ed., s.v. "metal," "gold."
2. *Columbia Encyclopedia*, 4th ed., s.v. "gold," "silver," "goldwork," "silverwork."
3. *Columbia Encyclopedia*, 4th ed., s.v. "metalwork," "Neolithic period."
4. *Columbia Encyclopedia*, 4th ed., s.v. "metal," "Iron Age."
5. *Columbia Encyclopedia*, 4th ed., s.v. "lead."
6. *Columbia Encyclopedia*, 4th ed., s.v. "metallurgy," "copper," "Neolithic period," "metalwork."
7. *Columbia Encyclopedia*, 4th ed., s.v. "brasses, ornamental," "pewter," "metalwork."
8. *Columbia Encyclopedia*, 4th ed., s.v. "metalwork," "silver."
9. *Columbia Encyclopedia*, 4th ed., s.v. "metal."
10. *Columbia Encyclopedia*, 4th ed., s.v. "metal," "corrosion," "gold," "tin," "lead," "copper," "metal," "silver."
11. H. A. Plenderleith and A. E. A. Werner, *The Conservation of Antiquities and Works of Art*, pp. 197–202, 376–378.
12. Stephen C. Rees-Jones, "Some Aspects of Iron Objects from the Sea."
13. *Columbia Encyclopedia*, 4th ed., s.v. "tin," "allatropy."
14. *Columbia Encyclopedia*, 4th ed., s.v. "Britannia metal," "pewter."
15. *Columbia Encyclopedia*, 4th ed., s.v. "gold."
16. *Columbia Encyclopedia*, 4th ed., s.v. "gold."

SUGGESTED READING

Fales, Mrs. Dean A., Jr. *The Care of Antique Silver*. Technical Leaflet No. 40. Nashville: The American Association for State and Local History, 1967.

Gary, Ebenezer. "Brass Instruments: Practical Guidelines for Repair." *Technology and Conservation Magazine* 6 (Fall 1981): 38–46.

"'Gold' Is a Many-Alloyed Thing." *Technology and Conservation Magazine* 2 (Fall 1977): 10.

Lemmer, Geoffrey M. "The Cleaning and Protective Coating of Ferrous Metals: A Brief Survey." *AIC Bulletin* 12: 97–108.

MacLeod, Ian D., and Neil A. North. "Conservation of Corroded Silver." *Studies in Conservation* 24 (November 1979): 165–170.

Made of Iron. Houston, Texas: University of St. Thomas Art Department, 1966.

Majewski, Lawrence. "On Conservation: Silver." *Museum News* 51 (April 1973): 10–11.

Moore, N. Hudson. *Old Pewter, Brass, Copper, and Sheffield Plate*. Rutland, Vermont: Charles E. Tuttle Company, 1972.

Morris, Kenneth, and Jay W. Krueger. "The Use of Wet-Peening in the Conservation of Outdoor Bronze Sculpture." *Studies in Conservation* 24 (February 1979): 40–43.

Oddy, W. A., and M. J. Hughes. "The Stabilization of 'Active' Bronze and Iron Antiquities by the Use of Sodium Sesquicarbonate." *Studies in Conservation* 15 (August 1970): 183–189.

Organ, Robert M. "Conservation of Iron Objects." *Historical Archaeology* 1 (1967): 52–53.

Organ, Robert M. "The Consolidation of Fragile Metallic Objects." In *Recent Advances in Conservation*, pp. 104–110, 128–134. London: Buttersworths, 1963.

Plenderleith, Harold J., and Robert M. Organ. "The Decay and Conservation of Museum Objects of Tin." *Studies in Conservation* 1 (June 1953): 63–72.

Plenderleith, H. J., and A. E. A. Werner. *The Conservation of Antiquities and Works of Art: Treatment, Repair, and Restoration.* New York: Oxford University Press, 1971.
The "Metals" section of this reference may hold some hints for nonprofessionals, but many advances in treating degraded metals have been made in recent years, especially for archaeological specimens.

Rees-Jones, Stephen G. "Some Aspects of Iron Objects from the Sea." *Studies in Conservation* 17 (May 1972): 83–87.

Reisman, Shelley. "A Sparkling Solution: How to Clean Old Silver." *History News* 38 (August 1983): 22–23.

Stanbolov, Todor. "Removal of Corrosion on an Eighteenth-Century Silver Bowl." *Studies in Conservation* 11 (February 1966): 37–44.

Ternbach, Joseph. "Restoration of Bronzes, Ancient and Modern: *Bulletin of the American Group—IIC* 12 (April 1972): 110–116.

"Tin Helps Bring Back the Sound of Music." *Technology and Conservation Magazine* 3 (Spring 1978): 6–7, 10.
Restoration of metal pipes.

Van Zelst, Dr. Lambertus, and Jean-Louis Lachevre. "Outdoor Bronze Sculpture: Problems and Procedures of Protective Treatment." *Technology and Conservation Magazine* 8 (Spring 1983): 18–24.

Western, A. C. "The Conservation of Excavated Iron Objects." *Studies in Conservation* 17 (May 1972): 83–87.

12

Textiles:
Care and Conservation

With the exception of such things as wedding gowns and full-dress military uniforms, most old garments have had long, hard-working lives. Old rugs, old curtains, old quilts, and old blankets, too, are often worn, sun-faded, soiled, stained, or moth-eaten.

Speaking generally here—more specific information follows—caring for such textiles involves, from time to time, cleaning, strengthening weakened areas, and providing protection against further deterioration.

One should consider cleaning old textiles only if that will not affect the strength or color of the fabric. While there are a good many effective methods for removing ordinary soil and many stains, injudicious and indiscriminate cleaning of old textiles can cause shrinkage, distortion of form, color loss, or color bleeding. Proper care in choice of procedure, materials, and method may, on the other hand, improve the appearance of old textiles, kill any insects or insect eggs and larvae that may be present in the fabric, and protect the fabric by removing nutrient materials that attract insect pests.

Weak areas in garments and fabrics should be strengthened and reinforced by mending torn places, filling in small holes and thread losses, and providing support for "thin" areas and points of stress.

Protecting old textiles against further deterioration should include not only a careful and safe cleaning, insect-proofing, and mending, but the providing of proper storage conditions and exhibition care.

Some general suggestions for the safe care of old textiles include the following.

1. Do not subject old textiles to high humidity. Air that is too moist encourages the growth of mold and mildew, which can stain fibers and cause them to deteriorate. Elevated humidity also seems to promote insect activity, although drier conditions will not keep insects away. It is an excellent idea to inspect textiles regularly for mold growth or the presence of insects in either the larval or the adult stage.

Fig. 12.1. *Simple forms for display or storage of costumes may be made with hardboard supports, covered with polyester fiber-fill and washed, unbleached muslin. If a form is to be used, it must be made to fit the garment that will go on it.*

2. Low light levels should be maintained where textiles are kept; and in textile storage areas, darkness is preferred when people are not present.

3. Always handle all textiles with care: protect them from being touched while on display, and *never* allow anyone to wear historic garments. Physical handling of textiles should be done with freshly laundered white cotton gloves, to avoid transferring grime, perspiration, and skin oils to old fabrics. Support textile items as much as possible when they are being moved or placed on display. If fabrics must be folded, avoid old crease lines, where fibers are already weak; cushion fold areas with polyester batting or crumpled acid-free tissue.

4. Mark textiles with removable labels, such as sewn-in cotton tape. Never use markers or inks on historic textiles. Avoid pins, staples, and clips, which can tear and stain historic fabrics. Non-staining staples of Monel metal are available for use near artifacts.

5. Do not allow fabrics to come in contact with ordinary paper, cardboard, wood, or building boards. A "belt and suspenders" method of protecting textiles by lining wooden drawers or trays is suggested: place a sheet of archival polyester film next to the wood or paper. *Be sure that you are using materials of archival quality.*[1] This impermeable barrier will prevent migration of acids from wood to fabric. Then, to prevent any possible condensation between the artifact and the plastic, cover the polyester with acid-free tissue or heavier acid-free paper. Monel metal staples may be used to fasten the linings in place, if necessary.

Care of Woolens

Several characteristics of wool create the need in woolen fabrics for extra care in handling, whether in storage or on display. Wool fiber usually possesses a very high rate of extension—which simply means that it is very easily stretched. To compensate for this natural characteristic, woolen items on display should be carefully supported by some more sturdy fabric used as backing or by draping them on a panel set at an angle. Moreover, the capacity of woolen fibers to absorb moisture readily from the environment may cause expansion of even properly displayed woolen material. Especially on display, allow for flexibility in mountings for wool and provide sufficient space for the material's possible increase in volume. Since wool does not benefit from low humidity, a constant relative humidity level of 50 percent is considered best.

All woolens—as well as items of feathers, hair, and fur—must be checked for condition before coming into your collection areas. Clothes

moths, carpet beetles, and various insect larvae may remain alive—
though dormant—for several years under unfavorable conditions; and if
inspection of incoming fabrics reveals such infestation, these pests can
and should be eliminated, either by cleaning the material or through use
of poisons.

Cleaning Woolens

Before any woolen fabric is cleaned with water or solvents, it should
be freed of all loose dirt. One way to do that is to use a vacuum cleaner
on the material at low suction. Use either a low-powered hand vacuum
or a canister model with the venting slots open; and if the fabric appears
even the least bit fragile, place a piece of plastic screening over it to
protect it from fluttering or being strained by the stress of the vacuum's
suction.

Wet cleaning. Many woolens in good condition can be washed safely, if
proper precautions are taken. Test all colored materials before washing,
to see whether or not the colors will run. To do this, put a piece of clean
white blotter under each test area—each of the various colors—and
with an eye dropper, let fall enough drops of distilled water for it to go
through the material; then check to see whether a color stain has seeped
through the fabric onto the blotter. If the color areas tested show no sign
of reacting to water, the fabric may be washed in distilled or de-ionized
water, with a non-ionic detergent, and then rinsed—thoroughly.[2]

In drying wet-cleaned woolens, avoid any agitating or heating of the
fabric—those conditions tend to shrink wool fibers and cause them to
"felt," or mat together. Wet wool should never be hung up to dry,
because its own weight is heavy enough to pull it out of shape. Instead
of hanging a woolen item, lay the fabric out flat, on clean toweling,
shape it according to its original dimensions, and let it dry gradually.

One drawback to wet cleaning for woolens is that old, brittle woolen
fibers may be adversely affected by the necessary friction of the washing
and drying action. In addition, woolens with a high-twist yarn structure
or with special finishes should not be wet cleaned. Proprietary cleaning
agents should not be used, since their formulations are variable, and
they may leave in the fabric residual deposits that could cause deterioration later.

If you are considering wet cleaning for old rugs, get in touch with a
firm that specializes in rug-cleaning and repair. Rugs can present special
problems and are often quite difficult to handle, because of their size and
weight.

One final note on wet cleaning: *Never use a hot iron on wool or on any other old fabric.*

Dry cleaning. The usual solvents used in dry cleaning do not wet the fibers of wool; yet, they do dissolve greases, oils, waxes, and resins from woolen fabric. Modern dry cleaning solutions often include a small percentage of synthetic detergent and water, in an amount considered safe for woolens and silks, which increases the range of stains that can be cleaned from these materials. However, historic woolens should not go through the normal cleaning process, which involves too much tumbling and spinning for old fibers.

Woolen items should be hand-cleaned only, and that should be done by a professional dry cleaner, using fresh, clean solvent. Before dry cleaning begins, all colors in the material to be cleaned should be tested, as is done properly before wet cleaning; and dry cleaning should be undertaken for only the kinds of soil mentioned above—greases, oils, waxes, and resins.

Neither traditional nor modern methods of dry cleaning should be tried on historic textiles by an amateur. Two good reasons are that none of the solvents used in traditional home dry cleaning are considered safe to use without extraordinary precautions—the fire hazards, toxicity, and carcinogenic properties of those materials make them an unacceptable personal risk; and modern spot removers and sprays cannot be guaranteed as to their ingredients or their action, and so they should be avoided.

Whether the cleaning method decided upon be personal or commercial, however, it should rid the fabric not only of soil and stains, but of unwanted insects, larvae, and eggs. Proper cleaning before storage or exhibition is the best and most practical insurance for the well-being of all fabrics.

Ridding Woolens of Insect Pests

Cleanliness. Moths like dark, quiet places; thus, a periodic airing and sunning of woolen fabrics may discourage these insects, although it is not the best solution to such a problem and, over an extended period of time, it may require too much handling of fragile fabrics. *Woolens must also be kept clean.* It is grime—such things as scraps of food, droplets of grease, and similar kinds of soiling—that attracts moths to woolens. Cleaning processes therefore serve three purposes: they rid the fabric of unsightly stains, divest it of insect infestations, insect larvae and eggs, and remove the polluting nutrient material that would encourage future

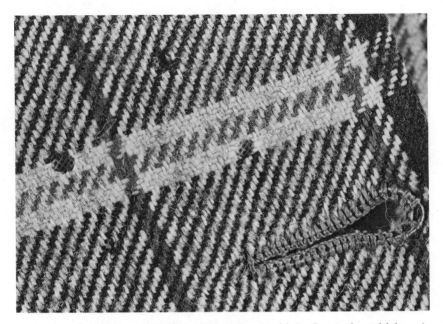

Fig. 12.2. Moths have destroyed part of this woolen fabric. Care and watchfulness in storage might have prevented this damage.

insect invasion. It helps to protect all fabrics if storage areas are also kept clean by regular—and frequent—washing, vacuuming, and dusting to eliminate the kind of uncleanly conditions that attract moths.

Sealed containers for storage of woolens. Cleaned woolens can be safely kept, rolled on acid-free tubes, in boxes, chests, or rooms that are sealed—but these storage places must be *tightly* sealed, as insect larvae can penetrate openings of one-sixteenth of an inch. Use tape seals on the outside of boxes and chests and in corners and doors of storage rooms. Cedar chests and closets lined with cedar wood should also be sealed; they may *deter,* but they do not kill moths; and they have no effect whatever on carpet beetles.

Insect poisons. Keep in mind that any substance that will kill insects is *poisonous* and that it will have some toxic effects on human beings. For that reason, few insecticides are considered acceptable for general use at present. Many traditional favorites, such as cyanide gas and DDT, have deadly effects that are now well known, and they are no longer available for general use. By all means, consult a good reference book, or, per-

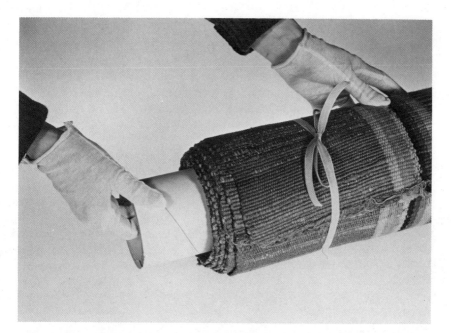

Fig. 12.3. Rolled storage for flat textiles: cover a large-diameter cardboard tube with a barrier layer of polyester film, then with acid-free paper. The object to be stored is then rolled onto the tube and tied with cotton or linen tape. In this instance, the object will be placed in a closed storage cabinet, so no outer-wrapping layer is needed. More delicate fabrics should be rolled with an interleaving layer of acid-free tissue, so that friction and snagging will not damage fragile fibers.

haps, a local agricultural extension agent, to help identify your insect problems and the possible, acceptable remedies available.[3]

As this book goes to press, there are two generally acceptable materials for control of insects, although only one is registered for use in public buildings. The two are *dimethyldichlorovinylphosphate* (DDVP) and *paradichlorobenzene* (PDB). Strips containing DDVP are available under a variety of trade names for general use. Moth crystals composed of PDB are widely used, but this substance is *not* an approved and registered material. Thus it is important to keep up to date through various periodicals for the restrictions and suggestions issued for the safety of the public by the Environmental Protection Agency and other testing agencies.

Using DDVP insecticide strips is quite simple, although one should

Fig. 12.4. Paradichlorobenzene moth crystals in a muslin bag or insecticide strips containing dichlorovinyl dimethyl phosphate may be used to control insect infestations.

observe all recommended safety procedures. Gloves should be worn as protection against skin contact with the poison itself. Placed in its hanging container, the strip is merely put in a storage closet or box. *DDVP should not be used to treat a room that is used regularly by people.*

Moth crystals should be of the paradichlorobenzene (PDB) type, rather than the naphthalene type, since the latter does not kill some insect pests. The crystals should be placed in a cloth bag at the highest possible level in a storage closet or cabinet, since the vapors are heavier than air. Check to see whether either poison has an adverse effect on any paints, finishes, or colors of artifacts being treated. Because of potential reactions with materials, the insecticides should be used *as needed,* not on a constant, long-term basis; and they should not be placed in direct contact with artifacts.

Notes on Silk

Silken fabrics, which are generally more delicate than woolens, should also be treated with meticulous care. Many kinds of insects destroy silk, so collections should be surveyed carefully. Old silks often become quite brittle, and friction or sharp folds will break the fibers. Both infrared and ultraviolet energy have deleterious effects on silk. In collections or display areas, the ultraviolet component of sunlight or fluorescent light should be shielded or filtered to prevent damage to silk and other materials; and heating devices or strong lights, which also produce infrared energy, should be kept away from silk. A bit of preventive care can protect silken objects from greatly accelerated effects of aging.

Old silk must be supported and must not be hung free. Frequently, garments or flags made of silk can be couched or stitched between two layers of fine, almost invisible silk or synthetic netting.[4] But determining whether this can be done with a specific piece and seeing the job itself through to completion are for conservation experts.

During the nineteenth century, silk was sometimes weighted with tin salts, to give it more luster. Old dresses and flags so treated eventually fall to fragments and dust, and there is, as yet, no known way of halting or reversing the deterioration.

Along with protection from strong light and heat, a moderately low humidity level is beneficial to silk. A relative humidity level of 40 percent will help silk survive, although that is a lower R.H. level than is acceptable for other organic materials. And one should take greater care in handling silk under such conditions, since the fibers will be slightly more brittle than they would be in higher humidity.

Water spots on silk are caused by small amounts of water dissolving natural or synthetic gums on one part of the fabric. Water spots are not damaging to the material, although they can be very disfiguring. Professional help is usually needed to remove these blotches from silk.

Care of Cotton and Linen

Since cotton and linen are not affected by moths, and their fibers do not "felt" (mat together) and shrink to the same degree as wool fibers do when washed in hot alkaline solutions, a proportionately greater amount of cottons and linens survives in public and private collections.

Unfortunately, these sturdy materials are often treated in a rather cavalier manner, as if they would last forever: old curtains are hung up on display and left up indefinitely—until, one day, when they are taken down for washing, it is discovered that they are not only sun-faded, but sun-rotted, as well, at the point of falling to pieces if put through a washing. Note also that some insects are attracted to starches and sizing in fabrics, as well as to cotton and linen fibers themselves. Some thought, then, should be given to proper care for cottons and linens.

Exposure to sunlight or strong light for a short period may reduce stains and yellowing in these fabrics, but prolonged exposure leads to the fading of dyes, more rapid oxidation, and embrittlement of the fabric fibers. Some dyes add to the deterioration of cotton and linen fibers, and strong light accelerates that effect.

A constant relative humidity level of 45 percent is beneficial to cotton and linen, but a range of between 50 and 55 percent R.H. is acceptable.

Cotton and linen items may be cleaned in much the same way as woolens. Bleaching of fabrics can be a complicated task and should be avoided. Also, bleaches, sizings, starches, and other laundry aids may leave harmful deposits on old fibers, so none of these should be used.[5] It should be kept in mind that *any substance that comes in contact with an artifact has the potential for causing deterioration. Check everything in proper references, and do not use home procedures on items of historic value.*

NOTES

1. *Polyester Film Encapsulation* (Washington, D.C.: Library of Congress, 1980), pp. 21–23.
2. Harold F. Mailand, *Considerations for the Care of Textiles and Costumes*, pp. 8–9, 20–21.
3. Stephen R. Edwards, et al., *Pest Control in Museums*, pp. A–1 to A–30, B–1 to B–20.
4. Karen Finch and Greta Putnam, *Caring for Textiles*, pp. 30–43, 69–90.
5. Mailand, *Considerations for the Care of Textiles*, p. 90.

SUGGESTED READING

Annis, Zoe Katherine, and Barbara M. Reagan. "Evaluation of Selected Bleaching Treatments Suitable for Historic White Cottons." *Studies in Conservation* 24 (November 1979): 171–178.

Birrell, Verla Leone. *The Textile Arts, a Handbook of Fabric Structure and Design Processes: Ancient and Modern Weaving, Braiding, Printing, and Other Textile Techniques.* New York: Harper, 1959.

Bogle, Michael M. *Technical Data on Textiles,* Numbers One through Twelve. North Andover, Massachusetts: Merrimack Valley Textile Museum, 1979.

Craft, Margaret Loew, and Timothy Vitale. "Economical Textile Storage, Part I: Rolled Storage." *Museum News* 58 (November/December 1979): 71–77.

Craft, Margaret Loew, and Timothy Vitale. "Economical Textile Storage, Part II: Flat Storage." *Museum News* 58 (January/February 1980): 59, 61–62, 65–66, 68.

Edwards, Stephen R., et al. *Pest Control in Museums: A Status Report (1980).* Lawrence, Kansas: Association of Systematics Collections, 1981.

Finch, Karen, and Greta Putnam. *Caring for Textiles.* New York: Watson-Guptill Publications, Inc., 1977.

Harris, Karyn Jean. *Costume Display Techniques.* Nashville: The American Association for State and Local History, 1977.

Keck, Caroline K. *Care of Textiles and Costumes: Adaptive Techniques for Basic Maintenance.* Technical Leaflet No. 71. Nashville: The American Association for State and Local History, 1974.

King, Dr. Rosalie, and Richard Bisbee. "Preservation of Navajo Woven Textiles: Care and Cleaning Procedures for Rugs and Blankets." *Technology and Conservation Magazine* 5 (Spring 1980): 40–43.

Mailand, Harold F. *Considerations for the Care of Textiles and Costumes.* Indianapolis: Indianapolis Museum of Art, 1980.

McHugh, Maureen Collins. *How to Wet-Clean Undyed Cotton and Linen.* Information Leaflet No. 478. Washington, D.C.: Smithsonian Institution, 1967.

Peltz, Perri, and Monona Rossol. *Safe Pest Control Procedures for Museum Collections.* New York: Center for Occupational Hazards, 1983.

13

Ceramics:
Care and Conservation

The term *ceramics* refers to a variety of baked-earth materials, ranging from the coarse-textured cooking pots of the Iroquois Indians to fine Dresden china figurines. Related materials include plaster of Paris busts and chalkware, which can be mended in a similar manner.

Vitreous Ceramics

Vitreous ceramics are high-fired, hard-glazed, and usually rather thin in cross-section. They are chemically stable, they resist the elements, and except in undergoing sudden extreme thermal shock—or being dropped—they present few problems. Occasionally, dust or stains accumulate in a crackled glaze, giving the affected area a brownish discoloration. Washing the area with a strong detergent, followed by application of bleaching-strength hydrogen peroxide (sold in drugstores as "20-volume") will bring out as much of the stain as is possible with household chemistry. The area treated should then be thoroughly rinsed to remove all traces of detergent and peroxide.

When thin ware, such as porcelain, is broken, a powerful adhesive is needed to give holding strength to the mended area. Consequently, the new two-part epoxies and "instant" cyanoacrylate adhesives, instead of the older nitrocellulose adhesives, are often used to mend thin ware.

The disadvantage of most of the new resins is that, once set up, they can be dissolved only with the greatest difficulty, or not at all. Thus, anyone who uses them must plan ahead very carefully, when a complicated repair is being made, to be certain that all the parts involved will go together in sequence.

The irreversible adhesives also contradict one of the basic guidelines of conservation—that all treatment should be reversible, if possible, to facilitate any future treatment that may be needed. In making these

178

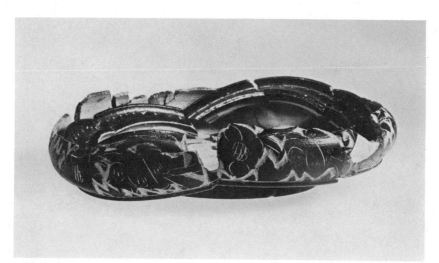

Fig. 13.1. The result of using an inappropriate adhesive on this bowl would be amusing, if it were not so difficult to reverse. The glue used here sagged after the repair had been made—and then set, rock-hard.

types of difficult repairs to ceramic objects, the type of adhesive to use is an important decision. Advice from a conservator and a review of the currently available materials is essential before attempting repairs on important porcelain objects.

Catalogues such as those from TALAS and Conservation Materials, Ltd., listed in "Suppliers," offer a variety of adhesives and repair materials that may sound enticing because of their many positive properties. However, the catalogues are not intended to be do-it-yourself manuals, and unless you wish to spend a great deal of money in experimentation, it is far wiser to consult an expert, even by telephone, and then purchase your materials.

In repairing vitreous ceramics, it is important to work with as thin a glue line as possible. A box filled with clean sand or round glass shot will be helpful for supporting round pots or for putting plates at a convenient angle to glue on a shard and prevent the piece from moving while drying. Chemical supply houses, such as Fisher Scientific, sell glass and teflon beads for obscure chemical laboratory processes. These beads are inert and stable and would serve well as support material. Some of the cyanoacrylate adhesives of the instant variety require only that the pieces to be joined be held tightly together for a few seconds to form a

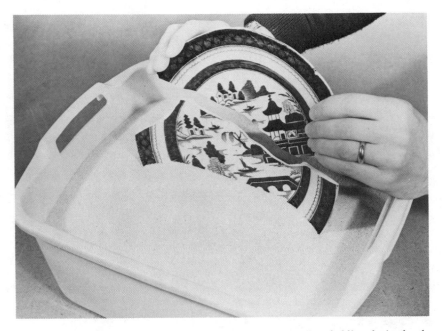

Fig. 13.2. A dishpan filled with clean sand makes an excellent holding device for the repair of broken ceramics of any shape.

bond, obviating the need for sand boxes, rubber bands, or clamps. Although solvents for these adhesives are available, they are dangerous materials, in themselves, and only with diligent application will they remove the cured adhesive.

Parts that stick out from the main bulk of a ceramic piece and have leverage exerted on them—such as teapot handles—or small cross-sections that support considerable weight—such as a figurine balanced on one foot—may need more reinforcement when being mended than just a good adhesive. Hollow parts may require dowel or wire reinforcement, and handles or spouts may need fasteners for extra support.

There may be other questions involved, as well, such as the future use of the object. If a piece of porcelain is a museum object or if it is destined only for display, the minimal, reversible treatment may be enough to repair it satisfactorily. For objects belonging to collectors or dealers, however, the repairs may be required to strengthen the piece as much as possible and disguise any disfigurement, so that the object may be used for its original purpose.

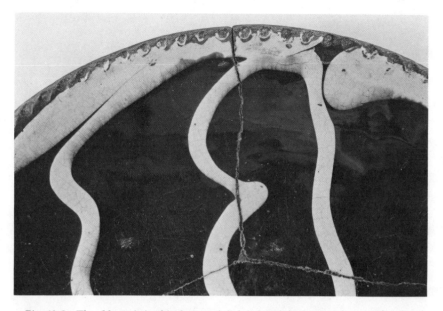

Fig. 13.3. The old repair in this decorated dish is best left alone, as long as the piece is holding together properly.

As with any other repair procedure, ceramics repairs that destroy or obliterate original parts of the object are to be avoided, since they detract from the historic and aesthetic quality of the object treated. With increasing numbers of trained conservators available, one would be wise to consult a qualified conservator of objects before attempting the repair of an important piece or taking it to a restorer who might use more traditional methods and materials.

High-Fired Earthenware

High-fired, thick-sectioned earthenware objects are a joy to the historian and the archaeologist alike. They are reasonably sturdy, and they are unaffected by heat, humidity, or insects. Through a study of their design elements, materials, and construction, the scholar can obtain information about past cultures. Given care in storage and handling, strong earthenware pieces should last virtually forever. Even a broken pot—if a reasonable number of contiguous shards can be found—can be reconstructed, through the aid of templates, to give the archaeologist or student the form of the original vessel. The detailed article by Eldon

Wolff mentioned in the reading list will give further information. Remember, however, that broken ceramics may release stresses within the material, with the result that even newly damaged pieces can be "sprung" and will no longer fit closely together.

Mending Pottery

Two important points must be observed in mending pottery: be certain that the edges of the shards are clean, dry, and free from grit; and work with as thin a glue line as possible.

Errors tend to be cumulative in a complex pottery repair job. It is best to start with a definite area, if possible, such as the shards of a broken base or rim, and watch your sequence carefully. Sometimes it is necessary to put the pieces together temporarily, with tape or a temporary adhesive, number and photograph them, and then proceed with the final gluing. Nothing is more irritating than finding out, when a difficult repair is almost finished, that the last shard will not fit in.

A suitable ceramics adhesive should remain tacky long enough to enable the repairer to correct the alignment of the shards; it should dry thin and hard; and it should be easily dissolved again if one botches the job. Remember to have a sand box—or shot box—for such mending operations, so that odd-shaped pieces can be held at a proper angle while the adhesive is drying.

Missing areas in a broken ceramic piece may be built up with plaster of Paris or other traditional materials, or they can be molded and cast from another section of the object or a similar item. Such restorations can be great fun, although obtaining good results is no easy task, and there exists the very real possibility of ruining the object if the filling in is not done correctly. A great variety of "archival quality" materials are now available, but the only way one can be sure of choosing the right one is to ask a conservator who knows from experience. And should you decide to undertake the compensation of missing parts yourself, by all means practice with *expendable* objects, first, and be absolutely sure that you record exactly what you have done and that the materials are reversible.

The philosophy of tinting mended areas varies among institutions and archaeologists. Some leave compensated areas white, in order to prevent confusion as to what is original. Others put a small amount of dry pigment in the repair mixture; and still others try, on aesthetic grounds, to match the background as exactly as possible. The choice will be determined by the needs of your institution or the nature and uses of your collection. Should you decide to tint reconstructed areas, acrylic artists' colors will prove easiest and best to use, in the long run: they do not change tint upon drying, they age well, and they can be made to produce a finish either matte or shiny. As with other skilled tasks, matching colors and designs is likely to be a frustrating experience, at first, and may well be better left to those with specialized knowledge and skills.

Special Problems with Ceramics

Soft-fired pottery and salt-laden friable software from archaeological sites present problems of their own. Frequently, such pieces will be crusted with limy deposits that obscure the design. If the pottery is hard and strong, the lime can be scrubbed off with a fiber brush in a solution of 10 percent sodium hexametaphosphate (laundry water-softener) in distilled water; the objects may be soaked in the solution to help loosen the deposits, to some extent. Acid solutions were sometimes used, in earlier times, for the same purpose, but in addition to the personal danger to the user such chemicals impose, they also carry a greater possibility of destroying the artifact, if the pottery is soft or if it has chalk or marble or limestone grit in it.

Even washing may cause low-fired friable wares to go to pieces. If it is necessary to wash the piece in order to remove salts from it, one may be facing a problem that is more complex than it might appear. Traditional methods called for coating the piece with one of a variety of resins that are protective of the object but still allow water and dissolved salts to pass through. However, after sufficient aging, it appears that some resin films may present problems of their own, in eventually causing the surface of the coated object to peel off.

The problem of the peeling surfaces illustrates the fact that even conservators may not know the long-term effects of materials used for repairs. Thus, when one can preserve the object without extra treatment, that is usually the preferred choice. Since the resins used in consolidating the softwares are soluble, at least the pieces that have not been adversely affected may be cleaned and otherwise treated, if necessary.[1]

A conservator or archaeological technician may have better suggestions for handling fragile items. At any rate, one must remember that sometimes ill-chosen repair procedures may make it all too easy to destroy the very objects that one is attempting to save.

Because the edges of soft-fired or salt-saturated pottery are so soft or friable, extra care must be taken in assembling them. Sometimes dipping

Fig. 13.4. Cheap and effective storage for small ceramic objects may be made of standard-sized boxes with strips of cardboard stapled in to form separate compartments for each item.

the edges in a thinned solution of adhesive will serve to consolidate the pieces. Then, when dry, they can be put together with full-strength adhesive. If the edges fit together poorly because of crumbling or wear, an adhesive with filler properties may be needed; but be certain that two poorly fitting shards supposed to be contiguous really do belong side by side—do not grind them to make a forced fit.

Gluing pot shards together can be quite easy—but ending up with a completed pot that fits correctly is not so easy. Do not be discouraged, however; work for a tight fit and proceed slowly.

NOTES

1. Catherine Sease, "The Case against Using Soluble Nylon in Conservation Work," *Studies in Conservation* 26 (August 1981): 102–110.

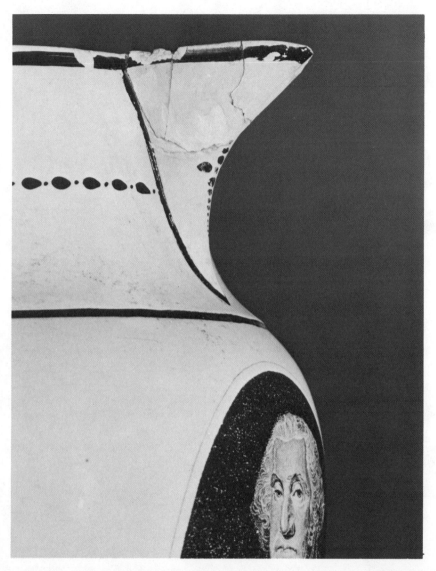

Fig. 13.5. Evidence of damage and inexpert repair is clearly visible on the spout of this pitcher. When a botched job like this turns up among recent acquisitions, find a conservator in the subject area and seek expert assistance.

SUGGESTED READING

Andre, Jean-Michel. *The Restorer's Handbook of Ceramics and Glass.* New York: Van Nostrand Reinhold Company, 1976.

Kingery, W. D. *Introduction to Ceramics.* New York: Wiley, 1960. The science and technology of ceramic materials.

Lanney, J. "Ceramic Restoration at the Victoria and Albert Museum." *Studies in Conservation* 16 (May 1971): 69–82.

Phillips, Morgan W. "Consolidation of Porous Materials: Problems and Possibilities of Acrylic Resin Techniques." *Technology And Conservation Magazine* 4 (Winter 1979): 42–46.

Pond, Thomas. *Mending and Restoring China.* New York: Avenel Books, 1970.

Wilson, Shari. "Restoring Pottery." *Curator* 11 (June 1968): 154–164.

Wolf, Eldon. "Pottery Restoration." *Curator* 3 (1960): 75–87. A practical working procedure, particularly for archaeologists who must try to conjecture the shape of a pot from a small number of shards.

14

Glass:
Problems and Solutions

Glass, in the traditional sense, is silica that has been fused with potash or soda ash. *Potash* or *ash* are crude alkaline carbonate salts obtained by leaching hardwood ash and evaporating the resulting solution. Addition to the silica-ash (or potash) mixture of a small percentage of lime, either deliberately or as an impurity in the ash, traditionally gave the glass stability. The inclusion of minute amounts of metallic oxide gave glass color—purple, for example, from manganese, and green, from iron.

To make glass, the mixture was heated until liquified, then formed—by being blown, drawn, or poured into molds—and then allowed to cool and stiffen; and, if the proportion of materials was in correct balance, the result was stable glass.

Sometime in the seventeenth century, it was discovered that if lead oxide were substituted for lime, the resulting glass, while softer, had a clear color and was brighter-looking than the potash-lime glass. The new product was known variously as *lead glass, flint glass,* or *crystal glass,* and it proved to be quite stable. But because it was more expensive than potash-lime glass, it was not used to make common glassware.

Devitrified Glass

Early glassmakers wanted a clear glass, so they often leached the ashes to purify them when making potash. Sometimes, as a result, much of the lime content was washed out and the glass became sensitive to moisture. An imperfect mixture of materials or incorrect proportions, such as an excess of alkali, could also lead to gradual deterioration of the glass.

Properly speaking, *glass is a stiff liquid, rather than a crystalline solid;* and under certain conditions, it will begin to *devitrify*—or change to a crystalline solid. The appearance of the glass that that happens to will vary, depending on the amount of devitrification that takes place. It may appear cloudy; or, as is sometimes seen in historical excavations, the glass may appear irridescent and quite beautiful. Under many environmental conditions, devitrified glass can be rather unstable, and it should be very carefully handled and monitored.

Glass that shows a severe surface crazing known as *crizzling* is a very unstable material, due to the drying out of a thin surface layer, followed by shrinkage and the opening of tiny fissures in that layer. *Crizzling* is the ultimate result of chemical and physical changes in poorly formulated glass, and it is not a reversible condition, at present. It was once thought that a dry environment would lessen the rate of crizzling in glass, but, in fact, a drier atmosphere accelerates the deterioration by drying and shrinking the surface layer of the glass. Crizzling eventually produces losses of tiny scales of glass, if the process is not slowed.

Another condition sometimes observed in unstable glass is often described as "weeping glass," because of the small amount of moisture that can be seen to accumulate on the surface of a piece of glass with that defect—which actually is incipient crizzling, and sometimes the beginnings of the surface fissures can be seen, in just the right light. "Weeping glass" occurs when poorly formulated glass has absorbed, from its environment, moisture in its surface layer, but the drying out that would cause the crizzling appearance has never occurred. Drying out a weeping glass object is the *worst* course of action one could take with it, since that would simply cause the shrinkage and cracking of the imperfect surface that has thus far been avoided.

The only treatment for crizzled or weeping glass objects is to store or display them in a stable environment with sufficient moisture to slow the decomposition. Because the material has what is sometimes called "inherent vice," one cannot hope to avoid or solve the problem, but only to slow its progress. Relative humidity levels of 45 percent to 47 percent are considered best for such glass items, but a stable environment of between 40 percent and 55 percent RH is acceptable.[1]

Broken Glass

The first step in dealing with a broken glass artifact is to bring together, carefully, all the pieces, in separate, relatively soft containers, such as the sections of an egg carton. Do not jumble the fragments together, or abrasion and chipping will make it more difficult still to obtain a tight fit when the pieces are assembled. Similarly, do not try to fit fragments together before it is time to make the repair, or you will only encourage further damage. Repairing glass is not the simple chore it might appear to be; new adhesives are continually being developed, and the choice should be made with care. Barbara Rottenberg's *Care and Display of Glass Collections* (AASLH Technical Leaflet No. 127—see the reading list) should help, or one might check with a conservator for up-to-date information on the most reliable adhesives for glass.

Fractured glass pieces are not only thin in cross-section, as a rule, but they present extremely smooth surfaces. Most directions for using adhesives say, in small print, "be sure to roughen edges before applying adhesive." That is more easily said than done, when one is working with small, thin pieces of a crystal goblet. On pieces where there are heavy cross-sections, solvent adhesives may not dry for an interminably long time, because the solvent is trapped between two nonporous surfaces.

Some glass may be so fragile or so shattered that it is not practical for an amateur to try mending it. If mending is attempted, generally the only adhesives that are likely to hold are two-part resins—like epoxy resins. Just remember that some of these adhesives are not dissolvable—be sure that you have a tight fit and thin glue lines, because you may not have a second chance at that spot. In recent studies, it has been discovered that edge-to-edge repairs made with epoxy may be severely weakened by relatively brief exposure to humidity levels of 70 percent to 80 percent RH. Since many facilities housing glass objects may be prone to such high humidity levels, under certain seasonal conditions, it is important to monitor pieces mended with epoxy resins.[2]

When using two-part adhesives, observe the working time or "pot life" stated on the label. In that way, you will know how much time you have for working on a piece before the adhesive begins to set. Avoid getting adhesives on your hands, as most of them are irritating to the skin, and some are capable of gluing fingers or eyelids together, if one is careless in handling them. Most adhesives should also give a date on the label to show the shelf life of the materials. Whether or not a shelf life is listed, it is good practice to mix and test a bit of the adhesive before using it on any valuable artifact. An adhesive that has outlived its shelf life may refuse to harden or may exhibit other ill effects.[3]

To help avoid the problem of having broken glass to mend, treat glass objects with the greatest of care. In storage or on display, sometimes something as simple as *a thin piece of padding*—such as expanded polyethylene—can help to prevent shocks when setting glass objects down, and it may also keep glass objects placed on hard surfaces from being jostled about by the vibrations that occur from time to time in most buildings.

Fig. 14.1. For safe washing of glass artifacts, use a plastic dishpan, even if you are working in a sink; the plastic provides a soft surface, in case the object is dropped.

If glass objects must be packed for storage, or for moving or shipping, always wrap them carefully. Wrap each item with tissue, first, and lightly pad all projections with bolsters of tissue. Cushion each piece with a layer of air cap or expanded polyethylene. Wrap glass stoppers or other small pieces separately, but make such packagings large enough to insure that they will not be overlooked in unpacking; colored tape on such small packed objects will help to differentiate between them and the cushioning material.

Cleaning Glass Objects

Organic deposits often dry and cling stubbornly to the inside of glass bottles and other containers—and of course they need to be removed, once discovered. Such ordinary materials as dried wine, dried milk or cream, or the remnants of most kinds of food scraps can often be removed by soaking the bottle overnight in a solution of laundry water-softener plus a bit of detergent. Then, with the bottle about half full of this cleaning mixture, carefully pour in some air-rifle shot (steel BBs from any hardware store), and *roll* the BBs *gently* around in the bottle to

Fig. 14.2. *A wick made of a twisted paper towel should be used to ensure that the interior of any small-mouthed container is thoroughly dried after washing. Be sure to leave plenty of towelling hanging out the top, so that the moisture can evaporate readily.*

loosen the deposits; then pour everything out and rinse the bottle with distilled water, to avoid further mineral deposits inside it. In using BBs to help clean glass pieces, *be very careful* that you *roll* the shot around inside the container, rather than shaking it, or you could very easily break fragile glassware. *If the glass is extremely thin, do not use the shot at all;* simply scrub the object as well you can with a bristle brush. It is also a good practice to wash glass items in a *plastic* wash basin, rather than a regular kitchen sink; plastic basins provide a much softer landing place if the glass being washed should accidentally be dropped.

In addition to the laundry-water-softener-and-detergent solution for cleaning glass, there are other types of cleaning solutions that can be used, if the first technique does not work. Complete instructions on the use of each product should be reviewed, however, before one proceeds to stronger materials.[4]

To dry the inside of a narrow-necked glass container, insert a long "wick" of paper or cloth toweling, leaving a good length of the material trailing over the outside of the container. It may take a day or two, but the toweling will absorb all the moisture on the inside of the vessel and funnel it outside the container to evaporate.

NOTES

1. Robert H. Brill, "The Use of Selica Gel for the Protection of Glass with Incipient Crizzling," *Journal of Glass Studies,* pp. 100–102.
2. Brill, "Protection of Glass with Incipient Crizzling," p. 111.
3. Barbara Lang Rottenberg, *Care and Display of Glass Collections,* Technical Leaflet No. 127.
4. Rottenberg, *Care and Display of Glass Collections.*

SUGGESTED READING

Andre, Jean-Michel. *The Restorer's Handbook of Ceramics and Glass.* New York: Van Nostrand Reinhold Company, 1976.

Brill, Robert H. "The Use of Equilibrated Silica Gel for the Protection of Glass with Incipient Crizzling." *Journal of Glass Studies* 20 (1978): 100–118.
Although rather technical for the most part, this article clearly describes the problem of crizzling and weeping glass, along with the proper care for glass objects.

"Making the Sum of an Object's Parts Equal a Well-Restored Whole." *Technology And Conservation Magazine* 3 (Summer 1978): 10.

Millard, Richard W. "Stained Glass Preservation: Guidelines for Repair and for Restoration." *Technology And Conservation Magazine* 4 (Spring 1979): 36–41.

Rottenberg, Barbara Lang. *Care and Display of Glass Collections.* Technical Leaflet No. 127. Nashville: The American Association for State and Local History, 1980. Information about general care, cleaning, packing, and adhesives for glass.

Tennent, Norman H. "Clear and Pigmented Epoxy Resins for Stained Glass Conservation: Light Aging Studies." *Studies in Conservation* 24 (November 1979): 153–164.

15

Artifacts of Bone, Ivory, and Animal Teeth

I n dealing with artifacts made of bone, ivory, or animal teeth, precise identification of the basic substance can often be difficult—and no wonder: such materials have commonly been sawn, carved, stained, or otherwise altered from their original shape, or they may be called by names that are ambiguous or misleading. Narwhal tusks, for example, were, in earlier times, often dyed a variety of colors by the Chinese, who used the tusks to make many kinds of decorative objects; and the substance called *whalebone* is not really bone, at all, but *baleen*, a horny, elastic material that hangs in flexible, fringed sheets from the upper jaw of baleen—or toothless—whales, which are filter-eaters; they use it as a food strainer.

T. K. Penniman's illustrated monograph, *Pictures of Ivory and Other Animal Teeth, Bone, and Antler* (included in the reading list) will be useful to those who may have difficulty in identifying the various materials in this category.

Animal teeth contain a hard, dense core of calcareous tissue called *dentine*—or dentin—with a fine longitudinal grain structure and an outer coating of enamel.

Ivory, usually categorized by the layman as the hard, white substance that makes up the tusks of elephants, is a form of dentine. It is also a term with varied interpretations. Some authorities say that *true* ivory is found only in the tusks of elephants; others note that, in the past, the unusually large or projecting teeth of many other animals, such as the hippopotamus, walrus, narwhal, sperm whale, and wild boar, were also called ivory.[1] Others define it as the dentine of any tooth.[2]

Bone is somewhat softer than ivory—or teeth—and of a coarser cellular structure. This is a good workaday definition, but until you have worked with these materials a great deal, there will still be pieces for which you will not be certain of having properly identified the basic material. If you are dealing with skeletal materials but are uncertain

194

Fig. 15.1. Ivory used as trim or inlay may be encountered in some unlikely places, as shown here. It often must be treated entirely differently from the surrounding materials.

whether the long bones included are those of a camel or a horse, or whether the small skull is that of a groundhog or a beaver, get in touch with the zoology department of the college or university nearest you; informative people there should be able to help you out with pointers about identification or bibliographical sources.

Bone, ivory, and animal teeth are relatively stable materials, but only in a carefully controlled environment. They can be decomposed by acids; and exposure to heat, high humidity, or burial in damp soil can cause them to crack and to deteriorate. The softer ossein, or collagen—the gelatinous, organic part of bone—is quickly decomposed by burial or by exposure to water. In some instances, it is replaced by salts; sometimes it becomes mineralized. In exhibiting artifacts made of these organic materials, avoid sunlit display space, and never place them in areas where a high temperature is maintained—such as near heat pipes or ducts, or in closed exhibit cases where heat builds up from lighted incandescent bulbs.

Warped Pieces

With the problem of warpage in objects made of bone, ivory, or tusks, one may hear the suggestion that such pieces be soaked in a variety of dilute acids, to soften and straighten out the organic structure to what may have been its original dimensions. That procedure should be avoided, however, because acids debase the material and alter its surface. Using procedures such as that, known to be potentially harmful, one can actually do collections items much more damage than good, and the possible cosmetic improvement in shape is never worth the destruction inflicted on the material itself. If you should acquire artifacts of these materials that show warpage, learn to live with them as they are—they will last a great deal longer if the basic substance remains undamaged.

Removing Grease Spots

Usually, a mild petroleum solvent like mineral spirits or benzine (not *benzene*), applied with a cotton swab, will remove reasonably fresh grease spots from objects of bone or ivory. If the grease has sunk in, make a poultice of fuller's earth and solvent, pat it gently onto the spot, and allow it to remain for awhile on the affected area, dissolving and absorbing the grease.

What To Do about Stains

Porous, bony material is easily stained by metallic corrosion products, paints, dyes, and other organic materials. The only safe bleach to use in attempting to remove stains on bone or ivory objects is hydrogen peroxide (20-volume) with a few drops of non-sudsing ammonia added per half-pint of peroxide. *Note that the moisture and the ammonia in this mixture could damage ivory especially.* If the hydrogen-peroxide-and-ammonia mixture does not work when applied very cautiously, do not try stronger bleaches; they are usually aqueous, strongly alkaline, or acidic, and therefore destructive to the basic material of the artifact. When collections items of bone, ivory, or tusks show bad stains, be prepared to leave really troublesome spots just as they are, or to consult an expert to determine whether further cleaning should be attempted.

Washing

Washing is not generally recommended for bone and ivory artifacts, especially if the soiled object is old and cracked, since removing from the object's cells and deep striations all the water used to wash it is almost impossible, and leaving it with a damp finish is likely to cause warping. Brushing such a piece gently with a dry bristle brush or a toothbrush is a safe way to remove loose surface dirt. If further cleaning is considered necessary, a piece of cotton wool or cotton batting barely dampened with a detergent solution (trisodium phosphate detergent, such as Soilax, in water) may be rubbed over the surface. Follow that by going over the object with a few dry cotton swabs, to soak up and remove any stray moisture.

Never allow objects of bone or ivory to become wet or to sit in water—with one single exception: objects salvaged from marine sites, where they have become impregnated with salts, should not be allowed to dry out. The salts can be leached out, in successive baths of fresh water, but the objects being treated should not be allowed to dry out.

Consolidation of bony materials, as with any other debased substance, is a matter of some complexity. Selection of the correct materials for each item to be treated and the proper procedure to follow should be left to an expert in that field. Home remedies or selection of the proper consolidant or cleaning method by guess might sometimes succeed; the more likely result, however, is the unnecessary destruction of a fragile, irreplaceable object.

Mending

Whether mending a broken piece of bone or ivory should be attempted and, if so, how it might best be done, is, once again, a situation in which the over-all condition of each individual piece must dictate the decision. The reason for this complication is that objects made of these materials, even when they are broken by mechanical shock, may have been subjected to other, earlier stresses and distortions, so that the freshly broken pieces may not line up neatly for reassembly. This problem, along with the difficulty of finding a suitable nonaqueous adhesive to use, can make the work of repairing bone and ivory more complex and more difficult than it might seem to be. One should also keep in mind the possibility that bony substances forced together and held for gluing and repair are quite likely to pop apart at another juncture sometime in the future, as wooden objects do, when forced together in mending. Warping and splitting are ways of relieving stresses on these organic materials, and they are not easily reversed.

Fig. 15.2. Miniature portraits are often found on ivory supports. This one was painted on a sheet of ivory so thin that it made repairs difficult and not altogether successful, even though the work was done by an expert conservator.

Working with Horn

Horn is a tough water-and-heat-resistant material, under normal conditions, and it will usually withstand prolonged exposure to a combination of heat and moisture before warping or beginning to deteriorate. However, horn is susceptible to the attacks of various types of beetles—especially dermestid beetles and cabinet beetles—and any horn artifact suspected of beetle infestation should be fumigated.

It has been observed that pieces of horn inlay or decorative work on old weapons shrink slightly with age. Under such circumstances, they are best left alone, as no soaking or rejuvenating techniques will re-enlarge their dimensions.

NOTES

1. *Columbia Encyclopedia*, 4th ed., s.v. "ivory."
2. *Columbia Encyclopedia*, 4th ed., s.v. "ivory."

SUGGESTED READING

Baer, N. S., et al. "The Effect of High Temperature on Ivory." *Studies in Conservation* 16 (February 1971): 1–8.

Majewski, Lawrence J. "On Conservation: Ivory and Bone." *Museum News* 51 (March 1973): 10–11.

Penniman, T. K. *Pictures of Ivory and Other Animal Teeth, Bone, and Antler.* Oxford: Oxford University Press, 1962.
Magnified photos that show how to differentiate among these often-confused materials. Primarily used for identification.

Werner, A. E. "The Conservation of Wood, Leather, Bone, Ivory, and Archival Materials." In *The Conservation of Cultural Property with Special Reference to Tropical Conditions*. Paris: The UNESCO Press, 1968, pp. 265–290.

16

Stone Artifacts

T he word *stone* is often used to refer to a good many different kinds of material. It is applied to objects as apparently unrelated as chalk sticks, marble tabletops, and limestone walls, and it includes related substances as apparently dissimilar as coral and slate, granite and pumice, plaster of Paris and alabaster.

Sometimes *stone* is used to mean the precious and semiprecious stones, or gemstones—diamonds, rubies, emeralds, jade, and others like them—used to make jewelry and other decorative items.

Speaking generally, some stones—the kinds used to line a roadbed, make a tombstone, carve a statue, or construct and ornament a building—are ordinarily regarded as types of rock. The kinds of stones used to make an ornamental box, a vase, a statuette, or a decorative clock case are usually those from among the gemstones—although there is a good bit of overlapping: some of these materials are so pleasing to the eye, so adaptable, and available in such quantity that they can be—and frequently are—used for both construction and ornamentation.

Objects of both gemstone and the rock types of stones may be found in collections of historical artifacts. This chapter deals with a very modest sampling of both, recommending the excellent source materials in the reading list and frequent consultation with the many kinds of experts who work with stone of one kind or another, in one or another of its many special aspects.

* * * *

It would seem that any kind of stone—dense, solid, inorganic, and regarded poetically as the last word in things impermeable and unyielding—might surely be one substance impervious to decay.

Yet, one has only to look at the worn, acid-pitted facades of stone buildings in industrial areas, the half-obliterated lettering on old gravestones, the erosion of coastal cliffs around the globe, and the deterioration evident in historic statuary, monuments, and architectural treasures worldwide, to realize that even a substance as durable as stone can be damaged by its environment.

Air pollution and the extremes of heat, cold, and moisture in ordinary weather cycles are the chief environmental enemies of stone.

How Air Pollution Erodes Stone

Carbon monoxide and nitrogen oxides from the fumes of gasoline-burning engines and other hydrocarbon fuels are primary offenders among airborne pollutants. Smoke, ash, soot, dust, hydrogen sulfide, sulfur oxides, and sulfurous acids, from the burning of garbage and the industrial use of the fossil fuels coal and oil, add other contaminants. These toxic substances, harmful enough in themselves, mingle with each other, with water vapor, and with the ultraviolet rays in sunlight to form additional poisons. Sunlight turns nitrogen oxides mixed with hydrocarbons into nitrogen dioxide and ozone, a powerful oxidizer. Sulfur dioxide mixed with water vapor or nitrogen dioxide produces a potent sulfurous acid and adds further strength to increasingly toxic acid rain, which already carries a high concentration of destructive acids. These airborne poisons not only bleach paper, burn off paint, decompose nylon, corrode metals, destroy plants, animals, birds, and marine life—they also endanger human life. And they steadily erode concrete, brick, mortar, and stone, damaging especially the kinds of stone commonly used for construction, statuary, and monuments—limestone in all its forms, marble, dolomite, cement, oolite, travertine, and chalk being the more familiar ones. All limestones are corroded by any form of acid in a liquid base, and so are particularly vulnerable to the acid-laden atmosphere common today in heavily populated areas.[1]

Water and Weathering

The destructive action of air pollution is intensified by the action of rainwater, dewfall, condensation, fog, mist, frost, and the seepage of water rising from wet ground. Moisture weakens and eventually will damage stone and stone conglomerates. The freezing and thawing of water in cold weather is especially destructive. Rainwater or frost particles accumulate in small cracks or pitted areas of stone or brick and freeze there, expanding as they freeze, and the force of that expansion often causes surface spalling (chipping, crumbling) or outright cracking

Fig. 16.1. *Extremes of environment and atmospheric pollution make the spalling and chipping off of stone surfaces almost inevitable in objects left outdoors. Such damage is initially difficult to repair and may not remain successful if the object must be returned to a harsh environment.*

of the stone or brick. Most of us have seen sections of stone walls a foot thick heaved over by frost after a hard winter, or buildings with walls cracked from shifting weight when poor drainage at or below ground level has leached out the mortar in masonry foundations.[2]

Even drops of dew, apparently quite innocuous, are destructive to stone: each dewdrop contains dissolved carbon dioxide gas, which forms a weak solution of carbonic acid particularly harmful on contact with such materials as mortar, concrete, chalk, limestone, and marble.

Add to air and moisture hazards the recurring ground tremors or vibrations from vehicular traffic and plant roots growing into cracked masonry, and the resultant weathering can gradually wear away the sturdiest stone. Porous, crumbly, rough-textured stone is especially susceptible to these forces, but all stone structures in an outdoor environment—buildings, monuments, statuary, fountains, courtyards, roadways, furnishings for patios and formal gardens—are vulnerable. The well-known tourist attractions of Luray Caverns, Carlsbad Caverns, and Mammoth Cave are there because they were carved out of enormous limestone deposits by underground streams carrying organic acids.[3]

Some Countermeasures

With odds that sound so unbeatable, what can be done to protect valued stone items? A great deal, really.

The first steps, in any instance, are to clean the object properly; make minor repairs that can be completed safely without expert help; and consult with informed sources about complicated repairs found to be needed. Then, whether the structure is to remain indoors or out, one should consider the available means for protecting the finish. Various kinds of waxes and surface sealers are available, and waterproofers for cement and masonry and several kinds of stone can be obtained from hardware stores or statuary supply houses.

Sources of Information and Supplies

An excellent way to obtain sound information about types of stone and ways to care for it is to visit the local monument works or marble company nearest you. The people who do hands-on work with stone know a great deal about their product and they can provide much practical information. They can also supply some of the specialized materials—sometimes hard to find—that are needed in working with stone; and they usually know the addresses of statuary supply houses where other hard-to-find supplies can be bought.

Detailed information about the proper care of marble and limestone can be obtained from the Marble Institute of America, 33505 State Street, Farmington, Michigan 48024.

The Vermont Marble Company and its affiliate, Vermarco Supply Company, both at Proctor, Vermont 05765, can provide information on stone care and protection and the supplies and equipment needed for it, as well.

So can the Wyandotte Chemical Corporation, a large conglomerate. Write to BASF Wyandotte Corporation, 100 Cherry Hill Road, Parsippany, New Jersey 07054.

*　　*　　*　　*

Differences in the structure of various types of stone make different procedures necessary for cleaning and protecting them. What is fine for a marble tabletop may be pure poison for a pearl necklace; an occasional washing with warm soapsuds is ideal for a jade vase or a jet ornament, but soap is the wrong thing entirely for marble and many other stones; and a statuette of plaster of Paris—powdered gypsum—should never be washed, at all; it should simply be dusted carefully—and regularly— and kept away from moisture.[4]

Because marble and stones very much like it are the ones most commonly found in collections of historical artifacts, the section that follows deals with their care. What to do about pearl necklaces, slate fireplace facings, and pieces of statuary follows, in the section called "Care of Miscellaneous Stone Objects."

Marble and Similar Stones: Cleaning and Care

Because of its great beauty and adaptability, marble, best-known of the several types of limestone, is nearly always found in historical collections more frequently, used in more varied forms, than almost any other stone. Cut and polished, marble ranges in color from pinks, reds, buffs, and yellows to green, gray, black, and snow-white. For centuries, it has been used worldwide to produce fine statuary, monuments, pillars, colonnades, and buildings, as well as wall paneling, wainscoting, floor tiles, wall slabs, building blocks, keystones, window and door sills, fireplace facings, hearthstones, and tabletops, and as a facing stone for buildings.[5]

Limestone, the basic sedimentary rock from which marble is formed, is also used extensively for both building and ornamentation. Buildings, decorative walls, and steps are made of it; it is used in paving, decoratively in rock gardens, as an ingredient in Portland cement, and as a source of lime.

The term *marble* is sometimes used—perhaps a bit loosely—to mean any kind of limestone that cuts well, takes a good polish, and can be used either as a building stone or for ornamental purposes. There is also some ambiguity in usage of the terms *onyx marble, Mexican onyx,* and *Egyptian* or *Oriental alabaster. Onyx marble* and *Mexican onyx* are often used to refer to travertine. Some authorities say that *Oriental alabaster* is, too; others say that *Oriental alabaster* was used in earlier times to mean, simply, marble, sometimes called "the alabaster of the ancients." In turn, the occasional vase or statuette sold as "Florentine marble" actually is Italian alabaster.[6]

Granite, bluestone, dolomite, and oolite are used primarily in building and construction. Travertine and alabaster, however, are used to make objects both large and small, many of them found in historical collections.

Typically a very hard stone capable of taking a high polish, granite is among the oldest rocks on earth and has been used as a building stone since earliest times. Ancient Egyptian obelisks were made of red granite; Roman builders used a gray for columns and colonnades; many varieties are used today for buildings and monuments.[7]

Bluestone, a blue-gray sandstone found in New York state, is widely used for building, veneer, paving, and making garden paths and roadways.[8]

Travertine—close cousin to marble, often beautifully colored and banded—was used by the ancient Egyptians to make vases and sacrificial vessels and to line the walls and ceilings of temples; today, it decorates expensive buildings and is made into vases, lamps, tabletops, and ornamental clock cases.[9]

Alabaster, a fine-grained, translucent variety of gypsum, is usually pure white or streaked with reddish brown. Soft enough to be scratched with a fingernail—and therefore easily broken, soiled, and weathered—alabaster is used to make statuary and smaller ornamental objects such as vases, decorative boxes, bookends, and lamp bases.[10]

The procedures below for cleaning marble can also be used safely and effectively to clean the other limestones—travertine (under all its names), dolomite, oolite, and limestone itself—as well as granite, bluestone, and alabaster.

Early Warnings

Since all the limestones, including marble, are porous and quite absorbent, extra care should be taken, from the beginning, to keep them as clean as possible, and so avoid leaving on them any foreign material that can seep through the surface and into the stone to create stains. An occasional washing with clean water and clean rags should be all that is needed for marble that has been kept clean and protected.

Metal objects should not be placed on or left in contact with marble or the other limestones. Metal—iron, particularly—causes rust stains. When such things as metal lamp bases, ash trays, tools, old keys, nails, bolts, metal fasteners, and so on, are left in contact with marble or any other limestone for more than very brief periods of time, especially if there is much moisture in the air, there is the risk of rust stains forming.[11]

Colored papers, marking pens, cold drink bottles, coffee cups, cigarette stubs, and other everyday items one may set down on a piece of furniture without thinking should be kept away from marble furniture, also; they, too, create stains that are hard to remove.

When marble artifacts need more than a mild cleansing—more than a once-over with clear water and a clean rag—the cleanser to be used is extremely important. Here are *four good things to remember about cleansers for marble and similar stones:*

1. Never use vinegar, lemon juice, or any other acid to clean marble and the several stones like it. Acid of any kind will etch the surface of these stones and cause irreparable damage.
2. Never use any of the common abrasive cleansers on marble and similar stones.
3. Never use soap to clean marble or any of the stones like it. Oils and other substances used in making soap cause soap cleansers to leave on stone surfaces a thin film or scum that is very difficult to remove, and soaps sometimes cause staining, as well. If more than clean water and clean rags are needed for cleaning marble and similar stones, use a good, nonabrasive, acid-free detergent. Sometimes, a mild household detergent will serve; a detergent made for laboratory wares should always work well, and these can be ordered from scientific supply companies. Good detergents are available in liquid, paste, and powder form; they work well in either hard or soft water, and they do not leave a film or scum on cleaned surfaces.[12] Lab detergents are excellent and are available from Conservation Materials, Ltd., and similar suppliers.

Fig. 16.2. Marble or limestone items like this little lamb may be easily cleaned, but beware of harsh cleansing agents—some are capable of dissolving the stone itself.

4. Always rinse more thoroughly than you ever thought might be necessary.

Routine Light Cleaning: Marble and Similar Stones

Since marble is quite porous, and must be protected from absorbing the surface dirt that you intend to scrub off it, the first step in cleaning it should be to flood the surface of the stone with water before applying detergent, so that cleanser and dislodged dirt will stay on the surface and will not soak into the stone.

Wash the surface with detergent, clean water, and clean rags or a clean fiber brush. Rinse quickly and well, with plenty of clean, hot water. If the stone is not clean after the first washing, wash and rinse again. Be sure that the final hot-water rinse removes all traces of detergent. Wipe the stone dry with a clean, lintless cloth, to avoid streaking, and polish gently with a clean chamois.[13]

Removing Stains: Marble and Similar Stones

Marble surfaces often are soiled by common, everyday things spilled or dropped on them: apple cores, orange peels, wet rings from the bottoms of soft-drink bottles, spilled coffee and overturned cocktails at reception time, bits of acid salads and oily dressings, cigarette stubs, ink smears, and so on. If such waste matter is discovered and removed immediately, little damage is done—the stone can be rinsed clean with clear water. Too often, however, harmful substances may go unseen for some time, left in contact with the stone until enough residue has seeped in to cause staining that becomes very difficult to remove. *Such stains are usually of three kinds: organic stains, rust stains, and oil stains, and different procedures are used to remove each type.*

Organic stains. Such things as spilled coffee, tea, wine, fruit and its juices, iodine, ink, cosmetics, or tobacco cause organic stains on marble. If the stained area is fairly fresh, pour on it enough hydrogen peroxide (17- to 20-volume strength, sold at all drugstores) to cover the stain; add a few drops of household ammonia, and let the mixture stand until the stain is bleached out. If the discoloration remains stubbornly visible, after the first treatment, make a spreadable paste—about the consistency of mayonnaise—of hydrogen peroxide and powdered whiting (sold at most paint stores). Spread a good, solid layer of the paste over the stained area and add to it a few drops of household ammonia, to start the reaction. Stretch a piece of household plastic wrap over the paste layer to keep it moist and leave it on the stain for several hours; then peel off the plastic, wash off the paste, and rinse the stone surface with lots of hot water. If the stain is still visible, repeat the poultice-and-rinse process until the stain is gone. Then rinse the surface thoroughly a final time with floods of clean, hot water and dry immediately with a clean, lint-free cloth.[14]

Rust stains. Rust stains are caused when moisture rusts metal objects left sitting on stone for some time. If rust stains are detected early enough, sometimes they can be removed simply by rubbing the area with a clean, dry cloth.[15] Rust marks that have been allowed to seep into the stone for some time are considerably harder to remove. *Do not, however, use commercial rust removers on them;* many rust removers contain acids and will quickly cause etching and surface deterioration in marble and the other limestones. There *are* special reducing agents available at some hardware stores, at most chemical supply houses, and through statuary supply houses, monument works, or marble companies. Any reducing agent should be carefully applied according to the manufacturer's directions.

Oil stains. Probably the hardest of all stains to remove from marble are oil stains. They are caused by any greasy household substance that comes in contact with the stone's surface. There are two or three reliable ways of treating oil stains.

Removing Oil Stains:

Method 1

You'll need household ammonia, plenty of clean, hot water, and an oil-removing solvent. These solvents can be bought from marble dealers or at some hardware stores, but you can make your own by mixing equal parts of amyl acetate and acetone with enough powdered whiting to make a paste. Amyl acetate is available at chemical supply houses; acetone can be bought at most drugstores; and powdered whiting, as mentioned above, is sold at most paint stores. Begin by washing the surface of the stone with non-sudsing ammonia, but watch out for the fumes. Rinse off the ammonia with floods of clean, hot water. Next, apply to the stain either the bought solvent or your homemade paste of amyl acetate, acetone, and powdered whiting. Put on a fairly thick layer of paste and let it get completely dry; then wash it off with hot water and rinse thoroughly with more hot water. Repeat the process, if necessary. If the stain still remains, after several applications of the poultice, try bleaching it out with hydrogen peroxide mixed with whiting, and rinse thoroughly with clean, hot water.[16]

Removing Oil Stains:
Method 2

Soak a white blotter in cigarette lighter fluid and place it over the oil stain. Let the blotter remain there until dry. Repeat several times, if necessary. If the stain remains stubbornly visible, make a paste of lighter fluid and powdered whiting and spread the paste thickly over the stain. Let dry. If the stain is still there, bleach with hydrogen peroxide to which a drop or two of ammonia has been added. Rinse thoroughly with clean, hot water.[17]

Removing Oil Stains:
Variations on Method 2

This method also uses the white blotter and a solvent. In addition to lighter fluid, other workable solvents include alcohol, acetone, and flammable cleaning fluids. Place the blotter, soaked in solvent, over the stain and cover it with a piece of glass or heavy cardboard. For stubborn stains, repeat these applications until the oil is drawn out; then bleach with hydrogen peroxide and a few drops of ammonia. Rinse thoroughly with clean, hot water.[18]

Smoke or burn stains, Method 1: For marble hearths or fireplace facings stained by smoking fires, sparks, or burn stains from popping coals, soak the stained area in very hot water; then scrub with detergent and a stiff bristle brush. Rinse well with clean hot water.[19]

Smoke or burn stains, Method 2. Some authorities advise scrubbing the stained area gently with powdered pumice and water. Some recommend using borax or baking soda and water. Mild burns on hearthstones made of limestone or sandstone *can* be cleaned by rubbing the burned area very lightly with a medium-grade abrasive paper. Conservators in general, however, frown on use of sandpaper of any sort on any artifact; use of fine abrasive powders, instead, will produce a polished effect on stone and will not significantly abrade the surface. Mild burns on hearthstones are the marks of normal use, and leaving them there is preferable to abrading away the surface of the material. And deep burns generally are impossible to remove.[20]

Protecting Cleaned Marble Surfaces

Polishing

Once your piece of marble is as spotlessly clean and free of stains as possible, you may find that its luster is dulled here and there by the cleansing, or the surface may be marred by small scratches or areas of roughness. If such blemishes are minor, correcting them is fairly simple; if the scratches are deep, however, or if the surface is badly etched or pitted, or if there are over-all imperfections and general roughness, the job will be difficult and quite time-consuming and for best results should be undertaken by a professional marble dealer, who has the experience, skills, and equipment needed for what is sometimes quite a complicated job.[21]

Light restoration of the stone's original luster after cleaning can be done with jewelers' rouge or rottenstone—and plenty of elbow grease, enthusiastically applied.

For removing small surface scratches and roughness, and repolishing a marble surface, two methods are recommended.

Polishing Marble:
Method 1

Wipe the area clean with a damp cloth, and wet the marble with clean water. Fold a clean, lintless cloth tightly into a small, firm pad; dampen the pad slightly in water and dip it into tin oxide powder—or jewelers' rouge—poured into a dish. (Tin oxide powder can be obtained from chemical supply houses and some large drugstores; jewelers' rouge, from jewelers' suppliers and arts-and-crafts dealers.) Rub the wet, abraded area briskly until it shines; then clean the spot immediately with a different clean, damp cloth. Tin oxide allowed to dry on a marble surface sometimes leaves a ring, which can be removed by rubbing the area lightly again with the powder on the dampened pad and immediately cleaning it off with a damp cloth.[22]

Polishing Marble:
Method 2

Small scratches and areas of roughness *can* be removed and surface luster restored to marble by rubbing the area affected with very fine abrasive paper, such as #600. See "Smoke or burn stains, Method 2," above, however; and remember that most, if not all abrasive papers will remove material and could harm surrounding areas. The finest papers can be hard to find, and any confusion could be the ruin of an artifact. Try tin oxide; and if the scratches are too deeply etched to remove that way, leave the job to an expert. When the spot feels completely smooth, brush the abraded dust away and wet the surface with water. Sprinkle a bit of rottenstone on a clean, dampened cloth and rub the marble briskly until a shine appears.[23]

Waxes and Sealers for Marble and Similar Stones

Once polishing restores its luster, marble can be protected by an appropriate sealer or a maintenance coat of top-quality colorless paste wax, buffed to a high shine with a soft, lintfree cloth or a lamb's-wool applicator.[24]

Waxes and sealers made to safeguard the finish of stone, brick, cement, marble, and tile can be obtained from statuary supply houses, chemical supply houses, monument works, or marble companies. Sometimes, sealers can be used in addition to waxes, and sometimes not; if the product you buy is one you have not used before, obtain—and follow—full instructions for its use. Better yet, for small artifacts, get advice from a conservator before using on them any material that might penetrate the material and be impossible to remove later.

Marble surfaces that undergo much handling or contact, such as floors, sills, or doors, can be coated with a sealer made especially for marble, once the surface is cleaned and buffed. Do not apply any other type of finish, with this treatment. Whenever the marble is washed, reapply the sealer.[25]

Reproduction of Stone Artifacts

Sometimes valuable original stone objects, designed to remain outdoors, cannot be brought inside for sheltering. In order to save artifacts of that kind—such as statuary or tombstones—a reproduction, cast from the original, may be an attractive alternative. Reproductions in various materials have been tried.

Once environmental hazards are removed, many kinds of stone constructions can be expected to survive outdoors for quite a long time. Adhesives, coatings, and consolidants used on outdoor stone artifacts may be expected to delay the inevitable, at best, however; and at worst, complications caused by protective coatings applied to the original may only hasten its deterioration. Thus, when it is the environment of the object that is the cause of deterioration in stone, the obvious, though often difficult, remedy is to change the environment. Molded reproductions of some objects may make that alternative a practical and workable one.

In making casts of an original stone artifact, always check carefully to ensure that separating compounds or the molding material itself will not penetrate the surface of the original stone, or staining or delamination of the object can occur.

Masonry: Consolidation of Stone

Burnt stone is commonly found in fireplaces, where heat has reduced either the lime mortar or the marble or limestone of the mantel to a crumbly, sugary texture. This effect is similar to the process of burning limestone, marble, or seashells to make quicklime: the carbon dioxide content of the stone is driven off, and a powder of calcium oxide remains. Attempts to give strength back to the resulting crumbly stone have been made with traditional and newer methods, but—to date—the test of time has not established a superior method for stone consolidation.

If old chimneys are to be restored for use again, it is unlikely that any method for consolidation of the burned stone will prove satisfactory, because of the enormous stresses involved, as well as the direct effects of a continuing high heat level. Fireplaces and flues that are required to be functional should therefore be rebuilt, at least on the inside, with modern materials.

Some consolidation materials may impart an objectionable gloss to stone surfaces; and there is also the chance that a new synthetic skin on the crumbly original stone may pull the surface right off the original. Then, too, there is the problem of water wicking up inside a stone outdoors when the stone has been waterproofed or consolidated on its outer layer—since the water cannot escape from the stone by evaporation, a hard freeze can cause the stone literally to burst apart.

Masonry: Salts, Efflorescence, and Encrustations

The whitish, powdery-looking deposits commonly seen streaking unevenly down brick or masonry walls have a technical name: they are called *efflorescence,* and they are caused by moisture dissolving and leaching the soluble salts out of the masonry. Traditionally, this happens with brick, soft sedimentary rock, and adobe. It can happen even after attempts to protect the masonry have been made by applying to it a covering layer of a soluble nylon coating. There is now evidence that soluble nylon is not so safe to use as it was once believed to be, however, so one should seek advice from a conservator of objects or a restoration architect before attempting to consolidate masonry surfaces and leach out dissolved salts.

The *stains* made by efflorescence can be removed from brick walls and most masonry surfaces by scrubbing with clean water, detergent, and a stiff bristle brush. Rinse thoroughly with clean water. This brushing and washing will remove the signs of efflorescence, but only by keeping the wall dry can one eliminate further occurrences.

Encrustations. Lichens, limy encrustations, or deteriorating old mortar have commonly been removed from brick and stone with a dilute acid solution. Since the acid will dissolve limey materials—including all types of limestone, of course—and since it is dangerous to handle, as well, it is not a suggested method for cleaning historical objects. Instead, water and detergent, applied with a bristle or nylon scrubbing brush, will usually remove all but the most tenacious encrustations. If problem areas remain, an expert in stone cleaning should be consulted before further or more drastic cleaning is undertaken. One must be very cautious to avoid destroying the material that is intended to be preserved.

Stone Floors: Cleaning and Care

Stone floors, usually set on a concrete base, may be paved with blocks of slate, bluestone, flagstone, magnesite, quarry tile, marble, granite, or terrazzo (a composite of marble chips mixed with cement and polished to a high gloss). Stone floors should be kept tidy by a regular going over with a soft broom, the floor brush of a vacuum cleaner, or a clean, dry, untreated mop. They can be washed lightly with clear water or with clear water and a mild detergent, quickly rinsed off.[26]

When they need a thorough scrubbing, remember that, except for granite, all of the above stones are porous, as is any cement base that may be used under them. This means that unless the dirty mop water used to scrub them is fairly quickly and very thoroughly rinsed off, some of it may seep down into the stone, carrying part of the dislodged dirt and impurities with it, to establish troublesome stains. When stone floors must be scrubbed, therefore, one should begin with plenty of clean water and *two* clean mops—one for mopping and one for rinsing. Use a detergent, instead of soap, which leaves a scum on marble and many other stone surfaces. *Some authorities advise using a powdered detergent, especially on marble floors, because a liquid detergent often leaves slippery places on marble floors, even though it is thoroughly rinsed off.* Work in small areas, mopping and then rinsing thoroughly, one section at a time, to prevent seepage of the mop water into the stone. If a section looks dusty or streaked after it dries, there are still traces of detergent left that must be removed by additional rinsing. If possible, use mops without metal parts, to avoid scratching the stone surface. If that kind of mop is not available, wrap the metal parts of the mop you use in cloth scraps to protect the surface of the stone flooring.[27]

Sealers for stone floors. Many newly cleaned stone floors can be protected with a cement sealer and waxed to provide gloss. Floors made of marble, granite, and limestone are exceptions—see pages 204–212, above, for material on cleaning and protecting marble and similar stones. A self-polishing wax is the type usually recommended for stone floors, because the self-polishing type is believed to leave the floor surface less slippery than waxes that must be polished.[28]

Care of Miscellaneous Stone Objects

Statuary

Outdoor pieces of statuary are usually made of marble, of one of the other limestones, or of granite—for proper care, see preceding sections on care and cleaning of these stones. Many *statuettes* and smaller pieces designed for display indoors are also often made of marble, related limestones, plaster of Paris, and alabaster. Alabaster is cared for in much the same way as marble: by washing in warm water with a soft cloth and a mild detergent, rinsing thoroughly in warm water, and drying with a lint-free cloth. *Remember never to use lemon juice, vinegar, or any other acid as a cleanser on these stones—acids destroy them.*

Statuary and other ornamental objects made of plaster of Paris *should not be washed.* They are made of powdered gypsum and should be cleaned with a soft *dry* cloth or a soft brush.[29]

Slate

Slate, a hard, fine-grained rock used for roof tiles, flooring, hearths, fireplace facings, and sills, can be washed with clean hot water and either a good, mild, low-sudsing detergent or washing soda—calcium carbonate, also called *sal soda* or *washing crystals*. Like marble and other stones, slate should not be washed with soap, because of the tough film soap leaves on the cleaned surface. After slate hearths and fireplace facings have been washed, well rinsed, and dried, a tiny bit of lemon oil rubbed in well makes the stone surface darker and more lustrous. Wipe off any surplus oil. As mentioned above, however, remember that anything that penetrates the stone can complicate matters later. The oil treatment is cosmetic only; and—it may attract more grime, as well as being impossible to remove. Also—never use wax on slate hearths or fireplace facings—the good effects that wax might have in other locations are negated by its reaction to fireplace heat.[30]

Objects Made of Gemstones

Like most other artifacts, objects made of gemstones—the precious or semiprecious stones—need to be kept clean, and the ways of doing that differ slightly, depending on the kinds of gemstone involved.

Jade, for example, often used to make vases, lamps, and other small decorative items, as well as jewelry, can do without a great deal of washing. Unless subjected to unusual neglect, jade retains its beauty well with regular dusting. If a new acquisition comes into your collection clearly in need of a good cleaning up, it can be safely washed in warm water, using a mild detergent and a clean cloth. Rinse well in water of the same temperature and dry carefully on a clean, lint-free cloth.[31]

Necklaces made of stone beads—crystal, amethyst, topaz, torquoise, and similar stones—can be cleaned quite nicely with dry baking soda and a small brush. They can also be washed, as can many of the decorative objects made with gemstones—in fairly hot water, using a good detergent and a small brush and rinsing thoroughly in hot water and drying with a clean, lint-free cloth or tissue paper. Putting necklaces into hot water repeatedly, however, is likely to weaken the thread on which they are strung.[32]

One of the caveats about cleaning pearl necklaces, as a matter of fact, is never to wash them in water, because water rots the thread that holds them. Clean pearl necklaces by going over them gently and often with a piece of soft chamois, rubbing the entire surface of each bead. Pearls set in rings or made into pins can quite safely be washed in water, though the water should be cool, not hot: *high heat damages pearls, acids dissolve them, and ammonia should never be put into the water the you wash them with.* Use a mild detergent with the cool wash water and rinse them thoroughly in water of the same temperature. Dry pearls carefully on a soft cloth or chamois.[33]

Decorative items made of the quartzes—agate, onyx, chalcedony, sardonyx, jasper, rose quartz, rock crystal, and others—can be safely scrubbed in hot water with a good detergent and a small, soft brush. Rinse in clear hot water and dry well with a soft cloth or tissue paper.[34]

NOTES

1. *Columbia Encyclopedia,* 4th ed., s.v. "air pollution," "limestone," "marble."
2. James Cheston Thomas, *Restoring Brick and Stone: Some Dos and Don'ts,* Technical Leaflet 81 (Nashville: The American Association for State and Local History, 1975); *Columbia Encyclopedia,* 4th ed., s.v. "weathering."
3. Thomas, *Restoring Brick and Stone; Columbia Encyclopedia,* 4th ed., s.v. "limestone."
4. Alma C. Moore, *How To Clean Everything* (New York: Simon and Schuster, 1961), pp. 87, 117, 147.
5. *Columbia Encyclopedia,* 4th ed., s.v. "marble."
6. *Columbia Encyclopedia,* 4th ed., s.v. "marble," "alabaster," "travertine," "stalactite"; Moore, *How To Clean Everything,* p. 114.
7. *Columbia Encyclopedia,* 2nd ed., s.v. "granite."
8. *Columbia Encyclopedia,* 4th ed., s.v. "bluestone."
9. *Columbia Encyclopedia,* 4th ed., s.v. "travertine," "alabaster."
10. *Columbia Encyclopedia,* 4th ed., s.v. "alabaster"; Moore, *How To Clean Everything,* p. 8.
11. Bernard Gladstone, *The New York Times Complete Manual of Home Repair* (New York: Macmillan Co., 1967), p. 419.
12. Moore, *How To Clean Everything,* pp. 151–152.
13. Gladstone, *New York Times Manual,* p. 418; Reader's Digest Association, Inc., *Reader's Digest Complete Do-it-yourself Manual* (Pleasantville, N.Y.: Reader's Digest Association, Inc., 1973), p. 459.
14. Stanley Schuler, *How To Fix Almost Everything* (New York: M. Evans and Co., 1975), p. 117; Gladstone, *New York Times Manual,* p. 418–419; *Reader's Digest Manual,* p. 459.
15. Gladstone, *New York Times Manual,* p. 419.
16. Gladstone, *New York Times Manual,* pp. 419–420.
17. Ralph Parsons Kinney, *The Complete Book of Furniture Repair and Refinishing,* New Revised Edition (New York: Charles Scribner's Sons, 1981), p. 82.
18. Moore, *How To Clean Everything,* p. 98.
19. *The Family Handyman:* New York: Universal Publishing and Distributing Corp., 1965), p. 407.
20. *Reader's Digest Manual,* p. 459; *Family Handyman,* p. 407.
21. Kinney, *Furniture Repair and Refinishing,* p. 81; Schuler, *How To Fix Almost Everything,* p. 116.
22. Gladstone, *New York Times Manual,* p. 420; Schuler, *How To Fix Almost Everything,* p. 116; Moore, *How To Clean Everything,* p. 98.
23. Kinney, *Furniture Repair and Refinishing,* p. 81.
24. Gladstone, *New York Times Manual,* p. 420; Schuler, *How To Fix Almost Everything,* 116; Moore, *How To Clean Everything,* p. 98.
25. Schuler, *How To Fix Almost Everything,* p. 118.
26. Moore, *How To Clean Everything,* pp. 97, 149, 154.
27. Moore, *How To Clean Everything,* p. 97; *Reader's Digest Manual,* p. 459.
28. Moore, *How To Clean Everything,* p. 154.
29. Moore, *How To Clean Everything,* p. 147.
30. Moore, *How To Clean Everything,* pp. 141, 149.
31. Moore, *How To Clean Everything,* p. 87.
32. Moore, *How To Clean Everything,* pp. 88, 117.
33. Moore, *How To Clean Everything,* p. 117.
34. Moore, *How To Clean Everything,* pp. 126, 87.

SUGGESTED READING

Bryant, Terry. "Protecting Exterior Masonry from Water Damage: Moisture Control Procedures and Products." *Technology & Conservation Magazine* 3 (Spring 1978: 38–42.

Conservation of Stone, II: Preprints of the Contributions to the . . . Symposium. 2 vols. Bologna: Centro per la conservazione della sculture all' aperto, 1981.

Grimmer, Anne E. "Masonry Conservation: Documenting the Condition and Treatment and Condition of Historic Building Materials." *Technology & Conservation Magazine* 6 (Summer 1981): 32–35.

Livingston, Richard A. "The Air Pollution Contribution to Stone Deterioration: Investigating the Weathering of Bowling Green Custom House, New York City." *Technology & Conservation Magazine* 6 (Summer 1981): 36–39.

Phillips, Morgan W. "Consolidation of Porous Materials: Problems and Possibilities of Acrylic Resin Techniques." *Technology & Conservation Magazine* 4 (Winter 1979): 42–46.

Plenderleith, H. J., and A. E. A. Werner. "Stone." in *The Conservation of Antiquities and Works of Art: Treatment, Repair, and Restoration.* New York: Oxford University Press, 1971.

Good outline of problems with stone objects; note that some treatments may be of questionable value by current standards.

Sramek, Jiri. "Determination of the Source of Surface Deterioration on Tombstones at the Old Jewish Cemetery in Prague." *Studies in Conservation* 25 (May 1980): 47–52.

Thomas, James Cheston. *Restoring Brick and Stone: Some Dos and Don'ts.* Technical Leaflet 81. Nashville: The American Association for State and Local History, 1975.

Weiss, Norman R. "Cleaning of Building Exteriors: Problems and Procedures of Dirt Removal." *Technology & Conservation Magazine* 1 (Fall 1976): 8–13.

Winkler, Erhard M. *Stone: Properties, Durability in Man's Environment.* 2d ed., rev. New York: Springer-Verlag, 1975.

17

Photographs

Photographic materials consist of many different kinds of images and supports, from those that are in nature comparatively stable to those that are transitory. Some of the more stable types of photographs are daguerreotypes, ambrotypes, and black-and-white paper prints of various kinds, as well as glass plate and "safety film" negatives. Materials now rather well-known for instability are nitrate films and color prints of all kinds, especially the earlier types; most early color images that have not received extraordinary care have now deteriorated beyond usefulness. Some archivists will not collect color prints because of the difficulties of their preservation.

It must be noted that even those materials that are said to be stable will deteriorate quickly under adverse conditions, and many are composed of very sensitive components that must not be given any amateur treatments.

All photographic methods depend upon composite materials that are usually emulsions deposited on a base, but may be a chemically impregnated carrier for the image. The base may be of glass, paper, tin plate, leather, or numerous other materials, and the emulsion is sometimes rather delicately adhered. Both the base and the image materials are subject to deterioration or separation from one another, and the thin, sensitive layer of the image is especially prone to damage by scratching and abrading, as well as chemical deterioration. Bear in mind that paper prints may be destroyed if the paper base deteriorates. Try to think about the care needed for each element of a photograph. For full descriptions of the numerous historical photographic techniques, see a general work on photography. Learn to distinguish between the different processes for sorting and filing purposes, as well as for care of the objects.[1]

Indeed, an adverse environment can quickly destroy a photographic collection that may have survived many decades intact. The worst enemy of photographs is high humidity, which encourages mold growth on many materials and will result in the destruction of many kinds of

Fig. 17.1. Even relatively modern photographic materials may deteriorate in odd ways. This large negative is undergoing separation of the subbing from the base.

photographic emulsions, as well as paper, leather, cloth, and other organic materials associated with the image-bearing material itself. Moist conditions may also directly affect the emulsion of the photograph itself, usually by softening it and making it very vulnerable to damage by scratching, abrasion, or even insect attack, or by chemical changes in the material.

Air pollution is another environmental problem, because of the foreign substances—often acids—that are brought into contact with the complex structure of the photograph. For example, pollutants coming in contact with daguerreotypes can cause rapid tarnishing of the silver image layer; in some instances the image may be saved by proper conservation treatment, but all too often the silver is corroded beyond saving. Other photo processes are similarly vulnerable to chemical attack from air pollution. It should be noted that cleaning daguerreotypes in particular is not recommended, since some of the image silver is removed in the process. Also, substances such as thiourea in the solution may cause later retarnishing, often in the spotty pattern known as "daguerrean measles."

Finally, keep light levels low when exhibiting historic photographs.

Physical handling of photographs requires still further caution, because of the numerous possibilities for needlessly inflicting damage

Fig. 17.2. *Unless a daguerreotype or an ambrotype has serious problems, it is often best left alone. If you are debating about it, seek advice from a conservator, since some cleaning methods may lead to later problems from residual chemicals.*

upon the materials. Obviously, constant shuffling, filing, and sorting of collections will result in bending and abrading of original materials after a short time. One must attempt to develop a system that will allow for protection of materials, yet continue to make them useful. Several possibilities, albeit expensive ones, include storing images on microfilm, microfiche, and videodiscs; however, collectors must face the fact that constant use of original materials will soon result in their destruction. One common procedure is to prepare a good-quality copy negative *and* a working negative of each image, along with a sufficient number of prints for filing and other uses; thus, the original negative or positive image need not be handled nearly so often. For the best copying of a historical negative image, a new negative should be made *directly from it,* rather than copying a print made from the old negative. This process saves some loss of tone and detail from the print-making stage, although it is no easy task. Clearly, even this process is an expensive and time-consuming one, but it will effectively eliminate excessive handling of irreplaceable original materials. Often, file images may be made on an ordinary copying machine (Xerox, Canon, Minolta, etc.) if sufficient detail can be obtained.

When the photographic materials must be moved about, or placed in new storage containers, one should wear a pair of clean white cotton gloves, to avoid smearing perspiration and skin oils on the photo surfaces. Disposable gloves are available from photo supply houses, since they are routinely worn for work with all kinds of film and slides; washable gloves may be found in some mail-order catalogues, where they may be identified as "sleeping gloves" or a variety of other names. Washable gloves must be very carefully cleaned when they become soiled, so that all of the embedded grime and oils are removed and the fabric is made as clean as possible.

The number one priority in working with any photographic collection is to identify any nitrate-based film that might be stored with other materials. Since nitrate film decomposes to form acidic gases, it should be stored well away from other materials; and since it may also ignite spontaneously, extra precautions must be taken to guard against fire. *Nitrate film should be stored in a place that is dry, cool, and well-ventilated,* for the gases of its decomposition will hasten its own demise. Identifying nitrate film is usually not difficult, since better film bases were boldly identified with the words "safety film," to set them apart. Aside from tests using various solvents, the flame test generally will confirm or deny the presence of a nitrate base: simply snip off a sliver of film, outside the image area, and touch a lighted match to it; if the film sustains a flame and burns with little ash, it may be nitrate; if not, it is the more stable film base. Regular examinations of collections will help to identify nitrate film by its characteristic deterioration, as well as by other means. The film begins by turning yellowish, then bubbling in the base material, next becoming darker yellow or brown and sticky, and eventually degrading to a powder.[2]

At present, there is no way to halt or reverse the decomposition of nitrate films, so as soon as they are identified in a collection, every effort should be made to have them copied immediately and safely stored, if at all possible, rather than disposing of them. Badly deteriorated film should be disposed of at once; usually, these sticky or powdery pieces of film are well beyond copying, anyway. If all these precautions sound a bit drastic, one should remember that fire from nitrate film has destroyed more than one great film library, although those disasters occurred in motion picture storage, where great quantities of nitrate-based motion picture film were stored in one place.

Once hazardous materials have been segregated from the main part of the collection, attention should be given to the environment in the collection area. All efforts should be made to stabilize temperature and humidity and to keep the relative humidity level below 50 percent.

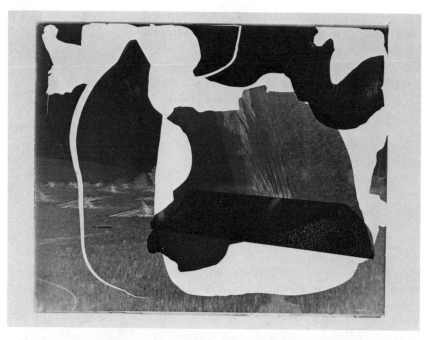

Fig. 17.3. Here, the emulsion is flaking off the glass-plate base it was placed on. Improper storage conditions may be the cause of this disaster.

Portable dehumidifiers may be a very effective means of gaining humidity control for many collections; try to allow dehumidifiers to be connected directly to a drain pipe, so that the machine can operate all the time and not be shut down by a filled-up water tank.

Low-temperature storage can help slow down the chemical deterioration of materials, and some archives now store their most important color films at temperatures below freezing. Suffice it to say, however, that *cooler* temperatures are preferred for photo storage, and one might consult with experts in the field for recommendations on the care of quantities of color images or other particularly sensitive photographs.

The environment for photo collections should also be clean, and free from dust and pollutant gases in the air. Frequent vacuuming of storage areas will help, but filtering the air may be necessary; although filters may be incorporated into air-conditioning systems, they may also be purchased as portable units, to service small areas. Beware of the type of filter that works by electrostatically removing dust from the air, since that process also may produce ozone gas, a strong oxidizer. Dry filters can remove dust from the air, and the addition of activated charcoal elements will help absorb polluting gases, as well.

Storage materials for photographs are continually being developed as a part of the nascent science of photo care and conservation. To begin with the storage room itself, dust-free floors and ceilings are necessary. Therefore, avoid housing your collection in unfinished basements or attics, where dust can infiltrate from all sides. Collection rooms should be as tightly sealed as possible. Concrete floors should be treated with sealants, painted, or covered with a suitable flooring to prevent concrete dust from being a constant and very serious problem.

Storage cabinets or shelves should be of metal, with a baked-on enamel finish, if at all possible. An alternative method utilizes acid-free boxes of convenient sizes, placed on whatever shelves are available. If wooden shelves must be used, cover the wooden surfaces with polyester film, to prevent acid migration from the wood to the storage boxes. It is best to seal *all* wooden surfaces to slow the release of acidic vapors in the storage room; epoxy coatings are best, but they are very expensive, so polyurethane varnish or a latex enamel applied over a proper undercoat may be used. Be sure to follow the directions for the product when using any paint or coating; then, allow several weeks for the coating to dry completely before putting photographs into the collection room. Avoid using wooden boxes or cabinets; they are acidic and will trap gases around your prized photographs.

Envelopes and sleeves for holding photographs may be made from paper, polyester film, or triacetate film, but they should not be of kraft paper, polyvinyl chloride, or glassine. Acid-free paper envelopes are most commonly used, because they are reasonably inexpensive and are very convenient to label. Paper envelopes should have a side seam, glued with an acid-free adhesive, or one can make seamless envelopes.[3] Place the emulsion side of the photograph away from the glued seam, to be on the safe side. Label the envelopes with pencil, India ink, or carbon typewriter ribbon; *never be tempted to write on an envelope while the photo is inside.*

Polyester film sleeves and envelopes are coming into wide use for storage, and improved methods and materials make them more attractive all the time. For example, one type of polyester is made so that it is less electrostatic than the normal formulation, and it is done without the use of coatings that would be unacceptable for archival use. Methods for adhering sheets of polyester film to one another have been improved; one may use double-sided tape to make envelopes, but commercially available folders and envelopes may be ordered with "welded" seams

Fig. 17.4. This photograph has been placed in a polyester sleeve, along with a piece of acid-free bristol board. The board adds stiffness to the package and provides a convenient, safe place to write a catalogue number.

that use no adhesive at all. There can be problems with polyester, such as the possibility of trapping moisture inside in high humidity conditions, the difficulty of labeling the slick surface, and the electrostatic properties of some varieties, which attract dust and grit. Sometimes, to offer extra protection in handling and examination of prints or negatives, polyester sleeves are used inside paper envelopes, or stiffeners of rag board may be inserted in the sleeve with the object. That way, one has the convenience and protection of paper, and the photo may be examined through the polyester cover without danger of contact with one's fingers.

Other storage materials are in current use, such as triacetate sleeves, and new ones are being tested; one new substance is *Tyvek* olefin material, which is a very stable synthetic that handles much like paper. Polyethylene may be suitable for holding flexible negative materials, although most polyethylene is treated with coating to prevent stickiness, and these can be harmful. One must be on the lookout for so-called *archival* materials, which may cause damage to photographic materials. One such item is colored mat board, which is sometimes considered safe to use with paper artifacts, but has been found to cause deterioration of the image silver of some photographic prints.[4]

The simplest method of photo print storage, and also the least expensive, is to interleave a small group of prints with non-buffered, acid-free paper, and place the group inside an acid-free folder. Several folders can then be stored in an acid-free document box, but avoid the temptation to squeeze too much into one container.

Glass-plate negatives are best stored standing on end; and folded envelopes, made without adhesives, are an inexpensive form of protection. If you already have regular acid-free envelopes, place the glass-plate negatives in them so that the emulsion faces *away* from the glued seam. Do not allow glass-plate negatives to lean or press hard on each other; use rigid dividers at close intervals on storage shelves to give extra support.

Considering the short time that photograph conservation has been explored, and the complex nature of the materials themselves, anyone working with a photograph collection would do well to begin the basic work of collection care at once; but one should read all available material on the subject, keep up to date on recent findings, and consult with a conservator in the subject area when problems are encountered. Remember the sensitive nature of photographs, and refrain from trying home remedies on valuable and irreplaceable images of the past.

NOTES

1. Weinstein and Booth, *Collection Use, and Care of Historical Photographs,* pp. 3–8, 208–210.
2. Weinstein and Booth, *Care of Historical Photographs,* pp. 190–191.
3. Weinstein and Booth, *Care of Historical Photographs,* pp. 136–141.
4. Mary Kay Porter, "Materials to Be Used with Photographs."

SUGGESTED READING

Bowditch, George. *Cataloguing Photographs: A Procedure for Small Collections.* Technical Leaflet No. 57. Nashville: The American Association for State and Local History, 1975.

Calhoun, J. "Storage of Nitrate Amateur Still-Camera Film Negatives." *Journal of Biological Photographic Association* 21 (1953): 1–13.

Daniels, V. "Plasma Reduction of Silver Tarnish on Daguerreotypes." *Studies in Conservation* 26 (May 1981): 45–59.

Gill, Arthur T. "Photographic Processes: A Glossary and a Chart for Recognition." Information Sheet No. 21. London: Museums Association, 1978.
Available from George Eastman House, 900 East Avenue, Rochester, New York 14607.

Noble, Richard. *Archival Preservation of Motion Pictures: A Summary of Recent Findings.* Technical Leaflet No. 126. Nashville: The American Association for State and Local History, 1980.

Porter, Mary K. "Materials to Be Used with Photographs." *A.I.C. Newsletter* 7 (August 1982): 12–13.
An example of "archival" materials that are not without their problems in some circumstances.

Vanderbilt, Paul. *Filing Your Photographs: Some Basic Procedures.* Technical Leaflet No. 36. Nashville: The American Association for State and Local History, 1966.

Weinstein, Robert A., and Larry Booth. *Collection, Use, and Care of Historical Photographs.* Nashville: The American Association for State and Local History, 1977.
An excellent compendium of information on the complicated subject of photo preservation. This area of conservation is in its nascent stages, but here is an excellent beginning for collectors.

Wilhelm, Henry. "Monitoring the Fading and Staining of Color Photographic Prints." *Journal of the American Institute for Conservation* 21 (Fall 1981): 49–64.

Appendix 1

Adhesives

There are thousands of adhesives on the market today capable of joining almost any combination of materials under a great variety of circumstances. No one adhesive product can do all jobs, however, no matter how optimistic the promotional literature sometimes seems. It is impossible to list all the adhesives on the market by trade names, although there are appropriate references on the subject, notably: Irving Skeist, editor, *Handbook of Adhesives*, second edition (New York: Van Nostrand Reinhold Company, 1977); also, Robert S. Miller, *Adhesvies and Glues: How to Choose and Use Them* (Columbus, Ohio: Franklin Chemical Industries, 1980).

Since many of the source books about adhesives are rather technical, it might be safer to address your questions to a conservation expert. Remember, if you are working on valuable historical objects, it is worth taking a little time to be sure that you have the right adhesive for the job, and not something that will cause eventual harm to a prized artifact. The following are some pertinent questions to consider in locating the right adhesive for a given situation.

1. What specific materials will be joined? It is important to know exactly what sorts of fabric, wood, metal, or other substances are to be in contact with the adhesive.

2. Will you have a tight fit, or do you need an adhesive with filler qualities, to compensate for two irregular surfaces with some voids? Many adhesives work best where the glue line is thin, but others do not.

3. Do you want a rigid or a flexible bond? You may want an adhesive or caulking compound that will allow for dimensional changes in materials as a result of temperature and humidity changes.

4. How will the article be used—in a static exhibit, or out of doors in live demonstrations? What stresses and environmental problems will be present after the object has been repaired?

5. How strong or permanent an adhesive is necessary? Bear in mind that the best course for the preservation of any object is to use reversible adhesives. Occasionally those types may be difficult to obtain, but permanent, insoluble adhesives should be used only as a last resort; and even then you might consider whether the object might not survive all right without being repaired for the moment.

6. Under what conditions will the adhesive be applied—indoors in a warm room, in an unheated shed, in outdoor cold, or in a wet location?

7. Do you want to apply the adhesive as a thin liquid, or as a paste or gel of stiffer consistency?

8. What tools do you need to apply it? Some adhesives may affect certain types of bristles or metals, or affect the skin in alarming ways.

9. How long a working time, or "pot life," is necessary, or how quickly do you want the adhesive to set? Anything from ten-second hardening to overnight hardening is available, and each has its own merits and problems.

10. Finally, an important but overlooked point: what is the shelf- or storage-life of the adhesive? There is no point in buying a year's supply of material if its storage life is only three months, or if it begins to break down in the container after it has first been used and exposed to air. Some adhesives are dated, so that you have a cutoff date for using them. To be sure that any adhesive will work properly each time you need it, test a little bit of it before attempting the important repair; at least you will know whether the material will set up at all, and how long that may take.

Some Adhesive Substances and Their Properties

The following list is not intended as a comprehensive guide to modern adhesives, but only as a brief orientation to some of the types available today. In the practice of conservation, very few of these adhesives can be recommended for general use, because of destructive properties, irreversibility, or other problems.

Pressure-sensitive cellulose tape. Pressure-sensitive cellulose tape is perhaps the most widely used adhesive substance on the market. Newer types of mending tape show great improvement over the older varieties, which dried out and turned brown in a few years. However, because of the difficulty of removing such tapes from any surface, and the permanent staining that sometimes accompanies the tapes' deterioration, they should not be used on any valuable object. Ironically, some of these tapes weaken and fall off the surface to which they have been applied, only to leave behind traces of dried adhesive and dark brown stains on vulnerable materials. "Archival" pressure-sensitive tapes are available, but none of them have been proven safe to use with irreplaceable papers (see "Wheat or rice starch pastes," page 230).

Pressure-sensitive laminating film. Resembling cellulose tape in appearance, pressure-sensitive laminating film comes in sheets or wide rolls, and is highly touted (by the makers) for preserving valuable documents and papers. Since there are safer—though more difficult—methods of lamination for severely weakened paper objects, this film merely adds unnecessarily dangerous adhesives over the whole surface of an object. Removal of these films from paper is even more difficult than loosening old cellulose tape. Though adhesive laminating films should not be used, there is no quick and easy solution to reinforcing weak, brittle paper.

Dry-mounting tissue. Either wax- or shellac-based in the past, dry-mounting tissues have been developed using synthetic hot-melt resins for greater usefulness. Some dry-mount tissues are removable, although the residue of adhesive or solvent left behind may be a problem. Indeed, even though some of the materials are said to be non-acidic, they are not recommended for mounting valuable papers or photos. Acid-free paper or polyester film photo corners adhered with the proper adhesive are the preferred alternative for mounting photographs.

Rubber cement. Rubber cement is one adhesive that should not be given houseroom. It stains paper quite badly and often permanently; and even though its adhesive quite commonly fails in use, the part you wish to remove is almost impossible to dissolve. It is not recommended for exhibition use, and definitely not for repair or mounting of artifacts.

Spray-can adhesives. Often rubber-based, spray-can adhesives in aerosol form also seem to suffer from the same defects as old-fashioned rubber cement: sometimes they hold like fury; other times they fail. Some may be potentially dangerous to use without good ventilation, because of the solvents in their formulae. They are usually considered to be useful in exhibition work, although many of them cannot be expected to hold well for more than a few weeks.

Wheat or rice starch paste. Wheat or rice neutral starch pastes are dry powders to be mixed with water and cooked. They are safer than commercial pastes, but make them in small amounts, for they will not keep long (see references under chapter on paper for recipes). They are useful on paper and cardboard because they hold well, but they can be safely removed if necessary. They are not strong enough for wood or metal.

Library paste. The commercial varieties of library paste have preservatives and other additives and are often acidic; they should never come in contact with paper artifacts. Neutral starch pastes may be obtained from conservation supply houses.

Contact cement. Contact cements are related to rubber cements and spray-can adhesives in that they have often used a latex base. Since they may have sulfur in them, these adhesives should not be used in exhibit areas where there may be lead or silver artifacts that can be adversely affected. Though contact cements often have great holding power, they are not recommended for conservation purposes because they are not reversible.

Melted waxes and resins. Stick shellac, beeswax, and various resin-wax mixtures have been used for centuries as mending materials; and along with newer synthetic waxes and resins, they are still valuable adhesives today. However, the use of these materials is usually an exacting and delicate process, and one that is confined to the laboratories of professional conservators.

Caulking compounds and mastics. Caulking compounds and mastics act as fillers and adhesives and are particularly useful when non-porous substances like glass and metal are to be joined. If there are irregularities in the two surfaces, the adhesive will fill in to give a more complete holding surface. They also give one the opportunity to wiggle the pieces to be joined or position the objects into place, a distinct advantage over quick-setting adhesives, at times. However, some of these compounds contain sulfur, and some are difficult to remove, once dry. Check the instructions carefully before using them.

Filler compounds. There are many filler compounds on the market. The traditional ones like gesso, putty, and wood fillers are made of inert materials like whiting, plaster, or wood dust, plus an adhesive. These are all useful for filling holes and cracks or for building up missing areas, and they adhere well to clean surfaces. They generally have little bonding power, and are not a substitute for adhesives. Some of the newer fillers, usually a two-part resin plus metal or fiberglass fillers, do have bonding power, but are rather expensive, and are not considered reversible in many instances.

Animal glues. Included in this category are fish glue, rabbit-skin glue, gelatin, and hide glue (carpenters' glue)—all traditional glues and still useful. Gelatin is used in various ways in fine arts conservation. Ready-made liquid hide glue is available and is considered by some to be the simplest and best adhesive to use on wood. Others contend that the dry hide glue is superior in strength, although it must be soaked, then cooked, and used while hot. Since hide glues do not stain wood, and are considered reversible, they are recommended for wood repairs where the joint will not be subjected to a great deal of moisture.

White glues (water-resin emulsions). White glues are useful for a variety of porous materials and are reasonably inexpensive. They are nontoxic to the skin, they can be thinned with water, if desired, and they give a good bond. But they should not be used where they will be subjected to high moisture conditions, nor with paper artifacts, nor with metal, which they will corrode. Once white glues have dried, they are no longer water soluble; usually solvents will dissolve the bond, but with age, that process becomes more difficult. The yellow varieties of these glues are essentially the same adhesive, except that they are faster-setting.

Clear adhesives of soluble resins. This category includes an enormous number of adhesives, most of which are labeled as "all-purpose, mends anything." Generally, they are resins in a quick-evaporating solvent ("Duco" and "Ambroid" cements are examples). The solid component may be a cellulose product, or one of a variety of other resins. Such adhesives are theoretically capable of being redissolved in their original solvents, but exceptions may occur under certain circumstances. Generally these adhesives are not as strong or as permanent as some of the more recently developed types designed specifically for the repair of certain materials, such as ceramic or glass repair (available from conservation supply houses).

Two-part synthetic resins. Typified by epoxy, polyester, or resorcinol, two-part synthetic resins are strong, waterproof, permanent adhesives, consisting of a resin plus a hardener and/or catalyst. These resins may be as thin as water, for impregnating rotted wood, or they may be the consistency of syrup, paste, or putty. Since most of the adhesives of this class are considered irreversible, once they have set, be sure that the pieces to be joined will *never* need to be taken apart again. Such adhesives are generally a last resort when one is dealing with valuable artifacts.

Appendix 2

Making Padded Coat Hangers for Historical Garments

A pattern for making padded garment hangers for historical wearing apparel was recently developed for the New York State Historical Association by Janet Susan Low, historical clothing consultant, and Elizabeth S. Warner, museum intern.

Such hangers are an improved storage aid for historical clothing that is not too weak and fragile to be hung; padding spreads the weight and stress of hanging and covers the comparatively sharp ends of the wooden hangers that are the basis of the new device.

The technique for making the padded hangers, shown below, step by step, has proven to be relatively quick and efficient, since it requires the use of just four materials, and there is no need for sewing or complicated cutting. And—the same pattern can be adapted for cut-down hangers of almost any size.

One word of caution, however: do not force even a padded hanger into garments that are smaller than average size.

Materials needed for making the padded hangers and suppliers from whom they can be obtained are these:

Unbleached, de-sized muslin fabric: Testfabrics, Inc.
P.O. Box 0
Middlesex, New Jersey 08846
Cotton twill tape: Newark Dressmaker Supply
P.O. Box 2448
Lehigh Valley, Pennsylvania 18001
Polyester batting: Upholstery supply outlets and some fabric stores

Varnished wooden coat hangers: Department stores and retailer furnishing suppliers

Directions and illustrations, step by step, follow.

For each hanger:

1. One piece of unbleached, desized cotton muslin,
   27 inches wide by 18 inches long.
2. One piece of polyester batting, 12 inches by 6 inches,
   with a 2½-inch slit in the center:

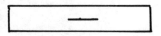

3. One piece of polyester batting, 20 inches by 6 inches,
   with a small hole in the center:

4. One piece of white cotton twill tape: ½ inch wide by 14 inches long.
5. One standard-sized coat hanger (styrene or varnished wood).

Step 1:

Place the piece of batting with the 2½-inch slit over the hanger's hook.

Step 2:

Place the piece of batting with the hole in the center over the hook and on top of the first piece of batting.

Step 3:

Cut a slit in the top of the piece of fabric. The slit should be centered and about 5 inches long:

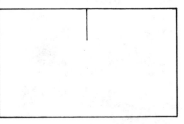

Step 4:

Place the padded coat hanger on top of the fabric, so that the base of the hook is at the base of the slit:

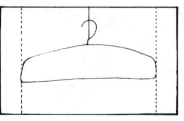

Step 5:

Fold the ends of the fabric over the ends of the hanger about 2½ inches—be sure that the ends of the hanger are well stuffed:

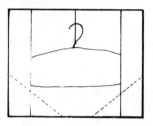

Step 6:

Fold the lower corners up to the center, as if wrapping a gift. Be sure the fold is snug against the bottom:

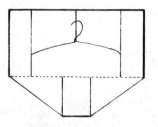

Step 7:

Fold the resulting lower point up to the hanger's hook:

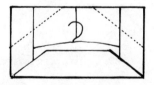

Step 8:

Fold down the outer corners at the top to the center—also as if wrapping a gift:

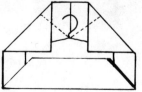

Step 9:

Fold down the inner corners at the top so that the result is this:

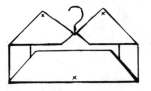

Step 10:

Poke holes at the places marked with X's in the drawing above, for Step 9. Thread the twill tape through the three holes:

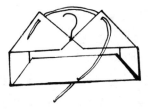

Step 11:

Draw up the ends of the tape tightly and tie in a bow-knot. *Do not tie any hard knots.* Tug, pull, push, and arrange everything so that it has a neat appearance. Be sure there's lots of stuffing in the ends. When you're finished, your padded hanger should look like this:

Design by Janet Susan Low
and
Elizabeth S. Warner

Suppliers of Materials and Equipment

The following list of suppliers is intended as a representative sample only of sources for materials mentioned in this book. In some instances, where very specialized materials are involved, there may be no other supplier; in others, where such things as tools or fire extinguishers are needed, your local telephone book should help you locate a source. In any event, be sure that you know specifically what you are looking for—be it a screwdriver or an archival envelope—so that you will not be talked into buying something else that will not do the job you have in mind.

For greater ease in finding a supplier who carries the product you are looking for, the suppliers listed here are grouped alphabetically under headings that indicate their products.

Many of the bibliographic sources listed with each chapter will be of help in determining specific materials to acquire, and perhaps some additional sources for them.

Above all, do not consider catalogues of various supply houses to be instruction manuals for the care of objects. There are many sorts of adhesives, resins, and other substances that may sound very enticing in the catalogue entry, though they are not considered suitable materials for many conservation treatments. It is all too easy to try a new material because its properties seem perfect for the job, only to find out that it is not equal to the task or that it has some unpleasant side effect you had not expected. If you have a job that apparently cannot be done, examine the bibliographic sources on the subject, or consult with a conservator who works with those materials on a regular basis.

Products and Suppliers

Air Filters
Research Products Corporation
1015 East Washington Avenue
P.O. Box 1467
Madison, Wisconsin 53701

Non-electronic, high-efficiency air filters.

Acid-Free Papers, Board, Conservation Supplies, Boxes
    Charles T. Bainbridge's Sons
    Rariton Center
    50 Northfield Avenue
    Edison, New Jersey 08817

    Acid-free and all-rag board, conservation-quality papers.

    Conservation Materials, Ltd.
    340 Freeport Boulevard
    Box 2884
    Sparks, Nevada 89431

    Acid-free papers and board, general conservation supplies.

    Conservation Resources International
    1111 North Royal Street
    Alexandria, Virginia 22314

    Acid-free, lignin-free storage boxes and materials; neutral pH boards, for
    photo and other archival storage and display.

    Crestwood Paper Company, Inc.
    Division of Willman Paper Company, Inc.
    315 Hudson Street
    New York, New York 10013

    Acid-free, all-rag mat boards.

    Process Materials
    301 Veterans Boulevard
    Rutherford, New Jersey 07072

    Acid-free and all-rag papers and boards, and associated materials.

Archival Storage Materials and Equipment. See Also Storage Cabinets, Furnishings
    Conservation Resources International
    1111 North Royal Street
    Alexandria, Virginia 22314

    Acid-free, lignin-free storage boxes and materials; lignin-free, neutral pH
    boards, for photo and other archival storage and displays.

    Hollinger Corporation
    P.O. Box 6185
    3810 South Four-Mile-Run Drive
    Arlington, Virginia 22206

Conservation-quality boards, polyester storage materials, archival boxes and cases.

Light Impressions Corporation
Box 3012
Rochester, New York 14614

Archival papers and boards, storage materials and equipment, tools, etc.

University Products, Inc.
P.O. Box 101
Holyoke, Massachusetts 01040

Wide variety of archival papers, board, boxes, tubes, and associated materials.

Art and Drafting Supplies
Art Brown & Brother, Inc.
2 West 46th Street
New York, New York 10036

Large catalogue of art and drafting supplies.

Dick Blick Company
P.O. Box 1267
Galesburg, Illinois 61401

Large catalogue of brushes, paints, and all sorts of art supplies.

Conservation Materials and Tools
Conservation Materials, Ltd.
Box 2884, #40 Freeport Boulevard
Sparks, Nevada 89431

Extensive catalogue of conservation materials and tools.

TALAS (Technical Library Service)
130 Fifth Avenue
New York, New York 10011

Conservation materials and tools of all sorts, but particularly for paper and book treatment.

Electric Lights and Lighting Equipment. See Also Photometers
Duro-Test Corporation
2321 Kennedy Boulevard
North Bergen, New Jersey 07047

Special-purpose and long-life light bulbs.

Filter Light Corporation
1910 East Wondover Avenue
P.O. Box 6292
Greensboro, North Carolina 27405

Fluorescent tube filter sleeves and associated materials.

Solar-Screen Company
53-11 105th Street
Corona, New York 11368

Filtering shades, film, and fluorescent shields, and light-reflective materials.

Verilux, Inc.
35 Mason Street
Greenwich, Connecticut 06830

"Color-balanced" low-ultraviolet-emission fluorescent tubes.

Nordest
206 Newbury Street
Boston, Massachusetts 02116

Miniature, battery-powered ultraviolet lights.

West Lake Plastic Company
West Lenni Road
Lenni Mills, Pennsylvania 19052

Rigid plastic ultraviolet filter tubes for fluorescent lights.

Fabrics
Pellon Corporation, Industrial Division
221 Jackson Street
Lowell, Massachusetts 01852

Nonwoven, inert fabrics.

Testfabrics, Inc.
P.O. Drawer O
Middlesex, New Jersey 08846

Fabrics, including some undyed and desized.

Fumigation and Drying Chambers
Vacudyne Altair Corporation
375 East Joe Orr Road
Chicago Heights, Illinois 60411

Fumigation and drying chambers.

Glass—Coated
Denton Vacuum, Inc.
8 Springdale Road
Cherry Hill, New Jersey 08003

Glare-reducing glass made with a durable, inert coating.

Glazing Materials, Polyester Film
Rohm & Haas
Independence Mall West
Philadelphia, Pennsylvania 19105

Acrylic glazing materials in numerous formulations from filtering to high-security.

Gloves—White Cotton, Washable
Vermont Country Store
Weston, Vermont 05161

Washable white cotton gloves.

Locks, Security Devices, Alarm Systems
H. Hoffman Company
7330 W. Montrose Avenue
Chicago, Illinois 60634

Locks, hardware, door alarms, and other security devices.

Magnifiers and Measuring Devices, Scientific Materials. See Also Photometers, Light Measurement, Temperature and Humidity Measurement
Edmund Scientific Company
400 Edscorp Building
Barrington, New Jersey 08007

Magnifying and measuring devices, variety of scientific materials.

Mat Cutters
H. F. Esterly Company
Industry Road
Brunswick, Maine 04011

Mat-cutting machines of high quality, generally for high-volume matting jobs.

Movers' Pads and Equipment
  Lawrence Piller, Inc.
  1930 47th Street
  Brooklyn, New York 11204

  Material-handling equipment, movers' pads, and other movers' paraphernalia.

Packing and Shipping Materials, Hardware
  Advanced Packaging, Inc.
  4303 Kenshaw Avenue
  Baltimore, Maryland 21215

  Cushioning material and transit cases for shipping, etc.

  Brown Cor International
  P.O. Box 21248
  Fort Lauderdale, Florida 33335

  Packing foams, tapes, and other materials.

  Simmons Fastener Corp.
  N. Broadway
  Albany, New York 12201

  Transit case latches, panel fasteners, other helpful hardware.

Photometers, Light Measurement Equipment
  International Light Company
  Dexeter Industrial Green
  Newburyport, Massachusetts 01950

  Photometers for measurement of visible and ultraviolet light.

  Littlemore Scientific Engineering Company
  Railway Lane
  Littlemore, Oxford OX4 4PZ
  ENGLAND

  Photometers for the measurement of visible and ultraviolet light.

Picture Frames, Framing Tools
  Kulicke Frames
  Division of A.P.F., Inc.
  601 West 26 Street
  New York, New York 10001

  Picture frames designed for display of fragile and valuable paper objects.

S and W Framing Supplies, Inc.
1845 Highland Avenue
New Hyde Park, New York 11040

Framing tools and a vast variety of special hardware.

Polyester Film Envelopes and Folders
Bill Cole Enterprises
P.O. Box 60
Wollaston, Massachusetts 02170

Heat-sealed polyester film envelopes and folders.

E. I. duPont de Nemours Company, Inc.
Wilmington, Delaware 19898

Polyester film, acrylic glazing materials, and chemicals.

Respirators for Solvent Vapors
Mine Safety Appliance Company
201 North Braddock Avenue
Pittsburgh, Pennsylvania 15208

Respirators for solvent vapors.

Safety Equipment and Materials-Handling Catalogues
Industrial Safety Supply Company, Inc.
574 New Park Avenue
West Hartford, Connecticut 06110

Safety equipment and materials-handling catalogues.

Scientific Apparatus, Laboratory Furnishings, Chemicals, Safety Equipment
Fisher Scientific Company
711 Forbes Avenue
Pittsburgh, Pennsylvania 15219

Scientific apparatus, laboratory wares and furnishings, safety equipment, and chemicals (eighteen branches across the country).

Silica Gel
Multiform Desiccant Products, Inc.
1418 Niagara Street
Buffalo, New York 14213

Silica gel in various packages and formulations.

Storage Cabinets, Furnishings, Display Materials, Lab Furnishings
Arrow Star, Inc.
637 William Street
Lynbrook, New York 11563

Storage and material handling equipment.

Construction Specialties, Inc.
55 Winans Avenue
Cranford, New Jersey 07016

Visual storage rack system for framed art works.

Interior Steel Equipment Company
2352 East 69th Street
Cleveland, Ohio 44104

Museum storage cabinets for all types of materials.

J. W. Murdock Industrial Products Guide
81 S. 2405 Waukegan Road
Deerfield, Illinois 60015

Storage and material-handling equipment.

Kewaunee Scientific Equipment Corporation
Special Products Division
Adrian, Michigan 49221

(Regional representatives)
Laboratory furnishings and museum storage cabinets and racks of various types.

ORO Manufacturing Company
P.O. Box 479
Monroe, North Carolina 28110

Storage racks for framed art works.

SHD (Standard Handling Devices)
P.O. Box 13N
Sycamore Avenue
Medford, Massachusetts 02155

Storage and material-handling equipment.

Steel Fixture Manufacturing Company
612 East Seventh Street
P.O. Box 917
Topeka, Kansas 66601

Museum storage cabinets.

Temperature and Humidity Measuring Equipment
  Abbeon Cal, Inc.
  123 Gray Avenue
  Santa Barbara, California 93101

  Hygrometers, thermometers, work lights, storage furnishings. and tools.

  Bendix Corporation
  Environmental and Process Instrument Division
  1400 Taylor Avenue
  Baltimore, Maryland 21204

  Psychrometers, thermometers, and other measurement equipment.

Tools
  Brookstone
  127 Vose Farm Road
  Peterborough, New Hampshire 03458

  "Hard-to-find" tools of all kinds.

  Sears, Roebuck and Company
  (Department store in local area)
  Tools, humidifiers, dehumidifiers, etc.

  Woodcraft Supply Corp.
  313 Montvale Avenue
  Woburn, Massachusetts 01801

  Large variety of hand woodworking tools, including many traditional types.

Illustrations Acknowledgments

Author and publisher wish to express grateful thanks to the New York State Historical Association for their kind permission to have photographs of items from their collections made and reproduced as illustrations for this book.

Index